EG00999

# IN FRONT OF THE CHILDREN

*Screen Entertainment and Young Audiences*

Edited by

CARY BAZALGETTE
and
DAVID BUCKINGHAM

BFI PUBLISHING

First published in 1995 by the
British Film Institute
21 Stephen Street
London W1P 1PL



The British Film Institute exists to promote appreciation, enjoyment, protection and development of moving image culture in and throughout the whole of the United Kingdom. Its activities include the National Film and Television Archive; the National Film Theatre; the Museum of the Moving Image; the London Film Festival; the production and distribution of film and video; funding and support for regional activities; Library and Information Services; Stills, Posters and Designs; Research; Publishing and Education; and the monthly *Sight and Sound* magazine.

British Library Cataloguing in Publication Data.
A catalogue record for this book is available from the British Library.

ISBN: 0–85170–452–2
0–85170–453–0 pbk

Cover design by Design & Art

Phototypeset by Intype, London

Printed in Great Britain by St Edmundsbury Press Ltd,
Bury St Edmunds, Suffolk

# ACKNOWLEDGMENTS

The idea of this book was first raised at a seminar organised by the British Film Institute's Education Department in conjunction with the Children's London Film Festival at the National Film Theatre, 26–27 October 1991.

We would like to thank Jim Cook and Marina Warner for their advice and support at the beginning of the project. We are also greatly indebted to the BFI Publishing production team: Roma Gibson, Dawn King and John Smoker, for their patience and professionalism. Thanks also to Tise Vahimagi for his perseverance in picture research.

*Cary Bazalgette and David Buckingham*

CONTENTS

**Notes on Contributors** ix

**Introduction**
The Invisible Audience
CARY BAZALGETTE AND DAVID BUCKINGHAM 1

Babes 'n' the Hood: Pre-school Television and its Audiences in the United States and Britain
MAIRE MESSENGER DAVIES 15

Watching with Mother in the Early 1950s
DAVID OSWELL 34

On the Impossibility of Children's Television: The Case of Timmy Mallett
DAVID BUCKINGHAM 47

'The Power is Yours': Agency and Plot in *Captain Planet*
GREG MYERS 62

Home Alone in the 90s: Generational War and Transgenerational Address in American Movies, Television and Presidential Politics
MARSHA KINDER 75

Unshrinking the Kids: Children's Cinema and the Family Film
CARY BAZALGETTE AND TERRY STAPLES 92

Once Upon a Time Beyond Disney: Contemporary Fairy-tale Films for Children
JACK ZIPES 109

Turtle Power: Illusion and Imagination in Children's Play
CATHY URWIN 127

Room to Dance: Girls' Play and *The Little Mermaid*
CHRIS RICHARDS 141

The Empire of Play: Emergent Genres of Product-based Animations
STEPHEN C. KLINE 151

Toy-based Video for Girls: *My Little Pony*
ELLEN SEITER 166

Moral Kombat and Computer Game Girls
HELEN CUNNINGHAM 188

Very Nearly in Front of the Children: The Story of *Alternity*
MARTIN BARKER 201

**Index** 217

# NOTES ON CONTRIBUTORS

**Martin Barker** is Head of the School of Cultural Studies at the University of the West of England, Bristol. He has been researching issues around the mass media since 1979, with a particular interest in the media and young people, and in panics about the effects of the media. He is the author of several books on these subjects, including *A Haunt of Fears: The Strange History of the British Horror Comics Campaign* and *The Video Nasties* (both Pluto Press, 1984), *Comics: Ideology, Power and the Critics* (Manchester University Press, 1989) and *Action: The Story of a Violent Comic* (Titan Books, 1991). He is currently working with Guy Cumberbatch on *The Intelligent Person's Guide to the Media/Violence Debate*, and with Roger Sabin on a study of the uses and adaptations of James Fenimore Cooper's *The Last of the Mohicans* as an index of 'the American Dream' (both forthcoming 1995).

**Cary Bazalgette** is Principal Education Officer at the British Film Institute, where she has worked since 1979. She has edited a number of teaching packs on media education, including *Reading Pictures* (BFI, 1981), *Picture Stories* (BFI, 1986) and *Screening Middlemarch* (BBC/BFI, 1994). With Oliver Boyd-Barrett, she led the BFI/Open University team that produced the distance-learning teacher training course *Media Education: An Introduction* (BFI/OU, 1992), and she has edited several books on aspects of education and the media including *Primary Media Education: A Curriculum Statement* (BFI, 1989), *New Directions: Media Education Worldwide* (with Evelyne Bevort and Josiane Savino, BFI/CLEMI/UNESCO, 1992) and *Report of the Commission of Inquiry into English* (BFI, 1994). She lives in London and has two children.

**David Buckingham** is a Lecturer in Media Education at the Institute of Education, University of London. He has extensively researched young people's use and understanding of media and has pioneered classroom-based research in media education. He is the author of *Public Secrets: EastEnders and its Audience* (BFI, 1987), and *Children Talking Television: The Making of Television Literacy* (Falmer, 1993); he has edited *Watching Media Learning: Making Sense of Media Education* (Falmer, 1990), *Reading Audiences: Young People and the Media* (Manchester University Press, 1993); and co-authored *Cultural Studies Goes to School: Reading and Teaching Popular Media* (Taylor and Francis, 1994). He is currently directing funded research projects on children's emotional responses to television, and on the role of practical production in media education. He has two sons.

**Helen Cunningham** is a Lecturer in Television Studies and Popular Culture at the University of Derby, where she specialises in youth cultures and new technologies. Her current research is on new communication technologies and uses of the Internet. She has also contributed to the Manchester Broadcasting Symposium.

**Máire Messenger Davies** is Director of Studies for Media Studies at the School of Media, London College of Printing, which is part of the London Institute. She is a former Associate Professor of Broadcasting at Boston University's College of Communication. Before becoming a teacher, she worked as a journalist for many years. She is the author of a number of books, including *Television is Good for Your Kids* (Hilary Shipman, 1989) and, with two psychologist colleagues, *Baby Language* (Unwin Hyman, 1986). She was one of the first holders of the Annenberg Research Fellowships at the Annenberg School for Communication, at the University of Pennsylvania in 1993, where she investigated media literacy in elementary school children. She is the editor of *The Journal of Educational Television*. She has four children.

**Marsha Kinder** is a Professor of Critical Studies in the School of Cinema-Television at the University of Southern California. Her most recent books are *Playing with Power in Movies, Television and Video Games: From Muppet Babies to Teenage Mutant Ninja Turtles* and *Blood Cinema: The Reconstruction of National Identity in Spain* (both from University Of California Press). Her current projects are an anthology on *Children's Media Culture* (forthcoming, Duke University Press) and a book entitled *Violence and Representation*. A long-time contributing board member of *Film Quarterly*, she also serves on the advisory boards of a wide range of journals including *Play Right*, a new magazine for the parents of video-game players. She is co-editor of a new book series called *Consoling Passions: Television and Cultural Power* (forthcoming, Duke University Press). At USC she is part of a collaborative research team developing alternative interactive narratives, including video games that address issues of racial and gender identification.

**Stephen Kline** is Professor of Communications and Director of the Media Analysis Laboratory at Simon Fraser University, Vancouver. His research interests are located broadly in the field of media analysis and audience research, including studies of consumerism, advertising, children's media, play and culture. He is the author of *Out of the Garden: Toys and Children's Culture in the Age of TV Marketing* (Verso, 1993) and co-author, with Leiss and Jhally, of *Social Communication in Advertising* (Methuen, 1986).

**Greg Myers** is a Lecturer in the Department of Linguistics and Modern English Language at the University of Lancaster, where he teaches on the Culture and Communication degree course. His current research is on environmental discourse as part of a project for the Economic and Social Research Council. He is the author of *Writing Biology: Texts in the Social Construction of Scientific Knowledge* (University of Wisconsin, 1990), and *Words in Ads* (Edward Arnold, 1994).

**David Oswell** is a Lecturer in Media and Cultural Studies at Staffordshire University. He is on the executive committee of the campaigning organisation British Action for Children's Television. He has just completed a PhD thesis entitled *Watching with Mother: A Genealogy of the Child Television Audience*. He is currently working on a book about historical audiences, and another on masculinity and sexual identity. His publications include, as co-editor, a collection of essays entitled *Pleasure Principles: Politics, Sexuality and Ethics* (Lawrence and Wishart, 1993). He has two daughters.

**Chris Richards** is a Lecturer in the Department of English, Media and Drama at the Institute of Education, University of London, and previously taught English and Media Studies in secondary schools and further education. He has published a number of essays relating to issues such as: questions of 'race' in teaching Media Studies; teaching popular culture; children's engagement with media texts. He has contributed to journals such as *Teaching London Kids, Screen Education, Screen* and *Changing English*, and to a number of books including *Watching Media Learning: Making Sense of Media Education* (Falmer, 1990), *English and the National Curriculum: Cox's Revolution?* (Kogan Page, 1992) and *Reading Audiences: Young People and the Media* (Manchester University Press, 1993). He is currently investigating and writing about the classroom study of popular music. He has two daughters.

**Ellen Seiter** is Professor of Telecommunications and Graduate Co-ordinator at Indiana University in Bloomington. She is the author of *Sold Separately: Children and Parents in Consumer Culture* (Rutgers University Press, 1993) and is the co-editor of *Remote Control: Television, Audiences and Cultural Power* (Routledge, 1989). She is currently completing an ethnographic study of television and video used in day care centres.

**Terry Staples** is a freelance writer and film programmer specialising in the area of children's cinema. He has programmed films for young audiences at the National Film Theatre, London since 1983, and from 1988–92 programmed the Children's London Film Festival. He is the author of the

*Piccolo Film and Video Factbook* (Piper Books, 1986) and has contributed articles, editorial work and research to a number of publications including *The Cinema Book* (BFI, 1985), *Cinema and the Realms of Enchantment* (BFI, 1993) and *Kinderkino in Europa* (Bundesverband Jugend und Film e.V., 1993). He is currently researching the history of children's cinema in Britain. He lives in London and has two children.

**Cathy Urwin** is a Child Psychotherapist. Before training she worked as a university lecturer in developmental psychology and as a researcher in child development. Her publications cover aspects of mother-infant interaction and early social development, the development of language and communication, and the history of developmental psychology and child analysis. She is co-author, with Henriques, Hollway, Venn and Walkerdine, of *Changing the Subject* (Methuen, 1984), and with Carolyn Steedman and Valerie Walkerdine she is joint editor of *Language, Gender and Childhood* (Routledge, 1985).

**Jack Zipes** is Professor of German at the University of Minnesota. He is also an active storyteller in public schools and has worked with children's theatres in France, Germany, Canada and the United States. His major publications include *The Great Refusal: Studies of the Romantic Hero in German and American Literature* (1970); *Breaking the Magic Spell: Radical Theories of Folk and Fairy Tales* (1979), *Fairy Tales and the Art of Subversion* (1983); *The Trials and Tribulations of Little Red Riding Hood* (1983); *Don't Bet on the Prince: Contemporary Feminist Fairy Tales in North America and England* (1986), *The Brothers Grimm: From Enchanted Forests to the Modern World* (1988) and *Fairy Tale as Myth/Myth as Fairy Tale* (1994). He has also translated and edited *Beauties, Beasts and Enchantment: French Classical Fairy Tales* (1991) and *The Complete Fairy Tales of the Brothers Grimm* (1987), and he has edited *The Penguin Book of Western Fairy Tales* (1991) and *The Outspoken Princess and the Gentle Knight* (1994). He co-edits *The Lion and the Unicorn*, a journal dealing with children's literature.

# INTRODUCTION

## *The Invisible Audience*

Childhood is often seen as another world. Although it is a world we have all visited, it has become inaccessible to us except through the distortions of memory. For most adults, there is an 'essence' of childhood that is unknowable, mysterious, even magical. We can only recapture it vicariously, through the imagination and, perhaps more commonly, through accepted and conventional ideas of what constitutes childhood.

These ideas differ from one society to another and have changed throughout history. In the European Christian tradition, children used to be seen as marked with original sin, and it was thought by most that they needed to be disciplined – sometimes savagely – into acceptable adult behaviour. It is still possible to trace echoes of this view. Many of the terms we use to talk about childhood reflect a notion of the child as an inadequate or incomplete adult: children are 'immature', 'undeveloped' and 'irrational'. But children are also often referred to as though they were not even human, as little monsters, devils or beasts; their capacity for unthinking cruelty may be remarked upon as unnatural and appalling but is often also seen as typical.

In contrast, the Romantics' vision of the child as natural, pure and innocent has functioned since the early nineteenth century as the basis for a more positive, even reverential, view of childhood. Here, the child is seen to lack all the negative aspects of the adult, such as guile, dishonesty, corruption and artifice. The Romantics' construction of the 'natural child' was an essential part of their wider critique of emerging capitalist industrialism. In this critique the child came to represent a sense of loss, of nostalgia for something more authentic, more natural. Later in the nineteenth century this nostalgia became sentimentalised and was drawn into the Victorians' contradictory and complex social myths about sexuality, innocence and gender. Fictional figures such as Dickens' Little Dorrit, childlike, pure and asexual, are nevertheless candidates for marriage: their very innocence renders them desirable.

Adults' ideas and feelings about childhood and children are therefore both powerful and deeply contradictory. Children embody hopes, desires and fears; arguments about how they should be treated, about their moral, intellectual and legal status, are rarely completely rational. In contemporary Western societies the positive values associated with childhood, and the emotions that are invested in them, can be mobilised in support of humanitarian aims: as they are, for example, in charity advertising. Yet they can also be invoked in support of various forms of repressive control, for example in social and educational policy-making. Debates about what children should and should not know, what they should be protected from or compulsorily taught, inevitably act as a focus of much broader moral, political and social concerns. Children represent both a threat and a hope for the future; we see them as both inheritors and usurpers.

**Childhood and the Media**

The media are also, for most of us, another world, albeit one to which we have daily access. We are certain of our own personal relationship to media such as cinema, television, radio and video, but most of us have not yet adjusted to the modern phenomenon of the mass audience. The fact that millions of others may be having the same experience at the same time is hard to comprehend, and threatens our sense of individuality. The most common response to this problem appears to be suspicion, an instinctive wariness; yet such fears almost inevitably seem to focus on 'other people' who are implicitly defined as less controllable and more vulnerable than ourselves. When those 'others' are a group about which we already have contradictory and powerful feelings, such as children, then the combination is explosive and simple solutions are sought. It must be the media that provoke delinquency and violence, cause moral depravity and undermine family life. It must be the media that reduce educational achievement, destroy children's intellectual and imaginative abilities, and brainwash them into racism, sexism and consumerism.

These responses run right across the political spectrum, and they have a long ancestry. The arguments being made in the 1990s about the harmful effects of computer games and violent videos echo those which have been made throughout history in relation to successive 'new' media such as theatre, the press, popular literature, cinema, radio and television. Perhaps the earliest recorded example of such concern is in the work of the Greek philosopher Plato, who proposed to ban the dramatic poets from his ideal Republic, on the grounds that they would have a damaging effect on impressionable young minds.

Such arguments inevitably invoke and rely upon broader ideologies of childhood. Indeed, contemporary media, particularly television, have often been seen as an attack on childhood itself, an invasion of the purity of the child that would inevitably lead to premature corruption. These arguments partly reflect familiar notions of children as innocent and vulnerable, and thus in need of adult protection. Yet as Martin Barker has shown,[1] they also incorporate the older view of the child as a potential monster. If the child is seen as inadequately or partially socialised, the media may have the power to penetrate the veneer of civilisation, and to release the darker, anti-social forces that lie beneath.

However, as Barker argues, it is particular kinds of children, and (by implication) particular kinds of parents, who are the focus of such anxieties.[2] Arguments about the effects of the media on children often hark back to a 'golden age' in which relations between adults and children (and by extension the whole social order) were seen as harmonious. This nostalgia for an imagined world of childhood innocence ultimately derives from a fear of social unrest brought about by 'other people' – that is, the working classes and their uncontrollable children.

Much of this concern has been focused on children's consumption of 'adult' media. The threat which has been posed by each successive technological development – most notably by television and video – has derived from the fact that they seem to offer less and less control for adults. Television has been seen to represent (to quote Neil Postman) 'a total disclosure medium' which effectively undermines adults' control over the knowledge and experiences that are available to children.[3]

Media produced specifically for children, which are the particular focus of this book, are subject to a different kind of moral policing. Producers as well as critics of children's media have been especially stringent in their monitoring of role models, of moral lessons and of stereotypes; and especially extravagant in their claims about the powerful effects of these upon children. The paternalistic approach of British public service broadcasting is perhaps the most obvious example of such pedagogical aims. But a similar premium seems to be placed on moral lessons and 'prosocial' outcomes in the more commercial environment of Hollywood or the US networks, even if this is sometimes seen to be at odds with other, more 'anti-social' aspects of the material, particularly violence. However, there are arguments, expressed most convincingly in critical studies of older forms such as the fairy tale,[4] which suggest that it is both pointless and damaging to exclude all violent and disturbing material from children's cultural experience. Children – like everyone else – need to be able to come to terms with the fear of annihilation, of power (their own as well as other people's), of anger, and of sexuality. Fairy tales, especially in their earlier, unsentimentalised versions, are prime examples of narratives which offer ways of facing up to fundamental dilemmas and anxieties through fantasy.

Whatever their motivation, arguments about the media in relation to children tend to conceive of them as powerful forces in children's socialisation, in some ways more powerful than parents and schools. Whether that power is used for good or evil – whether it does them good or turns them bad – it is essentially pedagogical: it is about instructing children in the ways of the adult world and their eventual place within it.

The problem with such arguments, however, is that they often seem to underestimate the diverse ways in which children themselves may actually make sense of the media and relate them to their other experiences. Such assertions often seem to take the material itself at face value, to assume that what adult analysts (or indeed adult producers) perceive or intend will necessarily correspond with what children perceive. A great deal of academic research on literature and other media over the last two decades has been concerned to challenge this idea, both by looking closely at how real audiences make sense of texts (we are including audio-visual products in this term), but also by looking at the often contradictory ways in which texts address readers.

According to this 'reader-oriented' approach, the text is no longer seen as the vehicle for a pre-determined 'message' that is simply delivered to the reader and can be recovered through critical analysis. On the contrary, the emphasis here is on the ambiguities and inconsistencies of texts, on the issues and questions they open up but cannot close down, on the possibility that the text is not all it claims to be. In order to gain a fuller understanding of texts produced for children, we need to reconsider our assumptions about children, and about how they will read.

**Studying Childhood**

Childhood has been subjected to a particular division of labour within academic study. While sociologists have concerned themselves with 'youth', children have predominantly been seen as the province of psychology, as if they were effectively devoid of social experiences. Children, it would seem, are implicitly regarded as asocial, or perhaps pre-social. This emphasis has had several consequences.

The psychological focus on development – and, more specifically, on cognitive development – has almost inevitably led to an emphasis on children's 'inadequacies' as compared with adults. The cognitivist notion of childhood as a steady progression towards the achievement of adult rationality is effectively based on the kinds of oppositions between adult and child we have noted above. Here again, children are defined in terms of what they apparently cannot do – such as think 'logically' – rather than in terms of what they can do. And it is supposed to be a condition of true adulthood that 'immature' and 'irrational' thinking is left behind.

Recent work in psychology has begun to indicate some of the limitations of this approach.[5] Development, it is argued, is inevitably and inherently a social process: the development of the mind cannot be separated from the social contexts in and through which it occurs. Furthermore, cognition (the intellect) cannot be separated from affect (the emotions). Psychoanalytic accounts of childhood[6] point to several problems with this separation, for example with the notion of childhood as asexual, as non-violent, or as innocent, and with the notion of adulthood as an achieved and fixed state.

The psychological emphasis in studies of childhood has also led to a neglect of the ways in which age functions not merely as a biological category, but also as a social category. Although children's bodies and brains do grow and develop, the meanings that are attached to this, and the ways in which 'development' is defined, are socially and historically variable.

Recent historical and sociological research has begun to offer plentiful examples of such variations. It is now a commonplace observation that our contemporary definitions of childhood, and the practices (of education, of child-rearing, and so on) that support them, are comparatively recent in origin – although there is considerable debate here both about historical accuracy and about the desirability of 'modern' Western notions of childhood.[7] Likewise, sociological research has suggested that such definitions vary substantially both between cultures and within cultures.[8] It is likely, for example, that within a given national culture girls and boys or working-class and middle-class children will be defined differently (and will define themselves differently) in relation to the categories 'child' and 'adult'.

Different social groups clearly possess different notions of how independent children should be, how far they should play a part in domestic labour and in labour outside the home. Particularly in the case of younger children, different ideologies of child-rearing involve different kinds and degrees of accommodation to adult requirements, which begin with the feeding of babies. As this research indicates, 'childhood' is partly a cultural and ideological construction. But it is also a construction that is reproduced and reinforced in everyday practices such as childcare arrangements, schooling, and in both private and public forms of regulation, from smacking (or not) to censorship (or not). Our assumptions about childhood – and adulthood – must be seen, therefore, in the context of our broader social relationships.

### The Child and the Text

In one way or another, however, definitions of childhood and adulthood will always express the power-differential between children and adults. The texts produced by adults for children – both 'literary' and other media texts – are inevitably bound up in these power-relationships. They are one of the primary means by which the respective positions of children and adults are staked out and defined. But they are far from simply coercive. The texts we produce for children also have to speak to children's perceptions of their own positions if they are to make any sense of them. They have to allow opportunities for children to think through their own positions in relation to adult power, and perhaps to offer fantasies of power and control that will enable them to think those relations differently.

Amid the extensive public debates about the effects of the media on children, very little attention has been paid to the material that is produced explicitly for them. Compared with film and television aimed primarily at adults, texts aimed at children have largely been neglected. Our principal aim in this book is to counter that neglect, and to indicate some starting points for a more informed critical debate.

Our focus is primarily on texts – and in particular on film and television – rather than on audiences. Yet perhaps particularly in discussing children's media these two aspects are inextricably connected. This is partly a result of the general academic move, described above, towards more 'reader-oriented' approaches to texts. Yet it also reflects the fact that these texts are defined primarily in terms of their audience. For example, children's television is one of the few areas of television that is thus defined: in Britain the BBC and many companies in the Independent Television network have Children's Departments, and there are three satellite channels exclusively devoted to children's programming. Likewise, many countries have foundations whose function is specifically to fund the production and distribution of films for children. As in the case of censorship, the existence and practice of such institutions is inevitably based on notions of what is appropriate or good for children, and on assumptions about the nature of child development.[9] As many of our contributors argue, the same is true of texts themselves – of the films and television programmes made specifically for children. Yet such texts are produced almost exclusively by people who are by definition very different from their target audience.

This point has been developed in relation to children's fiction in Jacqueline Rose's important study of Peter Pan, which is taken up in David Buckingham's chapter in this book. As Rose argues, 'There is, in one sense, no body of literature which rests so openly on an acknowledged difference between writer and addressee. Children's fiction sets up the child as an outsider to its own process, and then aims, unashamedly, to take the child in.'[10]

Analysing texts produced for children thus raises fundamental questions about how adults imagine the child audience. As well as asking what children want or need from the text, we can try to analyse what it is that adults, through the text, want or demand of the child.[11] Rose has shown how the image of the child can be used to deny our own difficulties and contradictions in relation to childhood, for example to do with language and sexuality. Similar tensions and contradictions have always been present in many visual representations of children. Patricia Holland has shown how images of children (and particularly of young girls) in advertising are often characterised by an underlying tension between notions of innocence and of sexuality.[12] But from cherubs and putti in Renaissance painting, through Victorian portraiture of wistful little girls, to Shirley Temple's mimicry of adult flirtation, erotic images of children have in the past been at least as explicit as they are now, if not more so. It is not condoning child abuse to recognise, and try to understand, the role of desire in adults' attitudes to children.

But the very idea of texts for children also raises the question of who 'children' are: as Rose argues, 'the very idea of speaking to all children serves to close off a set of cultural divisions, divisions in which not only children, but we ourselves, are necessarily caught.'[13] The idea that children, like other subordinate social groups, are somehow all alike in their tastes, interests and aspirations is powerful and widespread. Gender is now the only permissible subdivision of the child audience; and even this, as Ellen Seiter shows in her chapter in this book, can be subsumed by nervous marketing executives into a single, male category once it is realised that girls will accept products aimed at boys, but not vice versa.

However, we must beware of assuming that the 'child audience' actually makes its own purchasing decisions like other audiences. In the case of cinema, parents are clearly in a stronger position to mediate and select what their children watch, since at least in the case of younger children they generally have to accompany them to the cinema and pay for them to get in. Similar arguments apply to the purchase of books. In the case of video rental and sell-through, the economic power of parents is still a factor. But television is almost by definition less 'controllable' as a medium than the cinema or video, despite the encrypting of satellite signals and the availability of parental control facilities (or locking devices) on cable. Exerting control over your children's viewing also means either controlling your own or losing the precious time to yourself that can be gained by sending the children away – perhaps to their own room – to watch television. Now that being at home with the kids is often an option forced by poverty, unemployment or simply fear of violence outside the home, this is a price many parents find they are not prepared to pay.

One of the significant changes since the days of *Watch with Mother* – the BBC pre-school series described in David Oswell's chapter – is in the contemporary assumption that television is now unlikely to be mediated by the parent. However much childcare experts may recommend that you watch with your child, there is very little evidence that parents watch children's television. Indeed, as many of the contributions here indicate, a great deal of contemporary children's television seems to be designed precisely to exclude adults.

Nevertheless, as Rose implies, the effectiveness of this attempt to 'take the child in' to the text may well prove to be limited. Certainly in the case of television there is considerable evidence that the audience is not where the producers of television may imagine it to be. Viewing figures consistently suggest that children prefer 'adult' programmes, and (at least in Britain) children actually form a minority of the audience for their own programmes; the majority being adult groups such as the unemployed and the elderly.[14] More drastically, research has recently suggested that a majority of American children under the age of sixteen have never seen a complete television programme from beginning to end, perhaps largely as a result of the advent of the remote control.[15] Furthermore, as audience researchers have increasingly shown, texts do not simply 'position' readers, as if this were an inexorable, guaranteed process. Children have considerable power to determine their own readings and pleasures: they may well refuse to occupy, or even fail to perceive, the positions our adult analysis identifies as being marked out for them.

How therefore can we assess 'popularity' in relation to children's texts? The 'classic' Disney films, discussed here by Jack Zipes and Chris Richards, are perhaps the most obvious example of the extraordinary longevity of children's audio-visual culture. Tuning in to children's television in just about any country in the world, one is likely to find a familiar roster of US cartoons, many of which may be more than fifty years old. Is there something 'universal' about films like *E.T.* or *Home Alone* or *Teenage Mutant Ninja Turtles* that speaks to children across cultural boundaries, irrespective of other divisions between them? Or is this due to powerful marketing techniques and an absence of other options? For example, the films described in Cary Bazalgette and Terry Staples' chapter, which offer rather different constructions of childhood from those of mainstream Hollywood, are not generally distributed or shown, at least in Britain. Likewise, the worldwide dominance of US media, combined with the general underfunding of children's television, means that finance for home-produced television drama, even in countries like Britain and Australia, is often hard to find.

Nevertheless, the popularity of mainstream Hollywood films for children, and of US toy-based animation, cannot be explained simply in terms of cultural imperialism. Despite the contradictions Rose identifies, children are to some extent assenting to the positions adults mark out for them, not only because they have little choice in the matter, but also because those positions may offer power and pleasure. However patronising or sentimental we may find these images, we need to consider the very different pleasures they may be offering to children.

**The Struggle over 'Quality'**

At the present time, these kinds of tensions and contradictions have taken on a particular urgency. Here in Britain, the future of children's television has been seen to be particularly at risk in the impending transformation of broadcasting through cable and satellite, and through new delivery systems such as video by phone. Broadcasters themselves have argued that children are not a significant enough market for advertisers, so that it will become increasingly impossible to produce, for example, home-grown drama or broadly educative programmes in the new commercial environment. Instead, what has been threatened is an increased reliance on cheap, bought-in programming, largely from the United States. The example of US children's television – the so-called 'KidVid ghetto' – has been held up as an indication of the appalling fate that would await us: it is described as a kind of commercial wasteland, in which children are left helpless and unprotected in the face of a barrage of violence, sexism, consumerism and merchandising. At the same time, moral panics over violence and its effects have led to calls for yet more regulation of both video and television, despite the fact that Britain's existing legislation in this field is already the most stringent in Europe.

While attempts to defend media production for children are extremely important, they also raise some rather more problematic issues. Although much of the debate centres on notions of national (or 'European') identity and on the usual questions about media effects, the key concept that is always raised to counter these is 'quality'. Except in its eighteenth-century usage as a synonym for 'the upper classes', this used to be a noun that was virtually meaningless without a qualifying adjective such as 'high' or 'low'. Yet in the promospeak of late twentieth-century publicity, 'quality' has acquired an accepted meaning that tends to invoke the tradition of worthy BBC documentary and costume drama. In this area as in many others, judgments of quality are inextricably bound up with differences of social class.[16]

Yet, as a number of contributors here suggest, the opposite position appears to be equally untenable. Academic studies of media have historically moved away from evaluation on the grounds of aesthetic taste in favour of a kind of radical relativism – although of course they have been highly preoccupied with forms of ideological evaluation. However, recent debates in this field have pointed to the limitations of a 'populist' approach: the tide is now rapidly turning against the celebration of the 'oppositional' aspects of popular culture which was prevalent in the 1980s.[17] In this context, the issue of cultural value has returned to the agenda. As Charlotte Brunsdon argues,[18] judgments of quality are being made in a great many ways all the time; yet it is possible to recognise the diversity and social distribution of those judgments without assuming that they are completely relative and that therefore it does not matter what kinds of programmes are available.

Apart from anything else, the attempt to avoid the issue of cultural value provides no real basis for the urgent task of devising cultural policy.[19] Yet questions about the fundamental principles of any such cultural policy, and how it might practically be implemented, remain highly problematic.[20] Whose definitions of quality are to count? How are we to ensure good quality, or respond to poor quality? How should quality be related to funding mechanisms? And at what point are we to assess quality – in allocating resources for production, in analysing texts, or in considering the responses of audiences? We might want to assert, for example, that children (and perhaps particularly younger children) have specific 'needs' as an audience, which are related to their developmental level or to their broader emotional or social needs. And we might argue that those needs can only be met by specialist programming. Yet how are those needs to be defined, and by whom? And who is to determine what forms of programming will meet them? Media producers are obviously making these kinds of decisions all the time, but they do so on the grounds of professional intuition. There remains a significant lack of research which might actually inform their practice. The danger here, of course, is of seeing children as a unitary group. Yet we know even less about how the diversity of children's needs might be acknowledged and met by regulators and producers.

The issue of quality is thus problematic, particularly if the grounds for judgment are not made explicit. But it is ultimately unavoidable. In a sense, the real problem here is not with the notion of quality, but with the terms in which the debate has been conducted. In the case of children's television, there has been hardly any investigation into what children themselves might define as 'quality', and very little sense in which they have been able to participate in the debate: they are, in this sense, an invisible audience.

**In Front of the Adults**

This book is thus, inevitably, another book for adults about children's culture. It has been written by adults, and it contains adult readings of texts for which we are not the primary audience. While many contributors seek to question their own position, and to contrast it with that of children, none of us can simply claim to be writing 'on children's behalf'. Indeed, many of the contributors would not particularly want to do so. So limited is the general perception and level of argument about children's audio-visual culture, that it is a basic part of our project here to provide a wider and better-informed view of what is going on, and what has gone on, in production and programming for children. At the same time, we see it as vitally important to introduce new terms for debate about future possibilities for children's audio-visual culture. The themes we have developed in this Introduction will, we hope, become part of that debate.

**Quality, Public Service and the Market**

The troubled issue of 'quality', and whether public service institutions are better placed to deliver it than a market-driven production base, is, as we have pointed out, a constant theme in discussions of what is suitable for children. Several chapters in this book address this theme but in sharply different ways. For Máire Messenger Davies, the public service origin of *Sesame Street* and *Play School* is a key factor in guaranteeing broadcast provision that very young children can genuinely feel belongs to them; she cites adult nostalgia for such programming as validation of her argument. Likewise, Cary Bazalgette and Terry Staples argue for the necessity of public subsidy in supporting indigenous production of films for children outside the US, if children are to have the chance of encountering a genuine cultural range in their cinema-going. David Oswell, however, reveals a different perspective on the public service ethos when he finds the BBC's early programmes for pre-school children transparently ideological in their attempts to inflect family viewing practices.

Stephen Kline offers a view of life without public service broadcasting and uses content analysis to explore the nakedly commercial strategies of toy merchandising through broadcast animation for children, although he admits that this cannot give us the whole story and we need to explore such programmes from the children's point of view as well. David Buckingham takes this idea further in his reflections on the differences between the worthier kinds of children's television which he likes, and the zany nonsense of *Wacaday!* preferred by his own children, arguing that we have to accept the values that drive children's cultural preferences and, in doing so, acknowledge our own needs for triviality and fun. Jack Zipes distinguishes between different kinds of fun, attacking the versions of fairy tales provided over the years by Disney as formulaic and stereotypical, as opposed to the achievements of Jim Henson, Shelley Duvall and Tom Davenport in producing new versions of old tales that are progressive as well as entertaining. Looking at the pro-social message of Turner Entertainment's *Captain Planet*, Greg Myers' response is ambivalent: despite the programme's obvious ideological flaws, his own daughter's co-option of its themes and structures shows how textual analysis cannot reveal children's relationship to a text.

### Difference

Markets need to maximise audiences; there is thus a common cause between the commercial producer of texts for children and nostalgic adult notions about the universality of childhood. But several of the authors in this book dwell upon the essential theme of difference: the many ways in which the child audience may be differentiated culturally, historically, and on grounds of ethnicity and gender. The simple fact that children's interests and preferences are not necessarily the same as adults' is also a common theme. Ellen Seiter's study from a feminist perspective of the widely reviled *My Little Pony* stories argues against the easy assumption that they are merely exploitative, and in favour of considering the pleasures they may offer to very young girls. Similarly Chris Richards studies the ways in which girls appropriate the songs in *The Little Mermaid* and speculates about the ways in which this may allow an exploration of sexuality and adulthood through games and dancing. Like Richards, Helen Cunningham draws upon experiences from her own family in exploring the world of computer games and, again, resists the commonplace assumption that violent content guarantees an automatic appeal to a male audience in order to argue for the pleasures these games make available to girls. While these chapters deal with the relationship between text and audience, Martin Barker's production study of *Alternity*, a new comic that was not, in the end, actually published, reveals interesting detail about the relationship between producers and audiences and how the pleasures and preferences of the young male audience were courted by Fleetway publishers.

Fewer chapters are concerned with cultural and historical differences, and we hope that further publications in this field will take up the possibilities opened up here. Cary Bazalgette and Terry Staples' chapter touches on both: the divergence between the European-style 'children's film' and the US-style 'family film' is traced historically, and differences between European and 'third world' subsidised production for children are exemplified in their choice for detailed analysis of the Danish *Me and Mama Mia* and the Iranian *Where is My Friend's House?* David Oswell's chapter is wholly historical in its study of a key moment in British public service broadcasting, while Máire Messenger Davies offers a comparison between US and UK television; this is a valuable reminder that the two systems are not the same, and that temptations to apply research findings from one in the context of the other should be resisted.

### Childhood and Adulthood

Childhood and adulthood is, inevitably, the key opposition that has to be explored in any study of children's culture. How children are represented, to themselves and to adults; how children are addressed, and in what ways – or indeed whether – this has to be different from the way adults are addressed; how the family is constructed and reconstructed as the prime arena in which child-adult relationships are marked out: the social practices of generational difference are not natural and eternal but are maintained through processes like these. Marsha Kinder's chapter covers a wide range of both cinema and television in exploring the ways in which the drive to maximise audiences is breaking down the conventional markers of generational difference: children are seen behaving like adults, while adults are addressed as though they were children. This question of address is further analysed in other chapters. The ways in which casting, camera angle and editing style can be child-oriented or adult-oriented are discussed in Cary Bazalgette and Terry Staples' chapter; David Buckingham suggests that presentation styles which he finds offensively patronising maybe read by children as pleasurably complicit; David Oswell shows how, in the early 50s, point of view and voice-over function to draw in the adult viewer – the mother – to share television watching with the pre-school child. How families or parts of families share their cultural preferences or, alternatively, use them to establish boundaries, is a theme in these and several other chapters, particularly those by Chris Richards and Helen Cunningham.

**Fantasy**

Right-wing pressure to regulate and censor cultural production for children to 'protect their innocence' has been usefully countered in the realm of literature by writers such as Bruno Bettelheim, Margaret and Michael Rustin, Jack Zipes and Alison Lurie.[21] There is still a powerful need for similar analyses in the field of audio-visual culture. Four chapters in this book may be seen as setting the agenda for such work. Drawing on her experiences in child therapy, Cathy Urwin sees *Teenage Mutant Ninja Turtles* as a story rich in potential for nurturing children's psychic growth, were it not for the deeply unsatisfactory narrative resolution – motivated by commercial interest in possible sequels. Jack Zipes argues persuasively for allowing children to counter and subvert the oppressive versions of 'reality' constructed by adults who are caught within patriarchal and racist agendas. Zipes sees Disney as irrevocably caught up in these agendas, but Chris Richards argues that the domestic viewing context of video allows little girls to learn and appropriate the powerful fantasy world created in the song and dance sequences of Disney's *The Little Mermaid*, and hence to explore adult roles through their own dancing. A similar appropriation of the fantasy elements of animation is described in Greg Myers' analysis of the complex pattern of oppositions within the *Captain Planet* stories: he suggests that they may engender powerful ideas about co-operation, individual power and the potential for change, beyond the apparently bland ecological message.

This book developed initially out of the 1992 British Film Institute Summer School, *Borderlines*, and from a seminar held later that year in association with the Children's London Film Festival. At both events it was clear that informed study of audio-visual productions for children –

how they can be defined, how they are produced, circulated and received – is long overdue. It is about time that children's culture is taken seriously. We hope that this book is the first of many in a relatively unexplored field.

Cary Bazalgette, David Buckingham
London, June 1994

NOTES

1. Martin Barker, *Comics: Ideology, Power and the Critics* (Manchester: Manchester University Press, 1989).
2. See also Martin Barker (ed.), *The Video Nasties* (London: Pluto, 1984).
3. Neil Postman, *The Disappearance of Childhood* (London: W. H. Allen, 1983).
4. See Bruno Bettelheim, *The Uses of Enchantment* (Harmondsworth: Penguin, 1991), and Jack Zipes, *The Brothers Grimm: From Enchanted Forests to the Modern World* (London: Routledge, 1988).
5. See, for example, M. Richards and P. Light (eds.), *Children of Social Worlds* (Cambridge: Polity Press, 1986).
6. Most notably the work of Melanie Klein, e.g. *The Psychoanalysis of Children* (London: Virago, 1989).
7. See, for example, Philippe Aries, *Centuries of Childhood* (Harmondsworth: Penguin, 1973), and Lloyd de Mause, *The History of Childhood* (New York: Souvenir Press, 1974).
8. See A. James and A. Prout (eds.), *Constructing and Reconstructing Childhood: Contemporary Issues in the Sociological Study of Childhood* (London: Falmer Press, 1990).
9. For a discussion of this issue in relation to censorship, see Julian Wood, 'Repeatable pleasures: notes on young people's use of video', in David Buckingham (ed.), *Reading Audiences: Young People and the Media* (Manchester: Manchester University Press, 1993).
10. Jacqueline Rose, *The Case of Peter Pan: Or the Impossibility of Children's Fiction* (London: Macmillan, 1984), p. 2.
11. Ibid., p. 137.
12. Patricia Holland, *What is a Child? Popular Images of Childhood* (London: Virago, 1992).
13. Rose, *The Case of Peter Pan*, p. 7.
14. See Jay G. Blumler, *The Future of Children's Television in Britain: An Enquiry for the Broadcasting Standards Council* (London: Broadcasting Standards Council, 1992), p. 17.
15. A statistic quoted in Richard Kearney, *The Wake of Imagination: Towards a Post-Modern Culture* (Minneapolis: University of Minnesota Press, 1988).
16. See, for example, Pierre Bourdieu, *Distinction: A Social Critique of the Judgment of Taste* (London: Routledge and Kegan Paul, 1984); Kim Schroder, 'Cultural quality: search for a phantom', paper presented to the International Television Studies Conference, London, 1988; and Ien Ang, *Watching 'Dallas': Soap Opera and the Melodramatic Imagination* (London: Methuen, 1985).
17. This has been particularly apparent in the negative reception of the recent work of John Fiske, such as *Television Culture* (London: Methuen, 1987) and *Understanding Popular Culture* (London: Unwin, Hyman, 1990).
18. Charlotte Brunsdon, 'Problems with quality', *Screen*, vol. 31 no. 1, Spring 1990, pp. 67–90.
19. On the relation between academic studies and cultural policy, see Stuart Cunningham, *Framing Culture* (Sydney: Allen and Unwin, 1992).
20. For a thoughtful discussion of this issue, see James A. Anderson, Timothy P.

Meyer and Anne Hexamer, 'An examination of the assumptions underlying telecommunications social policies treating children as a specialised audience', in M. Burgoon (ed.), *Communication Yearbook 5* (New Brunswick: Transaction Books, 1982).

21. Bettelheim, *The Uses of Enchantment*; Zipes, *The Brothers Grimm*; Margaret and Michael Rustin, *Narratives of Love and Loss* (London: Verso, 1987); Alison Lurie, *Don't Tell the Grownups: Subversive Children's Literature* (London: Bloomsbury, 1990).

# BABES 'N' THE HOOD

*Pre-school Television and its Audiences in the United States and Britain*

MAIRE MESSENGER DAVIES

It's a beautiful day in the neighborhood, a beautiful day in the neighborhood . . .

Fred Rogers, *Mister Rogers' Neighborhood.*

Our audience is one child in a room.

Cynthia Felgate, Executive Producer of *Play School*, 1981.

Two years ago, at the American university where I was teaching, the graduation ceremony erupted when one of the guest speakers, Fred Rogers, presenter of the long-running pre-school programme *Mister Rogers' Neighborhood*, stepped to the podium. In sweltering heat in the university's sports stadium, thousands of red-robed graduands from all kinds of ethnic backgrounds threw their mortarboards into the air and cheered and yelled and whistled. Elderly professors on the platform looked bemused; Mr Rogers' fellow speaker, the Peruvian novelist Mario Vargas Llosa, looked amused. The ceremony seemed stalled, until Mr Rogers suggested: 'Shall we sit down and sing together?' (a line from his show). He and the students then sang 'It's a beautiful day in the neighborhood' and the stadium fell quiet, except for the occasional sob from a parent.

A colleague who heard the ceremony on local radio described the moment as 'magic', and so it was. The symbolic graduation from childhood to adulthood could not have been crystallised more appropriately – and it was spontaneous too, a live radio producer's dream. Other readings were excavated later. Cultural pessimists at the ceremony saw it as depressing evidence of American television's hegemony: all cultural differences reduced to a banal little song. Cultural optimists saw it more as an example of the often-failed American dream: the ability to unite disparate people in an unexpectedly life-enhancing way. It was certainly a striking example of the durable power of early experiences in children's lives, particularly when those experiences come in the form of entertainment.

Happily for the radio producers, too, the Mr Rogers episode gave dramatic resonance to the themes next addressed by Vargas Llosa, the main speaker. Referring to the Quatercentenary of the Columbus expedition – an extremely controversial topic on American campuses in 1992 – he talked about '*mestizaje*' – the assimilation of Europeans and Africans with native Americans, which had been rapid in South America and 'very slow' in the United States and Canada. 'In South America, all families have an Indian or African background . . . Whether we are Indian, white, black, mulatto or mestizo, when we Peruvians or Mexicans speak, we are enacting the rituals . . . of Incas, Aztecs and other pre-Columbian cultures.' He argued that *mestizaje* was 'irreversible' and that a 'quiet contempt for the *mestizo* condition' was the mark of the racist.

The opening credits of *Sesame Street*, the flagship pre-school programme in the United States, look like a demonstration of *mestizaje*. They are shot on film in the streets and Central Park of New York City, where the programme is produced. Young children from about three to seven are shown playing culturally universal games and activities: drawing on the ground; swimming; bouncing; throwing and hitting balls; trustingly holding hands with each other, and with an older person, who in this case happens to be Big Bird, a large yellow Muppet. The children are of different racial origins: African-American, Hispanic, blond and dark Caucasians, Asian, and mixtures of them all. However, they are all presented as natives of New York City in the United States of America, having been brought together by the common cultural experiences firstly of play and secondly of television. *Sesame Street*, like *Mister Rogers' Neighborhood*, is presented as a real location: a friendly place where children from different cultural backgrounds are welcome – and, above all, prioritised. It is their place: 'Where the air is sweet. Can you tell me how to get, how to get to Sesame Street.'

This chapter looks at the 'friendly places' made available for young children to 'visit' in the television systems of Britain and the United States, and compares them on a number of dimensions: their origins and purposes; their scheduling and broadcasting contexts; their content, including overtly educational content; their personnel; their style of addressing the child audience; their technical and other production effects. Underlying all these are assumptions about the nature of the audience, some of which have to be deduced from looking at the programmes (and are thus, as David Buckingham has argued, open to different interpretations). Others have been specifically articulated by the producers. Indeed, pre-school television is very unusual in having producers who see it as part of their job to be thoroughly well-informed about their audience, to the extent of having a large, sophisticated research operation in the case of *Sesame Street* and less formalised, but equally regular, forms of feedback in the case of British programmes.

The main sources of comparison in this chapter will be the US's *Sesame Street* and the British *Playdays/Play School*, with some references to other programmes. This choice of comparison, while recognising that the British broadcasting system gives much higher priority to children's programming than does the US system, is not intended to make a glib cultural contrast between US commercial glitz and UK public service purity. *Mister Rogers' Neighborhood* gives the lie to this stereotype, being very similar to *Play School* in its slow, conversational style, which has changed very little in twenty years; the astonishingly popular *Barney*, too, shows that US programme-makers need no help in producing simple (and, in this case, sugary and banal) programmes for the very young. In return, British children's television has long since caught up on the glitz front; a young American, weaned on MTV, would feel very much at home in front of the jazzy graphics and rock music accompaniments of much BBC and ITV children's programming.

The main points of similarity between *Sesame Street* and *Play School/Playdays*, are that they each have explicit prosocial goals, and are flagship programmes for their respective systems: they represent a philosophy of 'doing good' – the acceptable face of television to a public not always convinced that watching TV is good for children. *Playdays* is only one of a number of British children's television programmes with such a mission; *Blue Peter, Newsround* and a wealth of expensive drama on both BBC and ITV can also claim 'flagship' status in the UK. *Sesame Street*, on the other hand, although supported by a few other public service educational programmes for older children, such as *3–2–1– Contact*, stands virtually alone in American television as a cause for pride in children's programming – and even it comes under conservative fire from time to time, as in Lawrence Jarvik's scornful attack in a recent *New York Times* on the programme's 'waste' of public funds.[3]

*Sesame Street* and *Play School/Playdays* share a common target age group. They are both aimed at children between the ages of two and six, and they are both informed by an explicit philosophy of caring and nurturing which goes well beyond the standard broadcasting functions of informing, educating and entertaining. The BBC's nickname 'Auntie' might well be applied to both of them. Both, in their different ways, feature kind, grown-up advice about teeth-cleaning, and coping with new baby sisters, and finding one's way about in the world, which would be deemed unnecessary for older people. The imaginary neighbourhoods of *Sesame Street* and the Playbus route are intentionally happy, friendly places where people treat each other considerately, even though painful events such as illness or even death sometimes occur. A further similarity is that, despite their informative content, they are not intended to be viewed in an educational setting. They are aimed at the child at home, who turns to television primarily for entertainment. As such they are certainly 'pitching' for the child's 'friendship' in an approachable way – but since they are also part of the intensely competitive (particularly in the US) broadcast market, they have to take their chances in the audience ratings system.

When a programme is 'positioned' as entertainment, rather than as 'education' or 'schools programming', the main criterion for assessing its relationship with the audience is not what teachers or adults think, but whether the child likes it enough to watch it voluntarily. The producers have to know their audience, and how to encourage it to stay tuned in. They also need a rationale for serving this not very powerful group, which will attract funding and institutional support. In Britain, a sufficient rationale for pre-school programming, up to now, has been the general public service ethos of British broadcasting, particularly in the BBC. Such an ethos has never been available to support children's programmes in the United States.[4]

**Origins and Purposes**

A major rationale in the development of pre-school programming, especially in the United States, was to prepare children for formal schooling. Work on *Sesame Street* began in 1966 when TV producer Joan Ganz Cooney approached the Carnegie Foundation for funding for 'a revolutionary new preschool television program . . . that would seek to educate young children using the techniques and appeal of commercial television. Unlike previous educational TV programs, this one would be designed to address the needs of poor inner-city children.'[5] *Sesame Street* was unlike previous programmes in a number of other ways: in its desire to measure success 'by the extent to which it appealed to children', in Lovelace's words, as well as meeting educational goals; in its unique partnership between research and production; and in its use of the entertaining techniques of commercial television to attract the child viewer at home, which was, and remains, controversial.[6]

Remedying the deprivation of the 'lower-class child' was a key factor in attracting funding, including an initial grant of $4 million from the Federal government. According to Edward Palmer, one of the programme's founders, 'for children of low-income circumstances . . . it would provide a conceptually and verbally rich learning experience, and important early exposure to school related skills, all of which, we know, are less available to them in their homes, than to their middle-class peers in theirs.'[7] This 'deficit model' of poor children was at that very time beginning to be questioned: William Labov and colleagues produced their account of the linguistic correctness of Black English in 1968;[8] a summary of research challenging the 'myth of the deprived child' was produced by Herbert Ginsburg in 1972.[9] Nevertheless, the rationale for pre-school television provision, based on the need to prepare 'disadvantaged' children for the literacy and numeracy skills of formal schooling, has remained a major plank in Children's Television Workshop's case for support. Letter and number recognition continue to be major ingredients of *Sesame Street.* Its setting continues to be recognisably inner-city, where primarily poor people live.

The rationale for British pre-school programming was based on somewhat different ideas of the audience. In her history of children's television, *Into the Box of Delights*,[10] Anna Home, currently Head of Children's Programmes at the BBC, describes how *Play School* was created in 1964 to be 'a new kind of programme for pre-school children' on the new channel, BBC2. As with *Sesame Street*, part of the impetus for it came from 'a great deal of debate about the poor provision of nursery education'. But the way it was established seems to have been rather casual compared with its US counterpart. It had a precedent, in the cosy format of BBC Radio's *Listen with Mother*: 'Michael Peacock, Chief of Programmes for the new channel, invited Joy Whitby, formerly a producer of radio's *Listen with Mother*, to create a new daily programme for young children . . . The *Play School* team was relatively inexperienced in television terms.'[11] *Play School* had a huge stroke of luck when a power failure wiped out the opening night of BBC2 on 21 May 1964. Thus the 'modest new programme' was the first thing to appear on the new channel next morning – a promotional coup that no marketing strategy could have planned.

In the US, CTW's promotional techniques left nothing to chance. Adopting the marketing strategies of commercial television, they set out 'to prove that . . . a daily, hour-long educational program, directed to the preschool population, could successfully compete in the open television market-place against all that the commercial medium had to offer. It would achieve its educational goals by embracing the best of contemporary television entertainment techniques.'[12] The programme was to be aired on the public television network, then only recently (1964) established in the US, but it would still be competing with the much more powerful and successful commercial networks. In 1968, Joan Ganz Cooney and her assistant 'visited the top twenty-five markets . . . to achieve wide distribution in stations covering about 60 per cent of the population.'[13] Since then *Sesame Street*'s coverage of PBS station 'markets' in the US and its penetration of the pre-school audience has reached nearly 100 per cent. It also has a wide English-language international market and has been translated into thirteen other languages around the world. Because of this need to compete in the aggressively commercial environment of American broadcasting, CTW's idea of their audience had to be predicated on the concept of the market, a market to be attracted and held against commercial opposition. The programme had above all to be entertaining, or it would not attract viewers.

The British founders of *Play School* conceptualised the audience differently from CTW's concept of the market and the deprived 'lower-class child'. As Anna Home put it: 'One of the basic philosophies of the programme was to address the individual child at home, not the audience en masse, and it was important to encourage participation. Members of the production team used to visit children at home to assess how successful the programme was in this and other areas.'[14] Cynthia Felgate, the Executive Producer of *Play School* and the founder of its successor, *Playdays*, described the audience she and her colleagues were addressing as 'one child in a room'.[15] This personalised notion of the audience also gave rise to differences in production techniques and scheduling between the British and US models, discussed in more detail below. It could be argued that *Sesame Street* was conceived as a product, *Play School* as a conversation. (Neither conception, of course, was necessarily how the young child saw it, or how it actually worked.)

Despite wanting to supplement the lack of nursery provision, *Play School*, like most British children's television, defined itself institutionally as entertainment, not education – a distinction maintained in the structure of British TV, which has separate Children's and Schools departments in the BBC and some ITV companies. British children's producers fight very shy of the label 'educator'; for the Americans it is proudly worn. John Lane, a one-time director of *Play School*, in an interview described himself and his colleagues as 'adults from a number of different backgrounds – *not* educational or academic ones . . . *Play School*, to a child, is a place where two grownups live.' Unlike *Sesame Street*, too, the rationale for *Play School* does not seem to have made distinctions between children of more or less educationally deprived social classes, although it *was* socially representative. From the start it used presenters with different ethnic and regional origins. It was also the first British programme for young children to use male presenters.

The style of *Play School* and of other British pre-school programmes, particularly in their early days (*Andy Pandy* springs to mind), has been parodied for being too cosily middle-class. But there is no deficit model of working-class children behind it. In the Reithian tradition of raising the sights of the masses, *Play School* was aimed equally, if paternalistically, at everyone. In this tradition, producers do not pander to 'what consumers want'; they give people what they believe to be good for them. Working-class children thus get as good, or as bad, programmes as middle-class children do. State-of-the-art graphics, pop music on *Blue Peter* and grunge-clad presenters notwithstanding, this tradition continues strongly in British children's television, and runs very much counter to current technology-led trends in 'narrowcasting', with their specifically targeted markets.

**Scheduling**

The scheduling of pre-school programmes such as *Sesame Street* and *Playdays* reflects the assumption that the pre-school audience is at home in the daytime and that it gets up early: the first transmission of *Sesame Street* in the Boston market (where research for this chapter was done) is on WGBH's Channel 2, at 7 a.m. Another is shown at 12 noon, and another at 3.30 p.m. Boston can also receive New Hampshire public television, where *Sesame Street* is aired at 8 a.m. and 5.30 p.m. A young Bostonian could thus watch the programme almost all day long, but there is no way for her to know which programmes are going to be shown: whether they will include segments seen before or lessons about particular topics. Guest stars, such as Robin Williams or Candice Bergen, will sometimes be billed in the *TV Guide*, but otherwise there is little information in the *TV Guide* or in the form of programme trails or, as with *Playdays*, in the form of a predictable daily format about what to expect or why; the child tunes in and waits to see. This can be extremely annoying for those who like to plan their viewing. For instance, when Hillary Clinton, in a superb public relations coup both for CTW and herself, appeared on *Sesame Street* and was pictured on the cover of *TV Guide* with Big Bird in November 1993, there was no clear indication in *TV Guide* to tell us on which, of all the many screenings of the programme, she would appear. So we missed her. As is necessary in a system offering a choice of seventy channels, channel surfing or 'grazing', not content-led planning, has become the expected mode of viewing. You zap through the channels at around 12.30 and hope you will hit Hillary. If not, the other sixty-nine will offer something.

**Contexts**

On the public television channels, *Sesame Street* is part of a continuous daytime block of young children's programmes, including *Mister Rogers' Neighborhood, Shining Time Station* (a.k.a. 'Thomas the Tank Engine', complete with Ringo), and *Barney,* the purple Dinosaur, who seems to have started a trend in the relationship between the First Family and pre-school TV – he featured in President Clinton's Inauguration parade. The three commercial networks, ABC, CBS and NBC, PBS's national network competitors, show no children's programmes at all on weekdays, although they show cartoons at weekends. The Fox network (owned by Rupert Murdoch) shows cartoons during the day. So do the three other local stations in the Boston market not affiliated to networks. Disney and Nickelodeon, on cable, provide programming for older children. Despite recent legislation requiring commercial stations to provide informational programming for children, or risk losing their licences, the public network is still the main source of such programming. Thus PBS is virtually the only transmitter of non-animation young children's programming in the United States. They have cornered the 'market'.

*Playdays,* too, is part of a block of programmes, but these are distributed across BBC1 and 2, ITV and Channel 4 in a comparatively co-ordinated way. At the time of writing, *Playdays* is shown on BBC1 at 10 a.m.; the next pre-school offerings are *Sesame Street* on C4 at 12.30 p.m.; then there is original UK programming at 1.20 on BBC2 and 1.30 on C4. The next block of children's programming on BBC1 is between 3.50 and 5.35 p.m., with a variety of shows aimed at school-age children. ITV has an afternoon period of children's programming between 3.30 and 5.10. Satellite provides the Children's Channel and Nickelodeon all day; many of their programmes are British repeats or American imports, and there is a high proportion of animation.

*Playdays* is constructed as a weekly series and assumes a continuity in the audience from one day to the next and one week to the next. Each day's programme is built around a different 'Stop': the central link is a playbus going from stop to stop. Thus Monday is The Why Bird Stop (general knowledge); Tuesday is The Playground Stop (featuring real children); Wednesday, The Roundabout (games, magic, puzzles); Thursday, Patch Stop (location and Nature); Friday, The Tent Stop (fantasy, narrative drama). Each stop has its own presenter and regular cast of characters. Each day's programme is original, although some complete programmes may be repeated at holiday and other times. The same stories or songs may also be used in different ways over time. In keeping programming original, and fairly closely tied to contemporary and seasonal events, producers assume that the audience for Wednesday is pretty much the same audience as for last Wednesday, or for Tuesday. Thus it is assumed that audience and producers/performers are sharing common, contemporaneous experiences. It could be risky for producers to alienate the audience by repeating material they have only recently seen – rather like asking a child the same routine question about his day, when he's already told you an hour ago.

This recognition of the ongoing nature of the audience is much less the case with *Sesame Street*, where the same segment may turn up in two different programmes in the same week. The programme's format encourages mixing, matching and recycling of segments – and this is also cost-effective. *Play School, Playdays'* predecessor, relied even more on a sense of shared continuity with the audience. The same presenters would present a whole week's programmes, built round a single theme or a seasonal topic. Certain features of the set always remained the same – for instance the round, square and arched windows, which have passed into legend. The toys, too – Humpty, Hamble and co. – remained constant. In John Lane's words, '*Play School* and its presenters and characters may be one of the few sources of security children have in their lives.'[16] When *Play School* gave way to *Playdays* in 1988, there was a national outcry: 'Wicked Auntie Beeb is set to axe four of TV's top stars, Big Ted, Little Ted, Jemima and Humpty', cried the *Daily Star*.

This conceptualises the audience as a group known personally to the producers, sharing common experiences with them, as in an extended family. Linked stories and themes, as in *Play School*, or regular stops, as in *Playdays*, assume an audience which has been there before and will be there again. Such a conception is easier in a relatively small country like Britain. In the US, with its 250 million population and its three different time zones, it is simply not possible to assume that most of the nation's young children will be sitting down together at the same time, as can be assumed with *Playdays*. If Children's Television Workshop relied on reading out birthday greetings for members of its audience before each transmission of *Sesame Street*, as happens before *Playdays*, it would be swamped by the sheer number of greetings it would have to handle.

But the conception of the audience as part of a community, of which the producers are also part, demonstrates a difference of philosophy as well as a difference in population size. Within a public service system, which, despite deregulation, the British system still is, producers assume a quasi-parental role towards the young child audience (and indeed towards the adult audience too); the resultant illusion of personal intimacy with the audience gives rise to the characteristic chatty tone of British children's TV. In a commercially dominated system such as the USA's, the audience has to be defined in a more distanced way, as 'consumers' – the prize to be won from competitors – or as recipients of public munificence – the 'deprived'. Further, as Rowland and Tracey point out, the notion of public service broadcasting assumes a 'shared national culture' – and, in assuming it, helps to bring it about.[17] It is interesting that, despite the public service underpinning of the British *commercial* system, which until recently has been highly regulated, ITV's children's programming has found this sense of dialogue with the audience more difficult to achieve. Although commercial television has produced many successful and popular pre-school shows, such as *Rainbow* (Thames), *Pob's Programme* (Channel 4) or *Pipkins* (Central), the fragmented nature of the commercial system, with different companies competing for network space, makes the centralised administration of children's shows more difficult.

In the increasingly important game of 'niche marketing' in broadcasting, 'Children's BBC' benefits from being the unified product of one institution, and has succeeded in building up a very successful 'corporate image', complete with its own locale (the Broom Cupboard), its own menagerie (Gordon the Gopher, Edd the Duck) and its own peculiar range of shared references with its audience. BBC pre-school programmes such as *Playdays*, by sharing presenters, theme music and 'corporate logos' with the rest of the children's output, help to locate their young audience within the wider child community – the 'big kids' world of older siblings, friends and schoolfellows, the world of *Grange Hill*, *Live and Kicking* and *Newsround*. This world, with its deliberate microcosmic duplication of the adult output, begins to enculturate the child viewer into becoming an audience member of the grown-up world of British broadcasting. Whether 'Adults' BBC' will continue to be such a recognisable entity as 'Children's BBC', history will decide; at the time of writing (Winter 1993), its future is a matter of intense debate.

**Two Programmes**

To focus the differences and similarities between the US and British programmes, I chose to analyse two programmes: one edition of *Playdays* and one transmission of *Sesame Street*. Both were transmitted during August, school holidays in both countries. The *Playdays* programme was Tuesday's 'The Roundabout Stop', shown at 10.30 a.m. *Sesame Street* was shown at 12 noon on a Thursday in Boston. Although *Sesame Street* is shown in Britain too, I chose to watch it in the US to compare the way the programmes were 'framed' by their preceding and following output.

*Playdays* was preceded by a programme for older children, *Ipso Facto*, part of the BBC's holiday viewing for children (a repeat). *Ipso Facto* is an informational programme featuring topical, often controversial questions. This one dealt with death. It had a lively, young, female presenter and it included scenes of a funeral. It was a good example of the kind of programme that British children's television does outstandingly well, handling the topic in a forthright, sensitive way which is all too rarely found on adult television. A news bulletin followed, featuring an item about John Demjanjuk, accused of being 'Ivan the Terrible', the concentration camp torturer. Then there was the CBBC live link – with 'Philippa' reading out birthday greetings, in the approved confidential and somewhat frenetic style which has become the fashion for children's television presenters in

Britain (in contrast to the dignified Mister Rogers, and to elderly Muppets such as Bert and Ernie). There was also a puzzle involving mime, and children were invited to phone in their solutions. An automatic assumption of live and immediate audience interaction was established. This assumption is justified; CBBC gets many thousands of phone calls and letters every year.

*Sesame Street* was preceded by an episode of *Barney* the Dinosaur, in which Barney visited a restaurant accompanied by a female dinosaur with a breathy voice and long fluttery eyelashes. Then there was an announcement from the Corporation of Public Broadcasting, which finances public television, that the programme had been partially financed by the Lyons Group and by 'viewers like you'. Next there was an appeal from the local public TV station, WGBH, for $260,000 by 31 August from 'viewers like you'. A telephone number was given for viewers to 'make their pledges' with their credit card numbers. Then came the announcement for *Sesame Street*: 'Local broadcast of *Sesame Street* is made in partnership with McDonald's', accompanied by the McDonald's logo. Finally, the theme song of *Sesame Street* was heard – 'Sunny day, you can go miles away, on my way, to where the air is sweet . . .' – accompanied by its attractive, multicultural images of young children playing in New York's Central Park. The infant Bostonian, positioned in front of her TV set waiting for her favourite pre-school programme, could not have been sent a clearer message that in television, including public television, there is no such thing as a free lunch: consumers – 'viewers like you' – have to pay, and even Big Bird and his friends are only made possible through the corporate sponsorship of Lyons and McDonald's.

**Content**

Each *Playdays* programme opens with an animated credits sequence showing a playbus driving through both rural and urban scenes, with a childish, Northern England voice announcing the arrival of the bus at the day's stop. Each programme is introduced by its own regular presenter. The regular presenter of the Roundabout Stop is 'Mr Jolly', a bowler-hatted figure dressed like an old-fashioned fairground barker. He speaks in a stage-cockney style and provides a link for all the events in the programme.

The programme I saw opened with a shot of the roundabout going round, carrying half a dozen children aged five or six, and Mr Jolly's voice on the soundtrack saying ''ello, 'ello'. This programme used a regular format (again, relying on the audience's familiarity with the show) to set up a 'clue' on the roundabout; this clue was a cutout model of a large blue boot. Further clues were set up on the roundabout throughout the programme – a hat, a clown, a cardboard smile; they eventually led to a recognition of the programme's running 'mystery' theme which the children had to solve – a song about a laughing policeman. The climax to the show was the performance of this song by the presenters and the children. Mr Jolly was aided by another bowler-hatted character called the Giggler, played by a black actor. Both these characters had show-business connotations: the Giggler told vaudeville-type jokes and was dressed like Max Miller; Mr Jolly sang jolly songs and operated the roundabout. The whole programme, though punctuated by songs, rhymes, a sequence about the number 9 (as in *Sesame Street*), a puppet interlude and a craft session making paper hats, was integrated by the hunt for solutions to the 'mystery', which presumed that the audience would watch from start to finish.

Everything took place in the studio, with visual variety being provided by cuts between the action and musical sequences, and changes in lighting. At the end, when all the clues were assembled, a point was made of finding the words of the song in a book – another *Play School/Playdays* tradition, emphasising the importance of literacy. The programme closed with the children riding away on the roundabout. Afterwards, there was a trail for the following day's programme, The Patch Stop, a less studio-bound offering which takes children out on location.

*Playdays* has gone through some changes since it was first conceived by Cynthia Felgate. But her original unified conception of a weekly series of contrasting programmes, which supplement each other and hence assume a continuity in the audience, has not changed. Her original six aims were to incorporate: 'a variety of settings and styles of presentation'; 'attractive regular characters'; formats which combined both 'familiarity and innovation'; different relationships between presenters and viewing child; a combination of 'truthfulness and fantasy'; and a recognition of 'the very different circumstances in which the audience live and view . . . to let the lonely and less fortunate child find contact through the screen.'[18] There is a glimpse of 'a deficit model' here, but it carefully avoids expressing the deficit in terms of education or social class. A lonely or less fortunate child could just as easily be a middle-class child as a poor one. *Playdays*, both in conception and in execution, avoids any overt attempt to be seen educating children or compensating for educational deprivation. Number, books, concepts, language are introduced, but they are incidental to the overall storyline, which is couched in the form of a game, played between the TV characters, the children on the screen and the audience. The playfulness is underlined by making the presenters entertainers rather than instructors or adult hosts. The children on the screen could be from any social class (although they had clearly taken pains to look clean and well-behaved). They actually came from the Chicken Shed theatre company, a London-based drama group which integrates able-bodied and disabled children.

*Sesame Street* is more than twice as long as *Playdays* – it lasts an hour. The programme's own formative research in the 1960s indicated that children's attention decreases with longer items; an hour-long programme reflects an assumption by the producers that attention will not be sustained throughout, and that children will tune in and out of the show.[19] Thus *Sesame Street* is based on what John Ellis has described as the characteristic form of television – the segment (there were forty segments in the edition I viewed).[20] With this format, no attempt is made to create narrative unity between one section of the programme and another, although there may be some thematic unities. For instance, in the programme I analysed there was a running theme of performance, with recurring sketches featuring a Muppet character called Sir John Feelgood. This purely adult theatrical allusion is typical of the huge range of cultural references scattered through every episode of *Sesame Street*: this edition included references to Broadway, *Cat on a Hot Tin Roof*, *Hamlet*, classical choral singing, blues and jazz, Robin Williams doing a John Wayne impression, and a variety of artistic styles in animation. As negative critics have noted, such allusions make the programme more appealing to adults and older children than to the very young. However, a positive side effect of this is to encourage adults to watch with their children. Gavriel Salomon's research in Israel has shown that when mothers co-view *Sesame Street* with their children, the children learn more than when they view alone.[21] The only unifying concepts in *Sesame Street* are letters and numbers. Our programme was 'brought to you by the letters A and G and the number 13'. No particular link was established between A, G and 13. A sequence on the letter A followed Robin Williams's spot and was followed by an animation about a dog. The links, if any, had to be made by the viewer.

This fragmentary, unconnected way of presenting information has been one of the most controversial aspects of *Sesame Street's* production technique. The style was developed as a result of considerable research before the programme began; its rapid, constantly changing images, based on product commercials, seemed to be most effective for sustaining children's visual attention. Neil Postman, in his book *The Disappearance of Childhood*, expressed concern about what he saw as a contemporary shift from a print-based culture to an image-based one, and fingered *Sesame Street* as a prime culprit, offering a 'show business model of the world' and a 'high class act'.[22] He contrasts the 'slowed-down processes of thought required by [written] exposition' and 'the fast tempo responses required by a visually entertaining show.' Nevertheless, much research, including CTW's own, has shown learning gains from the show – although the gap between poor and better-off children was not closed as much as was hoped.[23]

Another criticism of *Sesame Street* has been made on the grounds of 'cultural imperialism'. The programme celebrates its quartercentenary this year (1994); it is available in English-language versions in sixty-five countries, and there are fifteen foreign-language versions broadcast in fifty other countries.[24] A programme which set out to cater specifically for under-privileged Americans, and was then actively solicited by 'producers in Canada, Australia, New Zealand . . . about the rebroadcast rights to the series',[25] can hardly be accused of aggressively pushing its products on unwilling foreign consumers. It could be argued that *Sesame Street* is imperialistic to countries trying to set up good children's programming in the way that Western water-purifying equipment is imperialistic to countries who have problems with water pollution – nobody minds it being of foreign origin so long as it is perceived as useful. Gregory Gettas, a producer with CTW's International Television Group, describes how the co-producers of the Arabic version, *Iftah Ya Simsim*, solved the problem of the seventeen different dialects among their audience by deciding to broadcast the programme in Modern Standard Arabic (MSA), the classical language of the Koran. This not only helped revive the classical language, but also gave rise to other MSA programmes about health and adult literacy. CTW's licensing policies require that 'all foreign adaptations of *Sesame Street* be produced to reflect the values and traditions of the host country's culture . . . any proposed alterations to the series would have to be approved, initiated and supervised by a local committee of educational experts, working in conjunction with the Workshop.'[25] CTW's licensing guidelines, unlike other culturally imperialistic enterprises, also forbid commercials in foreign adaptations of *Sesame Street.*

According to Gettas, the secret of the show's amazing success, for which there is no real parallel in British or in any other country's TV programming with the possible exception of the BBC World Service, is the flexibility of its format, which makes local adaptations easy and appropriate – Big Bird in Arabic, for instance, is a traditional camel character called No Man; in Israel it is a hedgehog called Kippy Ben-Kipod. Gettas also points out the universal success of the format with children: '[children] like its puppets and its fast-paced format; they like its emphasis on audience participation and the sense of mastery it gives them when they learn something new.' Local adaptations of the programme, Gettas argues, help children to 'appreciate the richness and diversity of their local cultures and traditions'.[26]

A further key to the appeal of the programme, overlooked by those concerned exclusively with the linear mental skills of reading or abstract thought, is the effectiveness for very young children of teaching through modelling that is offered by the visual, concrete and dramatic nature of TV. The medium's effectiveness as a role model is of course *another* cause of concern to critics, particularly where violence is concerned; a good recent review can be found in Comstock and Paik's *Television and the American Child.*[27] Modelling theories abound in studies of negative effects, but there is comparatively little on the positive models offered by programmes like *Sesame Street* and *Playdays*, and children's responses to the positive models they offer are undoubtedly under-researched, particularly in the case of British programmes (*Sesame Street* at least has its own research operation). For instance, early evaluative research on *Sesame Street* showed significant gains in positive attitudes towards those of different races after two seasons' viewing of the programme.[28]

One of the most proudly claimed virtues of the programme (as also claimed by Cynthia Felgate for *Playdays*) is that it is inclusive. Not only are its human characters multi-ethnic, but the Muppets embrace all kinds of colourful diversity too. Even plasticine can be enlisted to this cause: a dazzling 'number' in the episode I viewed was an animation of a blue blob called Cecile changing shape and singing 'I'm happy being me'. The children and adults featured on the show are diverse, and they include people with disabilities without comment. They show, in Edward Palmer's words, 'everybody relating to everybody else in warm and simple human terms'.[29] Everyone is welcome at *Sesame Street*, not just the literate or the privileged, which makes it very different from other strongholds of cultural excellence. Similarly, in its more modest way, anyone can ride the BBC's *Playdays* play bus.

The area where *Sesame Street* has fallen most short of its own high standards of inclusiveness is gender: the great majority of all its featured characters, muppets, cartoon characters and humans are, inexplicably, male. CTW have recognised this problem and have corrected it to some extent in the new 25th anniversary 1994 series, but male characters remain the norm. (The new series also seems to reflect transatlantic influences from the British style, with *Jackanory*-type storytelling segments and more 'real' people and children.) *Playdays*, like *Play School* before it, has a balance of males and females, among toys and puppets as well as humans. Another significant absence, despite both programmes' careful multiculturalism, is religion. People relate in 'warm and simple human', but secular, terms. The neighbourly environments to which these young children are invited have a humanistic ethos which may be rather different from the ethical environments of their own neighbourhoods. This is a problem for producers in multicultural societies like Britain and the United States, which is less likely to occur in, for instance, the Arabic versions of the programme. Watching young children's programmes in Britain trying to cope with Christmas has been quite an amusing spectacle.

**Addressing the Viewer**

Both *Sesame Street* and *Playdays* employ adult presenters who address the child directly. Direct address to the child, via the camera, is much more common in the British programmes – in fact it is a dominant feature. Children are asked questions, encouraged to join in and to help solve puzzles. The host's greeting to 'the one child in a room' opens each edition of *Playdays*. *Sesame Street* has a number of adult presenters, Bob (white), Gordon (black), Maria (Hispanic), and they do sometimes talk to the child at home. However, this has not been a ritualistic feature of the programme, until the changes in the current series mentioned above. Indeed, since segments from earlier years are regularly recycled, it may well be that the Bob we are seeing this week is in fact a younger Bob. This is not the case with the *Playdays* humans, who operate in real time and get older. *Play School* featured the same hosts for many years; when the oldest child in our family outgrew Brian Cant, an older, balder Brian Cant was still there for the youngest, eight years later. The use of real time is an inevitable feature of a programme like *Playdays* which is built round a daily, and weekly, structure and which addresses its audience as partners in a continuing enterprise. Apart from the occasional filmed interlude, people tell a story, or solve a puzzle, in the space of the programme's twenty-five minutes.

There is no 'real time' in *Sesame Street*. As each segment succeeds the previous one, the viewer has no idea whether the filmed sequence we are seeing (as in the case of my chosen programme) of children in a New York

City vegetable and flower garden was filmed last month or two years ago or five years ago. This enables many of the animation and number sequences to be repeated almost indefinitely – which obviously contributes to the programme's flexibility, and to its global marketability. The non-human characters allowed to address the camera are Big Bird, the large, simple-minded yellow Muppet who acts as the programme's mascot, and some of the regular Muppets such as Bert, Ernie and Oscar; of course, there is no problem with them ageing over time.

A favoured style of address in *Sesame Street* is the indirect one, where the human presenters or Big Bird or other Muppet regulars talk to children in the studio, and thus indirectly address children at home. Many sequences with real humans are sketches in which, for instance, Sir John Feelgood brings a toaster to be repaired in Maria's urban repair shop, and addresses it: 'Alas, poor toaster, I knew you well.' A discussion then follows about whether Sir John's sadness is real or acted. The audience is presumed to be overhearing this conversation, especially as it is uttered in loud, emphatic tones, but they are not part of it. Similar dramatic conceits are sometimes used in *Playdays* – the jokey sparring between Mr Jolly and the Giggler in the episode I viewed was like a music-hall cross-talk act, self-consciously aware of an audience but not addressing it. *Playdays* and *Sesame Street* illustrate John Ellis's distinctions between television and film's differing styles of positioning the viewer; *Sesame Street*, with its use of film and disconnected segments, invites a 'voyeuristic' response from the child at home – it is 'filmic'. *Playdays*/*Play School* (and also *Mister Rogers*) invite a direct response; they and the child are sharing an experience which appears to be happening now – the televisual mode of viewing.[30]

**Language**

Despite Neil Postman's criticisms of the predominance of images in television, both *Sesame Street* and *Playdays* contain a great deal of talk. Further, unlike the early days of pre-school television, there is very little 'talking down'. The audience is recognised to be young, but not deficient in understanding. The 'voyeuristic' approach, whereby the child viewer is positioned as a kind of eavesdropper, correctly recognises that this is an everyday situation for a young child. Being a spectator is not an aberrant position for a three or four-year-old, it is a permanent state of affairs. Children learn, not only by direct address, but also by being present at a very large number of conversations and events which don't concern them – family mealtimes, shopping trips and visits to their parents' adult friends. The language used by the adult presenters in both *Sesame Street* and *Playdays* accepts that children have limited world knowledge and vocabulary, but is otherwise the sort of language that adults normally use – straightforward and grammatical. The Americans are much bolder – and funnier – than the British in exploiting a range of colloquial registers and accents; again, with an eye on their sizeable adult audience. Comic stereotypes abound, most of them probably only recognisable to older viewers. There is, for instance, a little Southern Belle Muppet, who talks like Dolly Parton. Formal language is used by characters such as Sir John Feelgood, simple language by the childlike Big Bird, and the conversational style of a couple of Good Ol' Boys sitting on their porches is used by Bert and Ernie.

The use of Muppets was one of the most inspired features of the original conception of *Sesame Street*. It allowed the producers to extend the range of human types in many creative directions, entirely through voices. (The exception, as noted, is with female characters. There are no memorable *Sesame Street* females; the greatest female Muppet of all, Miss Piggy, never appeared in it.) It was not surprising that the Muppets were given their own, adult, show, which was also popular with young children. The transition from *Sesame Street* to *The Muppet Show* is characteristic of the leap that the young child audience has to make in the American TV system, once they outgrow pre-school. There is no intervening stage of viewing programmes specifically made for older children, such as the British-made *Byker Grove* or *Children's Ward*, in which children's concerns are dramatically central and taken seriously. The currently top-rated programme for six to nine-year-olds in the US is *Full House*, a prime-time sitcom in which children, including a pair of high-profile marketable little girl twins, are the prime butt of the humour. The laughter tracks on prime-time US sitcoms like *Full House* (and *The Cosby Show* before it) give a message to child viewers that the things children say, even when they arise from distress (as when Rudy Huxtable started menstruating), are not rational but comic. This use of 'cute kids' to create easy laughs (almost every US sitcom at the moment has young children in it) has provided one of the strongest contrasts in viewing experiences between the two systems for our family. My children were frequently outraged by the exploitation of child performers on US television; two days after our return from America, my youngest daughter (now fourteen) paused, astonished, in front of a *Newsround* story about the Sudan and said, 'I can't believe it! They're actually treating children like intelligent human beings!' Neil Postman had some justification for describing adult and children's television in the US as almost indistinguishable. But he would have found difficulty in categorising *Ipso Facto*. Intermediate, non-adult genres like this are not found in the US schedules. Hence a significant stage in 'audience-hood' is missed by American children. As viewers they go, as it were, from pre-school to junior high school – and, on the whole, they stay there.

### Audience Response

Both *Sesame Street* and *Playdays* set out to educate and inform their young viewers, in their different styles, within a framework of entertainment. These styles are predicated on different models of the audience and different expectations of audience response. In my experience of watching both programmes with young children in a domestic setting, children's behaviour doesn't differ all that much whichever of the two types they are watching. This is because, as a number of researchers have pointed out, attention is not just programme-driven.[31] Regardless of *Sesame Street*'s high-definition montage, or *Playdays'* careful construction of narrative, children may still be distracted by toys, other children, food, parents or mood – and these will vary greatly from one child to another or within the same child. Children may sometimes answer back to, and sing along with, the 'voyeuristic' *Sesame Street* and sit passively in front of the more directive style of *Playdays.* These kinds of behavioural observation are difficult to factor into research findings, but they are an inevitable feature of entertainment viewing in the home. Ethnographic studies of viewing behaviour in the home (for example, Morley[32] and Lull[33]) have not paid much attention to young children's behaviour, although Patricia Palmer[34] has pointed to the wide variety of children's social activities associated with TV viewing. Studies have revealed that, despite the relatively unstructured nature of home viewing, compared with school, formal learning still takes place. There is research evidence, particularly for *Sesame Street,* that children learn to recognise numbers and letters and books; gain knowledge of concepts and colours and shapes; and acquire social learning about different kinds of people and about themselves. The programme has also been shown significantly to improve vocabulary, independently of other factors such as parental education, gender and family size.[35] However, children themselves do not continue to tune into these pre-school shows because they want to prepare themselves for formal schooling or to appreciate 'formats which combined familiarity with innovation'. They watch because the programmes offer them something they want, or need, to see and hear. Very young children are as diverse in their 'readings' of, and gratifications from, television as anybody else – more so because the range of development between the ages of two and six is so wide – and more needs to be known about these readings.[36]

One valuable lesson offered to young children by programmes which have been made especially for them is that they, the very young, have a place-in-the-sun of 'quality' programming: they are an audience which matters. The wit, professionalism, star turns, cultural prodigality and general 'high-class act' of *Sesame Street* may indicate to Neil Postman an unfortunate descent into the values of show business; but to a child with no other access to the best performances in the culture these classy qualities say, as Lord Reith said. 'You are worth taking trouble over.' For the deprived, lonely children specified by the producers as part of their 'target audience', this may be a more useful lesson than learning about the letter G, or how to follow a trail of clues. It may be why young people look back so affectionately – and gratefully? – to their early experiences of pre-school entertainment. It is probably why the sight of a diffident elderly man in an ordinary grey suit produced such a rapturous response in a crowd of young men and women on their graduation day.

Since this essay began with the *Sesame Street/Mister Rogers/Play School* generation graduating from college, perhaps one of them should be allowed the last word:

When I was growing up, I would repeat the words spoken in Spanish on *Sesame Street*, count along with the Count, and dance to the music. *Sesame Street*, as well as my other favourites, was very unifying. All of my friends watched it and we could identify with one another more easily. To this day, many people of my generation can at least recognise if not sing the words of the theme song of the show: 'Sunny day. Everything's A OK . . . On my way to where the air is sweet. Can you tell me how to get, how to get to *Sesame Street*?'

(Janet Alvi, aged 20.)

NOTES


1. Máire Messenger Davies, *Television is Good for Your Kids* (London: Hilary Shipman, 1989).
2. David Buckingham, 'The Construction of Subjectivity in Educational Television. Part 1: Towards a New Agenda', *Journal of Educational Television*, vol. 13 no. 2, pp. 137–45; and 'Part 2: *You and Me* – A Case Study', *Journal of Educational Television*, vol. 13 no. 3, pp. 187–200.
3. Lawrence Jarvik, 'Getting Big Bird off the Dole', *New York Times*, 14 June 1992.
4. Edward Palmer, *Television and America's Children: A Crisis of Neglect* (Oxford University Press, 1989).
5. V. Lovelace, '*Sesame Street* as a Continuing Experiment', *Educational Technology, Research and Development*, vol. 38 no. 4, 1990, pp. 17–24.
6. See, for example, Neil Postman, *The Disappearance of Childhood* (London: W. H. Allen, 1982).
7. Palmer, *Television and America's Children*, p. 93.
8. W. Labov, P. Cohen, C. Robins and J. Lewis, 'A Study of the Nonstandard English of Negro and Puerto Rican Speakers in New York City', US Office of Education Cooperative Research Project No. 3288 (New York: Columbia University, 1968).
9. Herbert Ginsburg, *The Myth of the Deprived Child* (New Jersey: Prentice Hall, 1972).
10. Anna Home, *Into the Box of Delights: A History of Children's Television* (London: BBC Books, 1993), p. 58.
11. Ibid., pp. 68–9.
12. H. W. Land, 'The Children's Television Workshop: How and Why It Works'. Summary and Overview of Final Report for Nassau County Board of Cooperative Educational Services (Jericho, NY: 1972).
13. Ibid., p. 20.
14. Home, *Into the Box of Delights*, p. 71.
15. Cynthia Felgate, personal interview, 1981.
16. John Lane, personal interview, 1981.
17. W. D. Rowland and M. Tracey, 'Lessons from Abroad: A Preliminary Report on the Condition of Public Broadcasting in the United States and Elsewhere'. Paper presented to a joint meeting of the International Communication Association and the American Forum of the American University, Washington DC, 27 May 1993.
18. Cynthia Felgate, 'Introduction to Playdays', BBC press release, London, 1988.
19. D. R. Anderson and S. R. Levin, 'Young Children's Attention to *Sesame Street*', *Child Development*, vol. 47 no. 3, 1976, p. 806–11.
20. John Ellis, *Visible Fictions* (London: Routledge, 1982).
21. Gavriel Salomon, 'Effects of Encouraging Israeli Mothers to Co-observe

*Sesame Street* with Their Children', *Child Development*, vol. 48 no. 3, 1977, pp. 1146–51.
22. Postman, *The Disappearance of Childhood.*
23. G. Lesser, *Lessons from Sesame Street* (New York: Random House, 1974).
24. Gregory Gettas, 'The Globalization of *Sesame Street*: A Producer's Perspective', *Educational Technology, Research and Development*, vol. 38 no. 4, 1992, pp. 55–63.
25. Ibid., pp. 56–7.
26. Ibid., p. 56.
27. G. Comstock and H. Paik, *Television and the American Child* (New York: Academic Press, 1992).
28. G. A. Bogatz and S. Ball, *The Second Year of Sesame Street: A Continuing Evaluation* (Princeton, NJ: Educational Testing Service, 1972).
29. Palmer, *Television and America's Children*, p. 92.
30. Ellis, *Visible Fictions*, pp 24–5.
31. D. R. Anderson and E. P. Lorch, 'Looking at Television: Action or Reaction', in J. Bryant and D. R. Anderson (eds.), *Children's Understanding of Television: Research on Attention and Comprehension* (New York: Academic Press, 1982).
32. David Morley, *Family Television: Cultural Power and Domestic Leisure* (London: Comedia, 1986).
33. James Lull, *World Families Watch Television* (Newbury Park, CA: Sage, 1988).
34. Patricia Palmer, *The Lively Audience* (Sydney: Unwin Hyman, 1986).
35. M. L. Rice, A. C. Huston, R. T. Truglio and J. C. Wright, 'Words from *Sesame Street*: Learning Vocabulary While Viewing', *Developmental Psychology*, vol. 26 no. 3, 1990, pp. 421–8.
36. See Máire Messenger Davies, 'Art and Life: Stylistic Influences on Children's Reality Judgements about TV'. Report of research carried out under the Annenberg Postdoctoral Research Fellowship Program, University of Pennsylvania, 1993.

# WATCHING WITH MOTHER IN THE EARLY 1950s

DAVID OSWELL

The regular showing of television programmes with a distinct time slot for children under five is now commonplace in Britain. The BBC shows *Playdays* in the mornings between 10.05 a.m. and 10.30 a.m. ITV has a lunchtime slot in which it shows programmes such as *Tots TV* and *Allsorts*. And Channel 4 shows the US import *Sesame Street* daily at 12.30 a.m. Even though these programmes are relatively underfinanced and lack the status ascribed to other, adult and family, television, they are a fixed part of the schedule. Whether they will remain so in the present climate of deregulation is another question.

However, instead of looking at contemporary pre-school programmes I want to look at how this particular cultural form emerged in the early 1950s and at how these programmes fitted into the daily domestic routines of children's and mothers' everyday lives. In following this line of enquiry we can perhaps begin to unpack some of the accumulated ideas and pleasures that surround them.

## Television in the Home

Television's place within the home now seems almost natural and unproblematic, yet in postwar Britain this was far from the case.[1] The introduction of television into the home at a popular level in the late 1940s and early 1950s, far from simply being an object of hostility and phobia, attracted more contradictory responses. In 1950 Monica Dickens, in her regular column in *Woman's Own*, talked about television as a 'terrible extravagance' which would produce 'a nation, not of housewives, but of sluts!' Television was also associated with 'Americanness', poverty and squalor. Dickens was especially concerned about the effect of television on children:

> ht become a generation who couldn't read a book, or play
> t of doors, or amuse themselves with carpentry or trains or

butterflies, or the hundreds of hobbies with which a child can potter so happily.

In America, they're getting really scared of television. Doctors are saying that the children's health is suffering because they spend too long indoors.

Teachers are saying that their work is suffering, because they neglect their homework and sit up much too late to watch their favourite programmes.

Sociologists are saying that although TV may keep people at home, it is changing the pattern of family life, because it destroys conversation and domestic activities and concentration on any work or pastime.[2]

In her article Dickens argued that television was a dangerous and foreign medium which had no place in 'respectable' British homes.[3] However, only one in seven *Woman's Own* readers agreed with Dickens. Mrs Rostrum from Mangotsfield argued that television is an 'instrument of enormous possibilities for teaching young and old'. And Miss Collins from Manchester stated that:

> Today, there are so many interests and diversions taking people away from the home, that family get-togethers have become almost a thing of the past. I think television is the one thing that can bring back those family parties our parents always talk about and seem to have enjoyed so much.[4]

These readers were critical of Dickens's patronising argument about the new medium. They rejected the implicit injunctions of those experts to which Dickens refers and they rejoiced in the familial pleasures which television was able to introduce into the home.

The debate, though, was not simply divided in terms of those for or against television or between such authorities as social scientists, doctors, teachers or journalists and so-called 'ordinary people'. For example, Richard Strout, writing in the *New Statesman and Nation*, was more equivocal. He recognised television's spectacular magical power as potentially bringing both harm and joy into the home.

> The first effect of a home-owned television on the average family is much like that of a first cinema performance for a Hottentot. There is compelling fascination. World events simply pour out on the living-room carpet. The essence of television's magic, however, is not that it brings the outside world into the home but that it creates the illusion for the watcher of being himself at the scene that he is watching . . . The effect of this illusion is spectacular, and upon children it acts like a drug.[5]

Like any powerful magic, television was seen to need careful handling. The BBC, although concerned about the possible detrimental effects of television, was also aware of its future potential. Freda Lingstrom, who was Head of Children's Programmes, BBC TV, between 1951 and 1956, while concerned about the speed with which television could translate ideas from the television studios to the mind of the child, nevertheless conceived of children's television as providing a space of freedom outside the supervision of school and home. It was a space of learning, adventure and discovery. It was a space in which the child could travel to other, real and imagined, worlds.[6]

In the first major research into children and television, Hilde Himmelweit and her colleagues from the London School of Economics stated that 'there is no evidence whatsoever that television makes children passive'.[7] However, both Strout and Himmelweit and her colleagues pointed to the connections between television viewing and a vacation from the public sphere. Instead of the fear of boys roaming the streets in gangs, Strout was worried about the way television was able to reduce 'a gang of noisy unmanageable boys' to 'hardly speaking', sitting in front of the set for hours.[8] Himmelweit and her colleagues argued that the problem was not so much television but the way in which heavy television viewing acted as a barometer of a shy, retiring, insecure and maladjusted child. These children, the researchers stated, were 'often less intelligent than others (in the case of younger children from working-class homes)' and the 'solution of the problem is not primarily to restrict children's viewing, but to attack the various underlying causes.'[9]

Although there were a number of different responses to the introduction of television into the home in the late 1940s and 1950s, these responses circulated around a set of interrelated underlying problems about the making of television into a domestic medium and about the conduct of family life. The problem was not simply one of the power and effect of this new medium. In the rest of this chapter I want to look at how pre-school children's programmes emerged as a particular response to these broader problems.

## Imagining the Pre-School Child Audience

*Andy Pandy* was first shown in July 1950. *Bill and Ben* first emerged in July 1952. And together they were scheduled as *Watch with Mother*. Later in the 1950s they were to be joined by *Rag, Tag and Bobtail* and *The Woodentops*. What is surprising is that, even though the BBC had been making radio programmes for children since it started in 1922 and had been making television programmes for children since 1946, it was not until 1950 that it started regularly to broadcast radio and television programmes for the pre-school audience.[10] *Listen with Mother* was first aired on BBC radio in 1950, just before *Andy Pandy*.

While *Children's Hour* on radio had to some extent taken account of these younger children in the 1920s and 1930s, it had never taken them particularly seriously. Derek McCulloch (Uncle Mac), who had been Director of *Children's Hour*, said in 1942 that three to five-year-olds could not be 'catered for deliberately'. He imagined that this audience would merely enjoy a 'twinkly tune or certain sound effects, particularly domestic animals and everyday noises normally associated with the home'. The problem, though, was not merely that these children could only enjoy certain aspects of *Children's Hour*. More importantly for Derek McCulloch, and for the BBC generally at this time, this small audience was seen to come 'into no real category at all'.[11] The reason the BBC had not made regular programmes for pre-school children was that it didn't know how to *imagine* this audience. It had no category within which to think about it.

Both *Listen with Mother* and *Watch with Mother* did not merely address an audience that already existed. The emergence of these programmes signifies the *invention* of this small audience *for broadcasters* and *within the institution of broadcasting*. Of course, this is not to say that children under five didn't listen to the radio or watch television before 1950. That would be absurd. Nor is it to say that the construction of a pre-school child audience was effective or not. However, the distinctiveness and separateness of this audience for broadcasters was a historical invention. Likewise the demand to make programmes for this audience was something which emerged historically. It is in this sense that the pre-school television audience is not natural, but created. The argument I'm pursuing here does not lead to some inexorable determinism, but it does raise the question of how we can talk about the experiences of this small audience if we have no categories with which to separate this audience from other audiences. The question for me, then, is not whether certain discourses reveal or conceal the truth about this audience, but how the truth of this experience of pre-school children's television viewing is constructed as an object of governance.

Central to my argument is the question of how *Watch with Mother* emerged quite explicitly out of a set of questions about the mental and emotional well-being of the child posed in terms of the psychical dynamics of the family. In the planning stages of *Watch with Mother* there was clearly some reticence about the introduction of television programmes for very young children and concern about their effect on the proper mode of conduct within the home. An internal BBC memo noted that:

> We had a special panel to advise us consisting of representatives of the Ministry of Education, the Institute of Child Development, the Nursery Schools' Association, and some educational child psychologists, and I think they would be pretty sure to squeak if you were to publicise any Television programme for very young children as something that would set Mother free to get about her other business, even though that might in fact be what happened.[12]

It is evident that even in 1950 the relationship between television broadcasting and children was the site of various types of expertise and knowledge. There was a concern that the primary task of motherhood is to care continually for the young child and hence a demand that the BBC attempt to facilitate this relationship. But there was also a reluctant acknowledg-

however, but also directly addresses the audience at home. At times it is clear that she is addressing an audience of mothers rather than children. For example, when Peter the dog gets out of the bath and shakes the water off, she says, 'They always shake water all over you, don't they!' The inference here is that she is referring not only to the activities of excited dogs but also to the exuberance of small children.

Within such a discursive space the presence of the mother is at the cost of the voice of the child. Muffin and the other characters, who signify early childhood through their various gestures and activities, are spoken by the motherly narrator. Yet even though they are voiceless, the impression is given that they can speak. W. E. Williams in the *Observer* noted that 'Miss Mills has no truck with such vulgar devices as ventriloquism, but by repeating to us what Muffin the Mule has inaudibly whispered into her ear she convinces us that thus and thus did really speak.'[15] But while these texts do not display any vulgar ventriloquism, they do present the relation between mother and child within a specific relation of power: speaking, authoritative mother/silent, yet sometimes troublesome, child.

These programmes, however, were not specifically addressed to the pre-school child audience, although they were undoubtedly watched and liked by these very young viewers. *Muffin the Mule* was directed at children generally. It was not until 1950, four years after the start of *Muffin the Mule*, that the BBC specifically addressed a very young audience. *Andy Pandy* was created by Freda Lingstrom and her long-standing friend, Maria Bird. Lingstrom, while Assistant Head of the BBC's Schools Broadcasting, had been responsible for *Listen with Mother* and was asked to make a 'television equivalent on music and movement lines'. What Lingstrom and Bird wanted to do was to provide a friend for the 'very young viewer' at home. 'A three-year-old actor was out of the question, so a puppet was the obvious answer.' An old man in their home village – Westerham in Kent – made Andy Pandy for them, supposedly to the proportions of a three-year-old boy.[16]

Like *Muffin the Mule*, *Andy Pandy* had no linear narrative structure. Instead it presented a series of episodes with no apparent overall theme. In one programme Andy starts by playing on a swing, accompanied by Maria Bird singing 'Swinging high, swinging low . . .'. He is joined by Teddy. The camera then focuses on Teddy, who enacts the movements to the nursery rhyme 'Round and round the garden'. Finally, after a scene with Andy and Teddy playing with their cart and a scene with Looby Loo singing her song, 'Here we go Looby Loo', the two male characters return to their basket and wave goodbye, while Maria Bird sings 'Time to go home . . .'. The 'child' is not an agent within a story but is displayed within a series of tableaux of early childhood: playing on the swing; mother singing and child acting out nursery rhymes, and so on.

The programme was designed for three-year-olds and it was intended to bring these children 'into a close relationship with what is seen on the screen'.[17] This pre-school childhood world was a space of play, nursery rhymes and 'movement'. The children were 'invited to watch the movements of a simple puppet, naturalistic in form and expression.' And it was expected that from time to time they would 'respond to his invitations to join in by clapping, stamping, sitting down, standing up and so forth.'[18] It was a space in which children could 'build for themselves a heritage of traditional and other stories' and through which both pre-school children could be constructed as a community for television and pre-school childhood could be 'normalised'.[19]

*Andy Pandy* draws upon the language of play in order to make itself, and hence also television, homely: 'the puppet comes to the child in the security of its own home, and brings nothing alarming or contradictory to the safe routines of the family.'[20] In *Andy Pandy*, and also in *Bill and Ben*, the fictional world of pre-school childhood was represented within the confines of the domestic. Andy, Teddy and Looby Loo were always represented within the garden or the sitting room. Likewise in *Bill and Ben* the characters were represented within the garden and in close proximity to the little house which opened each episode. In *Andy Pandy* we hear nothing of the outside world. And in *Bill and Ben* all we hear about is the gardener: the function of his character, never seen or heard, is to signify the limits of this imaginary childhood world.

At the same time, though, these programmes use the language of play and the image of domesticity to present a picture of 'normal' childhood. In the scene in which Andy is playing on the swing Maria Bird addresses the audience saying, 'Andy likes swinging, don't you?' She then asks, 'Have you got a swing in your garden?' and exclaims, 'I expect some of you have!' The audience is immediately divided into those with gardens with swings and those without. The connotations of this division do not need to be stressed here.

As with *Muffin the Mule* the characters are voiceless. Maria Bird not only speaks to the characters, she also speaks for them. Andy, Teddy and Looby Loo play, dance and do childish things, but they are unable to articulate their own thoughts, desires or troubles.[21] Unlike contemporary makers of pre-school children's television, who recognise the importance of giving children a voice, the BBC in the early 1950s considered it important to set up clear lines of authority between mother and child and to establish childhood as a space spoken and, as I go on to say, supervised by the mother.[22]

In *Muffin the Mule* the world of children's play was carefully watched over by the 'mother' in the text. However, in *Andy Pandy* the mother is not physically represented. Instead, the mother is signified as outside of, and constitutive of, that narrative space. We do not see the mother. We hear her and we see what she is seeing. She is far from being a disembodied voice; her voice and gaze are productive of the childhood space of *Andy Pandy*. The mother 'in' *Andy Pandy* is presented as an omniscient and omnipotent narrator. Her voice constitutes the characters' thoughts and actions. And the gaze of the camera follows the voice of the narrator. Her command of the characters within the text is replicated in her direct address to the child viewer at home. Through her maternal commands to Andy, and her questions and invitations to the children at home, the viewer is brought within the terms of this maternal gaze: a gaze which is panoptic but not voyeuristic. It is the gaze of the mother as supervisor.[23]

I emphasise this here because the making of television into a domestic medium is at the same time the gendering of that viewing space. It seems obvious and uncontroversial to us now to say that 'good mothers' will supervise their children's television viewing.[24] It is only when we imagine that other viewing scenarios are possible that we recognise the constructedness and normalisation of this present viewing space and the role of the broadcasters in constructing it. However, instead of seeing television's normalising mechanisms as sinister (as Big Brother, or perhaps even Big Mother) and as a medium of domination and manipulation, we see that in the 1950s this discourse, concerned with the pre-school child audience, was intended to facilitate the freedom of the child and to form the child as a healthy and well-adjusted future citizen. It was thought that only in a properly supervised space could children properly exercise their freedom. Implicit in the argument of Himmelweit and her colleagues is the notion that the proper discriminating use of television is formative of good citizenship. The problem, in their view, is that in working-class homes parents fail to reflect critically upon their own and their children's television viewing. These families are all too eager to praise the good things about television.[25] Jan Troke in her regular column in *Everywoman* stated that 'Psychologists say that the right use of leisure turns on one thing, and one thing alone: discrimination. At school you have to learn what you're told. In free time, you choose – and learning to choose is the real secret of a full life.'[26] In *Andy Pandy* and *Bill and Ben* the construction of the mother outside of, yet constitutive of, the narrative space allows the childlike figures freedom within a protected space. And yet in these programmes the supervised freedom of the child is articulated with the child as a silent subject. It is only in the later programmes that the childlike figures are given some form of voice.

In 1953, partly as a result of the televising of the Coronation, television became more firmly embedded in everyday British popular life. In the same year *Rag, Tag and Bobtail* was scheduled within *Watch with Mother.* Unlike *Andy Pandy* and *Bill and Ben, Rag, Tag and Bobtail* has a male narrator, a storyline and characters who are given a voice. The characters – Rag the hedgehog, Tag the mouse and Bobtail the rabbit – are placed within the classic fairytale tradition which starts the narrative with 'Once upon a time . . .' The adventures and experiences of the three little animals are presented within the context of a story being told to the child audience at home. But what is interesting is that, even though the characters are given a voice, their voices are spoken by the narrator. The narration is in the third person and the narrator uses indirect address. He impersonates the characters, giving the impression that they have an identity distinct from that of the narrator at the same time as constituting their identity within his voice. Even in 1953, then, there is a certain hesitancy about animating the child as an autonomous speaking subject.

In 1955 *The Woodentops* was first shown on *Watch with Mother*. There is Mummy Woodentop and baby, Daddy Woodentop, the two twins, Willy and Jenny, Mrs Scrubbit, 'who comes to help Mummy Woodentop', Sam, 'who helps Daddy Woodentop', and Spottydog. And they all live in 'a little house in the country'. The image of rural domesticity appears, but this time as the backdrop to a fully formed 'normal' family. In the programme the narrator is motherly and authoritative. She sets the scene and tells us what is happening, but we also see the characters being given a voice of their own. Even Spottydog has a bark. Although very different from contemporary pre-school children's television, both *The Woodentops* and *Rag, Tag and Bobtail* are also markedly different from *Andy Pandy* and *Bill and Ben*. It is as if television has become safe for the pre-school child, so that now the mother, although not completely absent, can at least sit more easily while television shows its stories.

**Rituals of Viewing**

The textual devices used within *Watch with Mother* and the power relations which they constitute were deployed in conjunction with the use of scheduling as a specific extra-textual 'time-space ordering device'.[27] In the same way that a railway timetable coordinates passengers and trains across time and space, the schedule coordinates the routines of broadcasters within the BBC and the routines of individual viewers at home. Undoubtedly, viewers could, and did, operate different schedules. Domestic viewing is not ultimately controlled and planned from above. Yet if viewers, like train passengers, don't follow the rules, they miss the train. In this sense, power lies not in the medium of television itself but in the power relations (the rules of formation and the construction of authorities) within which television is embedded.

Initially *Andy Pandy* was shown in the afternoon, between 3.45 p.m. and 4 p.m., as part of *For Women*.

> It appears to be in the interest of the child that the series should be attached to a women's programme and separate from the Children's Hour. The performance should be seen at a time when older children are at school, so that the very young can look without the disturbance of the reactions of older children. If this can be achieved both the pre-school child and his mother may come to feel that this programme is especially theirs.[28]

The schedule was a way of dividing certain audiences and bringing together other ones. Through regular announcements, before women's programmes such as *Shop at Home* and *Women of Today*, mothers were informed about the programmes for their three to five-year-olds later in the afternoon. In placing *Andy Pandy* after women's programmes, the needs of the pre-school audience could be connected to the television pleasures of mothers at home and separated from the disruptions of older children.

The scheduling of the programme was initially done with the consent

line Rose's arguments quoted above. I will consider primarily factual programmes screened on British television, aimed at children roughly between the ages of five and eleven. These programmes seek to combine 'education' and 'entertainment' in varying forms and combinations. They are mostly studio-based, and often adopt a magazine format linked by a presenter or a team of presenters.

Despite the evident differences between this material and the established classics of children's literature, I want to argue that these programmes are characterised by tensions and contradictions similar to those identified by Jacqueline Rose. Although there is certainly a considerable degree of diversity here, there is also a shared uncertainty about how the child is to be addressed and 'taken in' to the text, which is manifested particularly in the roles of adult presenters. As in the very different case of *Peter Pan*, this uncertainty seems to reflect a much broader unease about adult power and about the impossibility of fixing or positioning the child viewer.

At the same time, the material I will be considering offers none of the seductive charm which adults often perceive in children's literary classics. In fact, I want to concentrate particularly on a programme (*Wacaday*, presented by Timmy Mallett) that I personally find enormously irritating – although I suspect that my views are shared by many parents whose children insist on watching it. My loathing for Timmy Mallett dates back several years, although it has certainly been intensified by my viewing of a substantial stack of videotapes for this chapter. On one level, I am trying to offer a theoretical and political rationalisation of these feelings. Yet I also want to raise some questions about what it means to generate such apparently rational academic discourse about a form of popular culture which is aimed, not at adults like ourselves, but at children.

**The Imaginary Family**

In his study of the BBC children's magazine programme *Blue Peter*, written in the early 1970s, Grant Noble describes the way in which the presenters appear to serve as a kind of surrogate family.[2] He argues that the programme offers an 'illusion of intimacy', in which the child viewer is invited to regard each of the presenters as a potential parent or older sibling. The particular family roles the presenters are seen to occupy are partly a function of their age, yet they are also manifested in a range of other personal characteristics – the formality of their dress, for example, or their tone of voice – and in the types of activities they are involved in and the kinds of knowledge and expertise they display. In different ways, all these characteristics serve as potential markers of the *difference* between adult and child, and of the distance between the presenter and the viewer.

There is evidence that this notion of the surrogate family has been a conscious strategy on the part of children's programme-makers. Edward Barnes, Head of BBC Children's Television during the 1970s and early 1980s, once described it as follows:

We try in all our programmes to integrate them into our kind of family:

> to make them feel that they belong, and to make them feel . . . that they have some say in what happens . . . I think it must do more good than harm to children from deprived homes, who feel at least they have a sense of belonging somewhere, rather than nowhere whatsoever.[3]

As this quotation suggests, 'our' kind of family is explicitly regarded as quite different from 'theirs' – from the 'deprived' families of the working class. Television is seen to act as an alternative parent, 'doing them good' by compensating for the emotional deprivation of their real parents.

In an article written in 1982, entitled 'Why I am a paternalist', Barnes responds directly to the charge that BBC programmes are too middle-class: 'If by middle-class they mean paternalistic, and if paternalism means being a loving and caring parent, I accept the charge.'[4] For Barnes, one key aim of this paternalistic approach is to defend children against the 'easy' popular entertainment offered by the commercial channels, such as the soap operas and situation comedies. Children's programmes should seek to lead children on to 'quality' adult programmes – although, again, this is defined in explicit class terms:

> One of the primary functions of a Children's Programmes Department is to teach children how to watch television, before they are conditioned to believe that they are *Crossroads* fodder and that programmes dealing with art and science and costume drama are not for them. This will be even more important when cable and satellite offer them 30 channels to choose from. Our children must not be the proles of tomorrow's television.

As the flagship of BBC children's programming, *Blue Peter* has carried much of the burden of this public service tradition. Where other long-running BBC programmes such as the serial *Grange Hill* have come under attack for representing young people as violent and disrespectful – and thus, its critics allege, encouraging them to follow its example – *Blue Peter* has largely remained true to Barnes's paternalistic vision. As such, it has inevitably served as an easy target for ideological criticism.[5]

In terms of its content, for example, *Blue Peter* has retained its emphasis on animals, charity appeals, sports and familiar hobbies. In line with its anti-commercial tradition, it continues to instruct children how to make cheap presents and useful household items from discarded toilet rolls and yogurt pots – whence derives the timeless expression 'And here's one I made earlier'. Perhaps the most notable recent example of this was its plan for a 'Tracy Island' (based on the children's puppet show *Thunderbirds*), costing a fraction of the shop price, which resulted in the programme being deluged with requests for instruction leaflets. As Stephen Wagg has argued, these emphases reflect a fundamental anxiety about the potential *passivity* of viewing: according to the Reithian tradition, the child is encouraged 'to be *active*: to make, to mend, to collect, to care for animals and to help other people'.[6]

Yet, however minimally, *Blue Peter* has changed. Compared with the distinctly parental figures I recall from my own childhood, its presenters are younger, less formally dressed, in some cases still in their teens. Surrogate mothers or fathers have been banished in favour of trendy older brothers and sisters, who readily make fools of themselves and profess to share their viewers' enthusiasms for pop stars and TV entertainment.

Similar changes can be detected in that other BBC flagship, *Newsround*, the children's news programme. Its rapidly greying presenter John Craven has been replaced by much younger, trendier presenters, who have emerged from behind the newsdesk and now sit casually perched on stools. And if children themselves still occupy a fairly marginal role in *Blue Peter* – appearing mainly in order to demonstrate unusual achievements – *Newsround* has recently instituted an access slot in which children present their own news stories.

## From Adult to Child

Admittedly, these changes are marginal, but when one looks more broadly across the range of children's programming they appear to be writ large. At least outwardly, children's TV in Britain seems to have thrown off the legacy of paternalism and adopted a much more egalitarian address to the viewer. It appears to be attempting the impossible task, to speak *for* the child, and in some cases *against* the adult.

This is partly manifested in the broad mix of 'entertainment' and 'information', and in how the relationship between them appears to be defined. Of course, such distinctions are inevitably problematic, and within the range of programmes considered here they are more a matter of degree than of kind. If *Newsround* lies at one end of the spectrum and a children's game show like *Fun House* at the other, there are many programmes that attempt to blend these different dimensions. Weekend morning shows like *Going Live*, *Parallel Nine* or *Ghost Train* will sometimes insert 'news' items, advice or interviews with experts (for example on an ecological theme) into their main diet of cartoons, celebrity interviews, pop videos and competitions. Even *Blue Peter* occasionally acknowledges such elements of popular entertainment, and not only in order to lead viewers on to 'better things'. Indeed, many children's broadcasters tend to argue against such distinctions, stressing the need to blend 'fun' and 'facts', although such formulations often seem to betray a conviction that 'facts' can never be 'fun'.[7]

Nevertheless, there have been changes in this respect also. The rise in popularity of the 'entertainment' magazine programme in the 1980s appears to have coincided with a decline in the proportion of 'information' programming for children, prior to the potential impact of deregulation.[8] Edward Barnes's notion that children's television should defend children against 'easy' popular entertainment seems to have been all but abandoned; on the contrary, many children's programmes now seem to take the form of a *celebration* of the 'proletarian' popular culture he was so concerned to resist.

Indeed, many of these programmes often seem to take place within an entirely mediated world. The guests who venture into the studio of *Going Live* or *Parallel Nine* are most likely to be pop stars, actors from other shows or even presenters from other children's programmes. Much of the humour of these programmes is based on a knowing mockery of other media genres and conventions, for example in the case of *Parallel Nine*'s 'Parallel Playback' (a game show played in reverse) or the antics of Trev and Simon on *Going Live*. In some cases – most notably with *Disney Club* – the programme appears to be little more than an extended advertisement for other media-related merchandise.

The implications of this are ambiguous, however. On one level, as Stephen Wagg implies,[9] there is a danger that children's television will degenerate into a kind of postmodernist nightmare of endless consumption. Yet at the same time, a great deal of children's television seems to be concerned with 'teaching children how to watch television'[10] – albeit in rather different terms from those preferred by Edward Barnes. Many of these programmes, and the continuity sequences that surround them, not only provide a considerable amount of 'behind the scenes' information about how television is made but also draw attention to their own production processes – or what in *Screen*-speak used to be called 'foregrounding the device'. There is no longer a realist taboo against showing the production crew or acknowledging the fact that the programme is rehearsed and scripted. The signs of amateurishness – the wobbly cameras, the stumbling presenters, the awkward links between items – are emphasised rather than effaced. To be sure, this is a cultivated *appearance* of spontaneity – a highly managed form of chaos. Yet it also seems to derive from a kind of anxiety, or at least embarrassment, about the distance between the programme and the viewer.

This appearance of egalitarianism is also reflected in the changing roles of presenters, already noted in the case of *Blue Peter* and *Newsround*. For example, the dress codes of children's presenters seem to reflect one of two potential roles. The preferred style is that of the trendy older brother or sister – cycling shorts, trainers and casual designer sportswear. The alternative option, of which Timmy Mallett is perhaps the most extreme example, is the adult-as-clown – polka-dots, luminous stripes and bright primary colours. Yet in different ways both seem designed to efface the markers of adult authority, and thus to minimise the differences between adults and children. In effect, the presenters seem to be masquerading as children: they are adults in drag.

Particularly in magazine programmes with studio audiences, like *Going Live* and *Ghost Train*, the presenters have the difficult task of exercising control while simultaneously adopting the appearance of childlike spontaneity. We're just kids like you, the presenters seem to be saying. We can make fools of ourselves, but we just don't care. We may have been let loose in a studio with a few million pounds' worth of equipment, but we're just having fun. We're not boring grown-ups who are going to teach you things or tell you how to behave. We're just *playing* at TV.

In this respect, the roles of the presenters seem to reflect a construction of the child, not as innocent and docile, but as wild and anarchistic – although of course this notion of childhood has its own history, both in television and in children's literature.[11] Nevertheless, the roles of children themselves within these programmes remain highly circumscribed. Real children participate largely as onlookers rather than participants. The studio audience cheers wildly on cue, yet it serves primarily as a kind of *mise-en-scène*, a backdrop to the crazy antics of adult presenters.

The one exception to this would seem to prove the rule. Uniquely, the BBC's *Why Don't You?* uses groups of children as presenters, although in fact they do not address the camera directly. Originally (and symptomatically) entitled *Why Don't You (Switch off Your Television Set and Go and Do Something Less Boring Instead)*?, this programme is very much in the worthy tradition of 'one I made earlier', in which children are urged to find Constructive Things to do in their spare time. Between acting out rather tame adventures, the children teach each other how to make recipes and useful household objects, and to play tricks and 'educational' games. Yet the wooden quality of their reading from the script reinforces the sense that these children are little more than ventriloquists' dummies, playing out adult pedagogical roles.

This unease about the relationship between 'information' and 'entertainment' is also reflected in programmes which lie more at the 'information' end of the spectrum. For example, the *pace* of 'information' magazine programmes has become much more frenetic in recent years, reflecting assumptions about children's attention span which seem highly questionable. A programme like *The Really Wild Show* makes a stark contrast with the much more sober natural history programmes I used to watch as a child: the average length of each item is around two minutes, and it is often hard to identify any thematic continuity as one animal 'turn' gives way to the next. Perhaps the most manic of all, however, is *Bitsa*, a version of 'one I made earlier' on amphetamines: here, the presenters rush furiously round the studio constructing a bewildering range of elaborate models from the familiar waste packaging, but with the added facility of electric drills and glue guns. Somehow, it is as if speeding up the process will deflect the suspicion that children's television might be doing anything as boring as actually *teaching* anything.

As I have implied, these characteristics of contemporary British children's television seem to represent a growing uncertainty about the traditional educative mission of public service broadcasting – and a partial retreat from it. The paternalism so proudly proclaimed by Edward Barnes would appear to have become an uncomfortable stance, and deference seems no longer to be a response that can be counted upon. The apparently egalitarian tone of contemporary children's television – and the carefully controlled impression of amateurishness that often accompanies it – derives ultimately from an embarrassment about the fact of adult power, and an effort to efface its more overt signs. Yet how effective is this attempt to close the gap between adult and child, and to speak on children's behalf?

**The Case of Timmy Mallett**

*Wacaday*, presented by Timmy Mallett, embodies many of the tensions I have discussed. *Wacaday* is a successor to an earlier children's programme, *Wide Awake Club* (WAC), which dates back to the early 1980s. Much of the appeal of the programme lies in its use of repeated in-jokes and references which 'Wide-awakers' (members/viewers) are expected to be familiar with. It is a club which, on one level, appears designed to exclude adults, and in this it would seem to be highly successful. Any passing interest parents might have in their children's TV preferences is unlikely to survive more than a single edition; and any theoretical commitments to the empowering potential of popular culture quickly fade in the face of Timmy and his interminable 'wackiness' (or craziness).

*Wacaday* was broadcast daily in school holidays by the now defunct breakfast TV company TV-AM, otherwise famous for the union-busting tactics of its Controller, Bruce Gyngell. The demise of TV-AM following the round of franchise awards at the end of 1992 was apparently a cause of great regret to Margaret Thatcher, who sent her personal condolences to Gyngell. For reasons one can only surmise, the instant rehiring of many TV-AM staff by the franchise winner, GMTV, has not yet extended to Timmy Mallett.

Nevertheless, Timmy remains a popular figure for children, and a source of extreme irritation for many adults. In 1991–2, he shot to the top of the pop charts with a cover of the old 1950s hit 'She wore an itsy-bitsy teeny-weeny yellow polka-dot bikini'; and he was featured in an advertisement for throat sweets, in a series including other noted media irritants Tony Blackburn and Jeremy Beadle – the joke being that if the hoarse Timmy were deprived of the sweets his voice would not return, for which we would all be immensely grateful.

*Wacaday* is very much dominated by the persona of Timmy Mallett. The only other 'characters' to appear in the programme are a budgerigar called Magic, who is occasionally let loose in the studio; a stuffed mallet called Pinky Punky, who is brandished in front of the camera, interrupting Timmy's monologue with jokes delivered in a grating, high-pitched voice; and Shaky the camera operator, whose hand occasionally comes into view but who is otherwise unseen (much of the programme is in fact shot on one camera). In addition, for several weeks in the summer of 1992, Timmy was joined by 'the Man from Manchester', a Northern stereotype with a flat cap and a Manchester United scarf, who would occasionally utter comments about 'black pudding' while instructing Timmy and his guests in 'wacky' versions of Olympic events (supposedly in relation to Manchester's bid for the Olympic Games). His incompetence and misunderstandings were explained on the grounds that he was from 'oop North'.

Two children, a boy and a girl generally aged 9 or 10, are introduced as guests on each programme. Aside from their introductions, in which they say their name, their home town and their interests, they generally speak only when questioned by Timmy or when asked to read from cue cards. There is no studio audience, although a tape of cheering children is occasionally played at key moments, accompanied by childlike whoops from the production crew.

As noted above, Timmy himself carries the clownlike persona of the children's TV presenter to its extreme. His typical outfit will include a luminous striped T-shirt and clashing, equally luminous Paisley shorts. One leg of the shorts is always rolled up, a quasi-Masonic sign of membership of the Wide Awake Club, which the guests are also required to adopt. Timmy also tends to sport two baseball caps, whose peaks point out at different angles: these 'Twin Peaks' are also required garb for guests. Perhaps the most striking feature of Timmy's appearance, however, is his 'outrageous' spectacles, drawn from a large repertoire of bright colours and designs which rivals that of Edna Everage. Film sequences tend to feature Timmy wearing different pairs of spectacles from one scene to the next, and he rarely wears the same pair two days running.

As this would suggest, Timmy is determinedly 'wacky' and never tires of reminding us of the fact. Apparently incapable of standing in one place, he typically lurches round the studio, gesticulating wildly as if attempting to encourage the participation of the imaginary studio audience. At the same time, he retains complete control of the studio space, often pulling the guests into position to deliver their lines. He leads the programme

*Timmy Mallett in* Wacaday. *Photo courtesy of John Miles Organisation.*

furiously from one item to the next, keeping up a steady stream of puns, jokes and catch-phrases, which guests and viewers (and the production crew) are urged to repeat. He appears to find his own jokes extremely amusing. Everything is 'absolutely brilliant' and 'completely and utterly amazing'.

Yet *Wacaday* also has educational pretensions. Each week, the programme takes a different country as a theme, which is developed in film inserts and in regular studio items such as games. Each episode lasts thirty minutes, and typically contains the following:

1. Introduction. Timmy welcomes the viewers, and asks Magic the budgerigar for today's 'Magic word', which is superimposed in a speech bubble.

2. The two 'Wide-awaker' guests are introduced. Each is expected to be wearing the requisite 'wacky' clothing and to bring clothes or gifts appropriate to the theme of this week's programme (for example, Viking horns). Their 'passports' (featuring photographs and information about themselves and their families) are inspected and their hands then stamped with a WAC rubber stamp by Shaky the camera operator.

3. Mallett's Mallet. This is a word-association game, played by the guests, in which hesitations or repetitions are rewarded by a hit from Timmy's large pink foam mallet, which registers their scores in 'squillions'. The winner and loser receive prizes, and the person who utters the magic word (often strongly cued by Timmy) is also rewarded.

4. Magic and Timmy. A story with cartoon captions, based on a different stop in Magic and Timmy's 'world tour'. This typically combines information about the location with puns and jokes.

5. Wac-Karaoke. The guests mime to a familiar pop song, whose words (displayed on screen) have been altered to include 'wacky' references.

6. A location film report from this week's country (generally different from the country visited in the Magic and Timmy item). This often features a historical story in which Timmy plays all the major parts, male and female. Timmy is frequently seen wandering in public places hitting the locals with his foam mallet, and they are occasionally conscripted as extras into the stories.

7. Wac-a-Make. *Wacaday*'s version of 'one I made earlier', in which the guests are instructed in making a model or a piece of clothing (a hat, for example) related to this week's country. Another option here is Mallett's Palette, in which Timmy instructs the guests in drawing cartoons (although he is never seen drawing them himself).

8. A second film report from this week's country.

9. Chat and Splat. A contestant is quizzed over the phone with five comprehension questions relating to the two film reports. If they are correct (which they invariably are, with considerable prompting from Timmy), a model representing a person of their choice (generally a relation or a teacher) is catapulted into a bowl of luminous green gunge.

10. The Wac-scrapbook. Images and objects relating to this week's country (often through more puns) are mounted in the scrapbook, in order to remind viewers of 'what we've learned on *Wacaday* today'. Timmy urges the viewers to tune in tomorrow to '*Wacaday* – the show your telly was made for!'

As this outline suggests, the menu of each episode is extremely rigid, which enables the presenter and the crew to operate effectively without a script. Only the bizarre interruptions of Pinky Punky occasionally seem to leave Timmy lost for words. This fixed routine also means that the pace can be kept fast and the appearance of spontaneous anarchy sustained.

**Why I Hate Timmy**

As this description suggests, *Wacaday* attempts to combine 'facts' and 'fun'. Indeed, the final items serve almost as a 'test', designed to assess and reinforce what has been learnt. Yet what does the programme attempt to teach, and how?

One difficulty here is that the 'facts' are often so deeply embedded in the 'fun' that it is hard to detect them at all. *Wacaday*'s history of the foundation of Norway, for example, featured the 'true story' of 'Harold Haircut' and his 'Fjord Escort', which found Timmy wandering through a shopping precinct dressed as a Viking, hitting passers-by with his pink mallet and demanding their treasure. 'Facts' there certainly are, but facts so lacking in context that they often appear quite meaningless.

In other instances, however, there seems to be a rather different kind of teaching going on. Timmy's visit to Russia, for example, was laced with the familiar puns – 'your mother will come russian in and start yeltsin at you' – and a very elaborate joke about 'Tartar-control toothpaste'. Yet it also contained some gems of political insight:

> Until a couple of years ago, Wide-awakers, Russia was a dull, grey, miserable sort of place to be. You weren't allowed to do anything or say anything without asking permission. And when you did, they just said 'Niet'. It was as if all the doors were shut and locked and there was NO FUN. And then along came Mikhail Gorbachev with a brand new word called 'Glasnost', and now Russia is moving from the darkness into the light.

The 'light' and 'fun' referred to here were represented (needless to say, perhaps) by the tourist souvenirs for sale in Moscow streets and the queues for McDonalds and Pepsi.

Timmy's visit to South Africa in 1991 saw him wandering around a black township (dressed in his familiar luminous 'wacky' shorts and glasses) collecting ingredients from the inhabitants to put in his 'melting pot'. South Africa, he announced, was also 'a melting pot . . . It's not perfect by any means, but it's getting there, slowly.' Other programmes from South Africa saw Timmy dressed in a Zulu warrior outfit and pith helmet, consulting a witch doctor, and then attacking the tribesmen with his mallet;

beating the locals in an ostrich race; and telling the story of the 'heroic bravery' of the British soldiers at Rorke's Drift.[12]

The point here, however, is not simply that Timmy Mallett is right-wing, or patronising towards other cultures, or even that he trivialises important political issues. While I personally find this offensive, I don't believe it makes very much difference to the children who watch the programme. I suspect the decontextualised, strangely metaphorical commentary I have quoted would simply be meaningless to most ten-year-olds, let alone my own six-year-old. It seems absurd even to entertain the idea that Timmy Mallett is a kind of political Svengali, mesmerising innocent children into ideological torpor.

My concern here is not so much the 'content' of the programme or any explicit messages it might be trying to deliver. What I find more problematic is the way in which it defines the child and the adult, and the forms of 'entertainment' and 'education' that are on offer. What is most striking about the 'educational' aspects of the programme is how self-referential they are. The facts the viewer is offered about other cultures seem strictly subordinate to the major focus of the lesson, which is to reinforce what a 'wacky' guy Timmy is. As I have suggested, this is clearly part of the programme's appeal. In-jokes, repeated rituals and running gags invite the viewer into a kind of pleasurable complicity, a membership of a club – albeit one whose primary activity appears to be reasserting that very complicity. Like many other children's programmes, this is television about television, not (as it seems to claim) about the world.

Ultimately, the programme positions the child both as somebody who enjoys 'fun' and as somebody who learns 'facts', but it defines both in its own limited terms. Facts, it would seem, can only be made palatable for children if they are served up with large amounts of fun: fun is the sugar and facts are the pill. Furthermore, the facts that count are those that can be tested: learning is about memorising and reproducing on demand, and it is encouraged through external rewards and reinforcements. However anarchic it may appear, fun is also about competition and is rigorously choreographed and controlled by adults. In practice, fun takes the form of a series of narrow routines, whose primary aim is to celebrate the 'childlike' persona of the adult presenter.

Thus, while the programme appears to address the child as an equal, it seems to be based on a form of contempt for its audience. An adult masquerades as a child, appealing to a definition of childhood which appears to value anarchy and disorder. Yet the roles allocated to real children in this scenario are highly circumscribed: they are little more than stooges, manipulated in order to display Timmy's infinite wackiness. The programme offers a routine spontaneity, a rigidly controlled appearance of anarchy, a codified form of madness. This may not be paternalistic, but it is certainly extremely patronising.

## From Child to Adult

In offering this account of my reactions to *Wacaday*, I have not sought to hide my irritation. For many readers who have seen the programme, I imagine it will be shared. Yet it also seems to me important to question what is going on here. What functions does this kind of academic criticism serve for us as adults, and where does it lead?

One of the major problems in writing about this kind of material is that one almost inevitably appears to be 'taking it too seriously'. While elaborate deconstructions of TV wrestling and game shows have become part of the stock-in-trade of academic Media Studies, there is still something faintly absurd and inappropriate about extending this kind of analysis to children's TV – or at least to programmes such as *Wacaday* that would undoubtedly fall well below most people's quality thresholds. Even here, for example, I have felt compelled to refer to Timmy Mallett as 'Timmy', not as 'Mallett' – let alone to adopt the academic mode.

The reason for this is partly because *Wacaday* is demanding – imploring, begging even – *not* to be taken seriously. Yet it is also because 'taking it seriously' almost inevitably positions me as an adult – and a rather concerned, over-earnest adult at that. What I'm doing is what adults *always* do: I'm being boring. In Timmy's terms, I am definitely 'NO FUN'.

On one level, I cannot deny this. The factual programmes aimed at children that I personally prefer are long-running series like *Cartoon Time* (presented by Rolf Harris) and *Hartbeat* (Tony Hart). In both cases, a comparatively elderly presenter instructs viewers in how to produce their own cartoons or artworks. The presenters display an enthusiasm for the material that I fondly assume to be genuine, and neither has to pretend to be a child. Both programmes give substantial space to children themselves to show their own work. Yet ultimately both could justifiably be seen as old-fashioned and paternalistic; and while they are certainly popular with children (as indeed is *Blue Peter*), my preference for these programmes may say much more about me than it does about the children who watch them, however much I may attempt to clothe it in the objectivity of academic discourse.

The danger here is that our own adult responses to television may effectively miss the point. What we find patronising may well not correspond with what children themselves find patronising – or they may be so used to being patronised by adults that they have developed ways of ignoring it. While I think I can see why children might enjoy *Wacaday*, I can't pretend to enjoy it myself. Indeed, it would be fairly surprising if a 38-year-old adult were to find Timmy Mallett amusing or admirable, since he clearly isn't trying to amuse me or to gain my admiration. As with a great many products aimed at young people, much of the pleasure seems precisely to *depend* upon the fact that adults are excluded. My six-year-old knows that he can happily sit singing along with Timmy, shouting out the catchphrases and practising his 'Wac-a-wave', without the slightest possibility of adult interest or interference. And if that enables me to have my breakfast and read the newspaper in relative peace, then I only have Timmy to thank.

As this implies, these definitions of 'adult' and 'child' are partly determined by the viewing context. While I wouldn't claim that my own family is in any way representative, a brief anecdote might serve to illustrate what I mean. The demise of *Wacaday* late in 1992 coincided with the arrival of Channel 4's *The Big Breakfast*, a programme that in many ways seems to represent the other side of the coin. If *Wacaday* features an adult masquerading as a child in order to address children, *The Big Breakfast* features adults masquerading as adolescents in order to address both adults and children. Both programmes draw from a limited repertoire of short items, which in the case of *The Big Breakfast* include celebrity interviews, competitions, location sequences and items about fashion, dieting and pop music. With the occasional exception of 'human interest' stories, *The Big Breakfast* resolutely avoids any taint of seriousness: the interviews between Bob Geldof (who is one of the owners of the production company) and high-profile political figures such as Nelson Mandela and Yasser Arafat which appeared in the programme's early days have been dropped. Like *Wacaday* and other children's programmes such as *Going Live*, *The Big Breakfast* cultivates an appearance of amateurishness and managed chaos: it is contrived to appear as though a group of twelve-year-olds have been let loose in a TV studio with a few million pounds to spend and told to get on with entertaining themselves.

*The Big Breakfast* has been extremely successful in terms of national ratings and is particularly popular with children; and, at least initially, it was a big hit in my own household. What it appeared to offer was a version of 'family viewing' that crossed the boundaries of age and gender. Prior to *The Big Breakfast*, I would personally prefer to read the newspaper while listening to the news on BBC Radio 4 – a station my partner refers to as Radio Boring Men. For her part, she would doze in bed listening to the breakfast programme on TV-AM, while the children (boys aged six and three) would opt for compulsive reruns of Walt Disney videos or the attractions of *Sonic Hedgehog*. *The Big Breakfast* seemed to provide a kind of common ground; and while its spontaneity has inevitably become routine, I have to admit that at first I found its amateurishness and stupidity almost liberating.[13]

On one level, *The Big Breakfast* is a prime example of what John Hartley refers to as the 'paedocratisation' of the television audience. It is a programme that effectively addresses its audience as children, with childlike preoccupations and concerns, and thereby seeks to unify that audience into a single constituency. According to Hartley:

> . . . broadcasters paedocratise audiences in the name of pleasure. They appeal to the playful, imaginative, fantasy, irresponsible aspects of adult behaviour. They seek the common personal ground that unites diverse and often directly antagonistic groupings among a given population. What better, then, than a fictional version of everyone's supposed child-

like tendencies which might be understood as predating such social groupings? In short, a fictional image of the positive attributes of childlike pleasures is invented. The desired audience is encouraged to look up, expectant, open, willing to be guided and gratified, whenever television as an institution exclaims: 'Hi, kids!'[14]

The problem with this argument, though, apart from the level of generalisation, is its assumption that this process is necessarily sinister and dangerous. Uncomfortable with triviality and 'fun', Hartley appears to want to escape to the seriousness of academic discourse, in which those of us who are truly critical and responsible can stake out the correct political positions on behalf of everybody else. There is a kind of puritanism here, not to mention a degree of arrogance.

What this criticism also seems to neglect is the element of irony which may be present here. Chris Evans, one of the main presenters of *The Big Breakfast*, seems to me to display this with a genuine degree of subtlety. Yes, he seems to be saying, I *know* this is completely childish and stupid but let's do it anyway. It is hard to point to signs of this irony, yet it is a quality which the most successful children's presenters – for example Philip Schofield and Sarah Greene of *Going Live*, or Andi Peters, the continuity announcer on Children's BBC – seem to me to possess, and which Timmy Mallett so signally lacks. Perhaps paradoxically, the problem I have with Timmy is that he is so resolutely *serious* about his 'wackiness'.

Finally, I would resist the implication in Hartley's argument that we should put aside 'the playful, imaginative, fantasy, irresponsible aspects of adult behaviour' – or indeed that we are able to do so. As Jacqueline Rose argues, our relationship to childhood is not fixed or stable: there is no childhood that is simply over and done with.[15] Children's television, like children's fiction, represents an attempt to impose order and cohesion, and to stave off the difficulties and contradictions of subjectivity. For all its claim to stand outside that process, academic criticism also serves to discipline and restrain 'the child' and to construct and reinforce 'the adult'. In the end, it is precisely the kind of thing you would *expect* grown-ups to do.

NOTES

I would like to thank Nathan Greenwood for his assistance in this 'research'.

1. Jacqueline Rose, *The Case of Peter Pan: Or the Impossibility of Children's Fiction* (London: Macmillan, 1984), pp. 1–2.
2. Grant Noble, *Children in Front of the Small Screen* (London: Constable, 1975).
3. Quoted in the Open University programme 'Social Integration: Children's Television' (BBC, 1981).
4. Edward Barnes, 'Why I am a paternalist', *Listener*, 4 November 1982.
5. See particularly Bob Ferguson, 'Black Blue Peter', in Len Masterman (ed.), *Television Mythologies: Stars, Shows and Signs* (London: Comedia/MK Media Press, 1984); and 'Children's television: the germination of ideology', in D. Lusted and P. Drummond (eds.), *TV and Schooling* (London: British Film Institute, 1985).

6. Stephen Wagg, 'One I made earlier: Media, popular culture and the politics of childhood', in Dominic Strinati and Stephen Wagg (eds.), *Come On Down? Popular Media Culture in Post-War Britain* (London: Routledge, 1992).
7. See Jay G. Blumler, *The Future of Children's Television in Britain: An Enquiry for the Broadcasting Standards Council* (London: Broadcasting Standards Council, 1992).
8. See the statistical analysis conducted by Chris Mottershead in Blumler, *The Future of Children's Television in Britain*.
9. Wagg, 'One I made earlier'.
10. For a discussion of this in relation to children's literature, see Margaret Meek, *How Texts Teach What Readers Learn* (Stroud: Thimble Press, 1988).
11. In the case of television, it is possible to trace this back to ATV's *Tiswas*, first broadcast in the mid-1970s and followed by its 'adult' version *O.T.T.* (Over the Top). Perhaps the most celebrated construction of the anarchistic child in recent children's literature is Maurice Sendak's *Where the Wild Things Are* – although here again, the lineage extends back at least to Richmal Crompton's *William* series.
12. Further examples of Timmy Mallett's acute political analysis may be found in *Timmy Mallett's Utterly Brilliant History of the World* – needless to say, a book regularly promoted on *Wacaday*. While not recommended for readers of an ideologically sensitive disposition, it has all the credentials for a National Curriculum History textbook.
13. It is important to note that these comments were written in 1992, well before *The Big Breakfast* was single-handedly responsible for resurrecting the career of the awful Keith Chegwin, and its main host Chris Evans went on to the Club 18–30 populism of *Don't Forget Your Toothbrush*. Discrimination in such matters must be sustained at all costs.
14. John Hartley, 'Invisible fictions: television audiences, paedocracy, pleasure', *Textual Practice*, vol. 1 no. 2, 1987.
15. *The Case of Peter Pan*, particularly Chapter One.

| secs | spoken words | images |
|---|---|---|
| | Our world is in peril. | Close-up of traffic.<br>Overhead shot of cloverleaf in city draws back to view of whole earth,<br>changes to pupil in eye of Gaia, |
| 05 | Gaia, the spirit of the earth, can no longer stand the terrible destruction plaguing our planet. | draws back to reveal Gaia, spinning, releasing dove and releasing lightning bolts to sky. |
| 10 | She sends five magic rings to five special young people: | Five spinning clouds become earths and then five rings of different colours.<br>The green ring enlarges to become a globe with longitude and latitude lines marked on it.<br>Five silhouettes appear in a bright light on the edge. |
| | Kwame, from Africa, with the power of earth, | Kwame (with earth in background) holds up green ring like a pistol and shoots a ray that puts him in silhouette and then becomes spreading waves; a scene of elephants and Land Rover; the rays hit the earth in a ring between the elephants, and a pillar of earth lifts the Land Rover. |
| 15 | from North America, Wheeler, with the power of fire, | Green-eyed mutant drives armoured car. Wheeler flies from left, fires a ray from a red ring that makes a circle of fire, melting the pavement, stopping the armoured car. |
| 20 | | |
| 25 | from the Soviet Union [now 'from Eastern Europe'], Linka, with the power of wind, | Tractor-feed computer paper billows out; pan to reveal a scene of tree stumps, logs on conveyor belt, and large machine with villains and computer, Linka's fist, then the badges on her jacket, then her angry face; she turns to fire her ring, which pro- |

| secs | spoken words | images |
|---|---|---|
| | | duces a whirlwind that wraps up the two villains in paper and carries them away. White |
| 30 | | out. |
| | from Asia, Gi, with the power of water, | Gi on surfboard, in green, shoots white ray at villain sitting on beach by a dolphin trapped in a net; |
| 35 | | a pillar of water approaches the villain, who holds an iced drink and wears pig swimsuit, carries away the smiling dolphin and the terrified villain; close-up of the huge wave, which withdraws revealing the villain in the net, bottle on head, and the dolphin leaping free into the sun. |
| 40 | and from South America, Ma-ti, with the power of heart. | Trees on fire, a parrot flies away, animals flee, Ma-ti enters and picks up monkey, a burning tree falls, a truck passes in the background; Ma-ti holds up a yellow ring. |
| 45 | When their five powers combine, they summon earth's greatest champion, Captain Planet. | Its ray divides into five, with one Planeteer in each cell. All shoot rays, which meet in the sky, producing a spiralling cloud, then lightning. The lightning strikes into the earth, a brown hand breaks up from the earth, then a brown head with brown shaggy hair. Breaking through shattered rocks and trailing rootlike clothing in air, the brown sheath falls away, revealing a body that is spinning in the |
| 50 | | air, first green, then red, then blue, then yellow; a close-up of the face shows a punk haircut, and he is revealed to have green hair, light green skin, a red jersey with a yellow |

| secs | spoken words | images |
| --- | --- | --- |
| | Planeteers: 'Go, Planet!' | emblem of an elliptical earth on his chest, red trunks and boots, an angry and worried expression. He flies away from viewer along a river with flames in a forest on the river banks; he |
| 55 | | flies at and then away from viewer, leaving a trough of water, a yellow-orange sky. Cut to scene of forest fire, with white streaks from left; |
| 58 | Captain Planet: 'The power is yours.' | Captain Planet flies down and towards viewer, then soars up, leaving the smoke clearing, and the trees green, seen between his legs. Cut to five Planeteers in front of blue grid-earth, surrounded by CAPTAIN PLANET; they lift rings; Captain Planet lands behind them; words appear below: AND THE PLANETEERS. Glow of light on their fists and across the letters. |

*The earth in peril.* The first potential actor presented in the introduction is the earth itself: 'Our world is in peril.' A critical linguist presented with this text would undoubtedly be struck first by the lack of an agent for the environmental damage. We are not told who or what imperils 'our world'. Cars in a traffic jam and on a motorway junction are icons that could be read as images of prosperity, or modernity, but here they can signify environmental peril in general, just as a yellow liquid pouring into a stream, or burning forests or a rubbish tip can in other episodes – they are all interchangeable on this level. Such icons make the threat instantly recognisable, but they also limit the possible threats to those we already know and can see (try to come up with an icon for nitrate pollution from fertilisers, or depletion of genetic diversity in seed varieties).

As there are two phrases for the planet, 'our world' and 'the earth', there are two images: the post-1960s view of the vulnerable blue, green and white earth as seen from space, and the traditional myth as personified in Gaia. The movement back from the traffic jam to the view of earth creates it as a thing, and it is then equated with Gaia's eye. Gaia is apparently an amalgam of several myths that need not be familiar to the viewers. Despite her Greek name, she is shown, I believe, as south Asian, and she speaks with Whoopi Goldberg's voice; she releases both a Christian symbol, the dove, and an Olympian bolt of her hand. There is another icon of the earth as well, the emblem seen on the chest of Captain Planet, the ellipse covered only by a grid, the mapped, human-marked earth. (Does this remind anyone of Turner's other enterprise, CNN?) In these images the earth is both the source and the terrain of all the action, but is always passive.

There are only two actions in the spoken narration: Gaia sends the rings, and the young people summon Captain Planet. These two delegations of authority are the basis for the agency in the plot, and also the problem, for agency can be attributed at the level of Gaia (the whole earth), the Planeteers (selected actors), or Captain Planet (their collective action). The invocation of superhumans can be seen as showing hope or despair – hope because it suggests we can work together to fight pollution, despair because it suggests humans themselves do not have the power to act decisively.

*The Planeteers.* The Planeteers and their rings are linked to the earth by a fast but crucial chain of images: Gaia's gesture creates spiral nebulae that form five earths which turn into the different coloured rings. Then the central, green ring enlarges into a grid-marked earth, and the five Planeteers appear as running silhouettes towering over it. Despite the fact that the Planeteers all look like Californians, and sound like Californians talking like foreigners, they are characterised by the narrator in terms of a system of differences in which each represents both a continent and an element. These are traditional allegorical systems (I think of the continents on the Albert Memorial), but they have been modified with significant additions to fit current ideas of the globe. The addition of the Soviet Union transforms the traditional continents into a union of East and West. (In more recent programmes, Linka is from 'Eastern Europe'). The addition of 'heart' transforms the traditional four elements into romantic nature, whole because it is seen through human affections. How do kids read this elaborate pursuit of balance? They may be familiar with these patterns from other plots. They may be aware of a group being used to represent the human race from such shows as *Star Trek*. They may be used to the magico-scientific explanation of superpowers. This reification of the emotions is common in children's cartoons, linking *Captain Planet* to *The Care Bears*.

In the fast editing of this one-minute sequence all the images are linked and defined in terms of a circular, spiralling movement. Our own perspective in each vignette is a swirling, crane shot-like motion. The spiralling movement begins with Gaia, goes to the spinning planets, to the action of the rings, which are shot like guns, and to the spiralling Captain Planet. The spiralling action of the magic rings, which create columns or tunnels of earth/fire/air/water, is important because it marks their action as disembodied, worked through the elements, and because it marks it as bounded, local. In any comic-book story of supernatural powers, or even in classical mythology, we must know the bounds of the special powers. But this visual definition of their powers also relates to a problem in dealing with environmental threats. The threat is always something spreading, and their action is always a sort of containing. Captain Planet's action is typically to return the spreading blight to its source, again a bounded, curving motion.

*The villains.* Since the pollution perpetrators have about five seconds each, they have to be instantly recognisable examples of environmental wrongdoing: killing elephants, destroying trees, killing dolphins, burning the rainforest. These icons portray environmental damage as something that happens to a victim nature, not as something that happens to us. Like the aristocrat driving over a poor person's leg at the beginning of *A Tale of Two Cities*, the wrong has to be obvious. Each villain is not just a person but a hybrid of human and machine, usually a big angular machine like those in *Star Wars*; however it is personalised, that cyborg creature is the basic source of environmental damage. These villains enable the viewer to trace environmental damage to a baddie, replacing the comic-book supervillains with figures bearing some resemblance to capitalists and scientists. But they are curiously redundant; we don't need supervillains to explain the hole in the ozone layer or the release of toxic wastes. Nikolas Luhmann has argued that there may be other dangers from the moralisation of environmental communication.[6] He sees communication about the environment as crucial in linking different social and natural systems that work in different terms and do not normally interact, but which must exchange information in crisis. The demonisation of one actor or another is, in Luhmann's view, noise that disrupts this feedback, putting all the different systems in univocal moral terms. For instance, if we demonise 'pollution perpetrators', we lose any chance of finding how our own daily activities cause pollution.

*Captain Planet.* Captain Planet is not just a union of their rings, he is also, like some other mythological heroes, a product of the union of earth and sky. Captain Planet emerges as powerful, old and brown, a figure from Blake's engravings; but he is quickly transformed into primary colours, a superhero rather than a threatening extension of the earth. In this opening sequence we see him, not fighting villains, but flying through a trough of water that quenches the burning rainforest. The forest then returns to its pristine green, which is characteristic of all environmental damage in 'Captain Planet'; it is all reversible. I wondered if viewers tried to analyse the colours, so I asked Alice why Captain Planet had green hair. It could suggest either the environmental movement or punk subculture. But she said it was green because his body was made up of the colours of the rings; she explains it within the system given by the introduction rather than by reference to other cultural systems.

At the end of the introduction, the cheering Planeteers form an emblem, Captain Planet landing behind them, the beam of light that linked the various images now glinting off its letters. For our purposes, the key part of this mythology is that it takes the five Planeteers acting as one to summon Captain Planet; he, unlike Captain America or other superheroes, is constituted by a group. In terms of the plot, this means that the Planeteers must work together. They need him and he needs them. If he is needed, it must be that these problems are not to be solved just through cooperation. But at the end of the introduction, as at the end of each episode, he says, 'The power is yours.'

This analysis of the opening shows some of the textual features that can be interpreted in terms of agency:

*Grammatical encoding of who does what, in a way that obscures or generalises actors.* ('Our world is in peril. Gaia can no longer stand the terrible destruction.')

*Changes in perspective that put the viewer inside or outside the action* (drawing back so that earth becomes eye/perspective on rings firing).

*Circular motions that bound and link the actions* (Gaia/earths/rings/earth/fire/wind/water/Captain Planet).

*Colours that signify characters' origins and allegiances* (Captain Planet emerging).

*Icons of environment as victim* (earth/globe/planet/traffic/elephants/dolphin/tree stumps/rainforest).

There is too much here, which is why there are openings for interpretations beyond any intended by the producers. The characters are not just a superhero and the earth. We have to have both ordinary polluters and the villains, Gaia and Captain Planet, the audience and the Planeteers, science and magic.

In one reading, the mythology outlined in the introduction to *Captain Planet* is profoundly disempowering: both good and evil action are put on to fictional characters, and our role is reduced to that of spectators. But the complexity allows for other readings as well, about the need for cooperation across East/West and North/South, the links between various environmental threats, the global nature of changes The question is how viewers consume this rich stew.

## The Superhero Plot and the Environmental Plot

The plot of *Captain Planet* grafts a framework of environmental action onto traditional superhero stories. Some of the tensions within *Captain Planet* plots arise from this clash of genres:

1. The superhero plot is initiated by the villains, while the environmental plot attributes agency to the audience.

2. The superhero fights for nothing less than the fate of the universe, while the environmental plot focuses on the small and local.

3. The superhero plot has a bounded episodic time-frame, which here clashes with the historical time of environmental change.

4. The superhero plot requires the use of supernatural powers, while the environmental plot emphasises natural and human powers.

5. The superhero invokes science, while the environmental plot leads to a critique of uncontrolled technology.

6. The superhero plot leads to a restoration of the status quo, while the environmental plot seeks change.

Let us consider the ending of one episode, 'Meltdown Syndrome'. In this, as in most episodes of *Captain Planet*, there are two battles. Captain Planet is invoked early on, and easily defeats the villain Duke Nukem, who has commandeered a nuclear power plant after an accident. He stops the leak and collects the spreading radioactive steam. But Duke Nukem, and more importantly the plant, remain. In the second cycle of a typical plot, Captain Planet is incapacitated by toxic waste or the Planeteers separated and thus powerless. There is, after all, no plot if the superhero is omnipotent. Alice explained this after a friend had been watching with her. 'She hasn't watched it before. She kept asking questions like is someone going to die. No one dies, only Captain Planet nearly sometimes. Captain Planet always comes twice, once before and once at the final moment.'

In this episode, the powerlessness is achieved by having the Planeteers locked in the reactor core so that they cannot summon Captain Planet. The subplot then involves the conversion of the scientist. The conversion of the natives is a common event in Captain Planet plots; they often end with the adults praising the Planeteers and testifying that they have been shown the error of their ways. After the scientist rejects Duke Nukem's plan of destroying the world with radiation, he breaks free and rescues the Planeteers, who summon Captain Planet.

There are then three endings. First, the fun part: Captain Planet vanquishes the villain. This is just a superhero at work, accomplishing the task while causing as much dramatic disruption as possible. Captain Planet, though, fights with incessant punning, a trait he shares with the villains but not with the Planeteers. It doesn't matter whether the puns are funny or not; what is important is that they mark a casual attitude towards the fight. It is also typical that he turns the villain's rays back on him, and that he fights using gaping holes and elemental forces, here earth and ice. The victory carries with it a sort of justice, a revenge of nature. Part of this revenge is a reversal of roles in which the bully is revealed as a big baby. All this is satisfying enough, and it may be all that younger kids pay attention to. But the villain always remains, as in other superhero stories; here he shouts, 'The world's still full of nuclear power plants and nuclear warheads. There will be other accidents. I will have my day. Then everyone will be like me!'

Duke Nukem's taunt reminds us that the plot has another level which has to be resolved too: the environmental threat, as well as the villain, needs to be removed. Captain Planet hurls the cooling towers of the plant into the sun. (I am told that this solution has been seriously considered by scientists, but for dealing with the reactors, not the cooling towers.) The scientist asks, 'But what will we do for power?' The answer, typically, is a technological fix (here, geothermal energy) that allows for another demonstration of superpowers (Captain Planet bores a well). The resolution, then, is both technical and natural.

The third, and for our purposes most important, resolution comes with the 'Planeteer Alert', in which Captain Planet tells the viewers directly what they can do. This is not just random environmental information; it is linked to the story rather as a moral is linked to a fable, repeating the main action on a different scale. As Ma-ti says, 'The little things you can do can make a big difference for our planet.' Here the message is that electrical power is essential but we must conserve it whenever possible. The words are spoken in turns by Captain Planet, Gaia and the Planeteers. The images invoke familiar icons of electricity: the power grid, street lights, stereos and televisions. The audience is no longer in the power plant but in the very living room in which they are watching the television. Surely this is as far as television can go towards giving young viewers a sense of agency?

But there are ways in which this conclusion seems odd to me, and these tensions might provide openings for wider thinking about agency. The first is just that it contradicts itself, for one of the things one could do to save power is not to watch *Captain Planet*, though he doesn't say you have to go that far. The contradiction reminds us that whatever advice we are given, we are still expected to take the consumption of large amounts of energy as an ordinary part of our lives.

The second oddity is in the shift of scale. In this episode at least the advice relates directly to the problem. But in other programmes, when they talk about hazardous waste this translates in the 'Planeteer Alert' into picking up litter. The effort to link these problems to children's lives is a useful one, but it often changes the problem into just a matter of good manners. The relation is one of metonymy rather than one of cause and effect.

The third oddity is that the 'Planeteer Alert', in requiring a sudden suspension of the fictional frame, may mark all that came before as fictional. It is not clear where viewers draw the line. We have a nuclear power plant visible from our house, so I asked Alice if this programme made her worry about nuclear power plants. She said, 'Don't be silly. There are no nuclear power plants. They're only on *Captain Planet*.' As with her other answers to my questions about the programme, she tries to make sense of the ground rules of the series, not to relate it to her own world.

The fourth and most important oddity of the 'Planeteer Alert' has to do with the *you* implied in 'The power is yours'. I took it to mean the viewers, who by working together could accomplish what Captain Planet has accomplished – we are to take the message out of the television show and into our own actions. But when I asked Alice, she said it meant, 'The power *is* theirs. He's giving the power back to the Planeteers. They gave him the power with their rings.' If on the other hand the *you* is to include, through the Planeteers, all the population of the earth, it leaps to a global population in which there can be no difference of interests over environmental issues. In one episode, the then forthcoming Earth Summit in Rio is sabotaged by an insidious villain who arrives in a spaceship and brainwashes the delegates into blocking environmental change. As it turned out, this was hardly necessary; quite terrestrial villains could do the job. But in the unified earth of *Captain Planet*, only such an evil plot could explain the failure to achieve unity.

### Playing Captain Planet

Current work in cultural studies focuses not on media texts themselves, but on the active construction of those texts by audiences.[7] It could be argued that the producers of Saturday morning cartoons have planned for this active construction, selling toys that enable the audience to re-enact the show and basing new programmes on licensed products so that they are hardly more than extended ads.[8] But much as we may deplore this extension of the toy market, it does not mean that kids play with these toys in the ways they are shown in the ads, or that their own play is determined by the programme-makers.[9]

When I asked Alice if she played Captain Planet, as she plays the Wizard of Oz, the Sound of Music, The Worst Witch, Five Children and It, or Narnia, she said, 'No, only sometimes in the car, Lauren and I practise with our rings. We have to get good at it. Then we'll have to have chairs to be Ma-ti and Kwame and Wheeler. Are there just two girls? I wish I had a big teddy bear like Theresa. Then he could be Captain Planet.' So her sense of the relevant actors is rather different from the one in my analysis – for her they are just the Planeteers, and in particular the girls. Gaia and Captain Planet and the villains are for her superfluous. In other programmes as well, such as *Thundercats* or *Dungeons and Dragons*, she seems to experience them only through a surrogate, and she watches carefully that there is some opening for a girl. It is gender over genre.

She also has a rather different view of the plot from mine. I asked her if she did play Captain Planet what she would play: 'I would just . . . I would just . . . I would . . . get all the rings and all the chairs and Lauren and I would put on our rings and call him and then it would be over.' The story, converted into play, becomes an elaborate tableau; the play is in setting it up, not in doing it. I was a bit surprised that the villains, whose defeat she had loudly cheered, did not make up part of this game. I asked her if she would fight anyone. 'No, because we can't think of anyone to fight and besides we haven't got a chair ugly enough.' All this was taking me far from what I was seeing as the main point of the programme, the environmental message to act in one's own life, the message that seemed to have an effect when she told me to throw things in the bin. So I asked her if she would play at stopping pollution. 'We don't know how to play that. We would go out to the *real* outside and look at the pavement and pick all that up. And then we'd go back inside and start playing the other game.' Of course this is just one viewer, and perhaps a younger one than the target age of the programme.

Whatever the larger pattern, the point remains that the environmental message does not just go out, encoded in the text. *Captain Planet* offers a range of sometimes contradictory embodiments of agency in environmental change. But they are picked up and made use of by children in their own enactments of heroes, of girls, of proper behaviour. Does this reading of *Captain Planet* tell us anything useful about the way adults read environmental texts? What is most important about this kind of text is that it asks us to imagine new kinds of environmental actors. The texts we have, such as green advertisements, tell us what actions to perform, but do not usually ask us to reconceive the social system. We are left with the same old heroes and villains. Underneath the cooling towers there are social systems providing the technology of certainty, the assumptions about the demand for power, the place of a plant in the community, the ways of thinking about the threat.

The identification of agency for good or ill leads to a view of environmental change. If there is no agent, the threat is treated as irreversible and the audience is rendered helpless. If villains are at the root of the evil, then environmental wrongdoing is removed from everyday actions. If it is inevitable human error, then the causes are treated in isolation, a matter of chance rather than system. If the machines are at fault, the implication is simple technological determinism.

Similarly, if the world is saved by Gaia, then our action is unnecessary. If only Captain Planet can save us, then our action seems hopeless. The Planeteers as agents suggest the need for concerted action, but deny the existence of different interests in different parts of the world. If machines solve the problem, as they do in this episode, the result suggests there is a technological fix. And if it is the audience that must finally resolve the problem, the ending encourages a sense of agency but also trivialises the problem to make it susceptible to this solution.

These readings are all double-edged, leading us to some insights into change, and some blindnesses. As Alice's responses show, viewers may still make something quite different from what a formal analysis suggests. But it is still important to see what possibilities, what limitations, the text contains. Then we can ask why we need Duke Nukem and Captain Planet, and what we can do with them.

NOTES

1. Claire Messud, 'Active Ingredient' (interview with Barbara Pyle), *Guardian*, 26 May 1992.
2. Toby Young, 'Little Brother is Watching You', *Guardian*, 14 August 1992.
3. Ariel Dorfman and Armand Mattelart, *How to Read Donald Duck* (New York: International General, 1975).
4. Steven Yearley, *The Green Case* (London: HarperCollins, 1991).
5. Richard Reynolds, *Superheroes* (London: Batsford, 1992).
6. Nikolas Luhmann, *Environmental Communication* (Oxford: Polity, 1989).
7. David Morley, *Television Audiences and Cultural Studies* (London: Routledge, 1992); Ellen Seiter, Hans Borchers, Gabriele Kreutzner, Eve-Maria Warth (eds.), *Remote Control: Television, Audiences, and Cultural Power* (London: Routledge, 1989); James Lull, *Inside Family Viewing: Ethnographic Research on Television's Audiences* (London: Routledge, 1990).
8. Tom Engelhardt, 'Children's Television: The Shortcake Strategy', in Todd Gitlin (ed.), *Watching Television* (New York: Pantheon, 1986), pp. 68–110. See also Stephen C. Kline, 'The Empire of Play', in this collection.

9. Ben Bachmair, 'The Function of Interpretation and Expression in Television Experience and Television Symbolism'; Ben Bachmair, Brukhard Hofmann, Michaela van Waasen, Martina van den Hövel, 'Media Analysis Within an Activity-Context – Understanding a Girl's Activities and Verbal Images', both in M. Charlton and B. Bachmair (eds.), *Media Communication in Everyday Life: Interpretative Studies on Children's and Young People's Media Actions* (Munich: Saur-Verlag, 1990).

*Acknowledgments*: Earlier versions of this paper were presented at the 'Domains of Literacy' Conference at the Institute of Education, University of London, and at the Centre for the Study of Cultural Values, Lancaster University. Thanks to Jonathan Potter, who said an analysis of environmental discourse must start with *Captain Planet*; to Bron Szerszynski, for discussion, references, clippings and a comic book; and to Alice, though she told me I couldn't talk about *Captain Planet* because it is a children's programme.

# HOME ALONE IN THE 90s

## *Generational War and Transgenerational Address in American Movies, Television and Presidential Politics*

MARSHA KINDER

> We are headed for a generational war, with the young against the old!
>
> Paul Tsongas, at the 1992 Democratic Convention.

> A blurring of the distinctions among children, teens, and young adults has taken place as children become increasingly more sophisticated and mature in their choice of entertainment.
>
> Standard and Poor's 1990 Industry Survey of the Toy Market.

> Television discourse addresses its viewers as children. . . . The bigger the target audience, the more it will be paedocratized.
>
> John Hartley, 'Invisible Fictions' (1989).

On election night in 1992, shortly after the Democratic candidates had been declared winners in the US presidential campaign, Vice President-Elect Al Gore announced that their victory represented a change not only of parties but also of generations, for this was the first time candidates born *after* World War II had been elected to occupy the White House.

A few days later, the President of MTV was asked if he could explain why the youth vote (those from 18 to 21) had overwhelmingly switched their support from the Republican to the Democratic party, a question he was supposedly qualified to answer since (as Bill Clinton would later acknowledge at the MTV inaugurative ball) his station 'had a lot to do with the Clinton–Gore victory'. He replied that the switch was due to the 'generational imagery' of the campaign. While he was referring to stunts like Clinton's performance on the popular late-night Arsenio Hall television show with saxophone and shades, I will argue that the Democrats were appropriating a marketing strategy that had already proved successful in the late 1980s and early 1990s – an exaggeration of generational conflict that paradoxically serves as an effective form of transgenerational address.

This chapter is a sequel to my earlier article on the 1988 US presidential campaign, 'Back to the Future in the 80s with Fathers & Sons, Supermen &

PeeWees, Gorillas & Toons',[1] where I argued that voters in that election had matched father-and-son pairs to pick from. Voters could elect either the formerly wimpish Bush appearing patriarchal and presidential next to his vapid young Quayle, or the diminutive Dukakis playing the successful son of poor Greek immigrants next to the tall, fatherly, experienced Bentsen. That essay positioned those reversible pairs against a cluster of optimistic oedipal comedies of the 1980s in which fathers and sons change places – films like *Big, Like Father, Like Son, Vice Versa* and *The Back to the Future* series. But in 1992 the voters were choosing *between* generations – between that supposedly unique generation of baby boomers whose development continues to be so doggedly tracked by the media and those aging veterans of World War II who are becoming increasingly obsolete. This choice, I will argue, should be read against those blockbuster comedies of generational warfare from the early 1990s, *Home Alone* 1 and 2, as well as MTV's successful children's cable television network, Nickelodeon.

In the 1992 presidential campaign the 46-year-old Clinton purposely accentuated the generation gap between himself and the 68-year-old Bush by picking young Gore as his running mate – that is, by using generational redundancy rather than balance to privilege that issue over those of class, regionalism, race, ethnicity, gender and ideology. This generational discourse was further underscored by the 62-year-old independent candidate Ross Perot, with his vice-presidential choice of the elderly Admiral Stockdale as running mate.

Clinton's campaign further emphasised generational conflict – by acknowledging that he was a fatherless son who had stood up against his alcoholic stepfather whenever he tried to abuse his mother or younger brother, and by picturing him now as a loving father doting on his daughter and as the husband of a woman who is a strong advocate for children's rights. Both in his television commercials and in his speeches, he frequently repeated the refrain, 'Unless we change, our children can become the first generation of Americans to do worse than their parents.' Both his and Perot's constant emphasis on the nation's staggering deficit led political commentators to use phrases like 'fiscal child abuse' and 'generational war'.[2] Shortly after the inauguration, the controversial issue of cutting entitlements was split along generational lines, with rumours that Clinton's new economic policy would guarantee *all* children free immunisations and would tax the social security benefits of comfortable seniors. Increasingly the media began to dub these two generations the 'needy' and the 'greedy' respectively, regardless of race, ethnicity, and class.

Like the juxtaposition of the three epigraphs that opened this essay, the Democrats' use of this generational imagery seemed to be contradictory or at least dialectic, for it suggested that the best way to prevent the 'generational war' was to exaggerate both the difference between baby boomers and their greedy elders and their over-identification with needy youngsters. As Clinton put it in his inaugural address, 'We must do what no generation has done before . . . we must provide for our nation the way a family provides for its children.' Thus, it was hardly surprising that young

*Home Alone* star Macaulay Culkin appeared at the inauguration-eve party (broadcast on CBS), quipping, 'This is the first inauguration party I ever attended and, I've been told, the first such *Democratic* event to occur in my lifetime!' The camera quickly cut to a close-up of the youthful Clinton and Gore laughing at his remark, as if this child star were somehow emblematic of their own meteoric rise to power. What such imagery and rhetoric achieved was a sense of dynamic change in the face of glaring continuities. In fact, one of President Clinton's first acts was to appoint the fatherly Bentsen (with all his traditional baggage) as Secretary of the Treasury. The issue of generational choice helped gloss over the fact that in the 1992 election, as in the past, voters were still choosing exclusively among matched pairs of white Anglo heterosexual males.

This generational strategy is commonplace in American commercial television, which, as Hartley has argued, tends to address its spectators as children precisely to avoid troublesome divisions of class, race, gender and ethnicity.[3] I will argue that this convergence of generations moves in both directions – not only are adult spectators 'paedocratised' but also young spectators are encouraged to adopt adult tastes, creating subject positions for a dual audience of infantilised adults and precocious children. These subject positions seem to provide an illusory sense of empowerment both for kids who want to accelerate their growth by buying into consumerist culture and for adults who want to retain their youth by keeping up with pop culture's latest fads. While this strategy appears to exaggerate generational difference, it actually constructs a transgenerational address that is profitable to sponsors, for (as Standard and Poor suggest) the same product (whether it is Macaulay Culkin, Ren and Stimpy, or Clinton and Gore) can be simultaneously marketed to both constituencies.

One might ask: what is the advantage of this simultaneous exaggeration of generational conflict and conflation? If a product appeals both to the young and the old, then why not simply omit any reference to generational conflict whatsoever? Such an alternative would fail to privilege 'transgenerational appeal' as a functional difference that distinguishes the 'product' from its rivals. Thus within this consumerist logic it is apparently more profitable to exaggerate generational warfare so that transgenerational address can come to the rescue. In the case of Clinton, that means solving an accelerating problem (like the generation gap or national deficit) which was not only ignored but also exacerbated by the Reagan-Bush administrations.

Yet, as if to complicate the dialectics, the popular press has recently highlighted not only the wonders of transgenerational address but also its potential dangers, suggesting that it threatens to erode the formerly 'naturalised' boundaries between adults and minors, parents and children, and the patriarchal laws and incestuous taboos that are propped on these distinctions. Nowhere were these dynamics more apparent and disturbing than in the Michael Jackson case (when he was accused of molesting a young boy), in the Woody Allen scandal (over his affair with Mia Farrow's adopted daughter and his alleged sexual abuse of his own child), and in the Amy Fisher trial (the teenage Long Island Lolita whose attempted murder of her lover's wife was the topic of three network TV movies). In all three cases the destabilised definition of childhood made it even more difficult to determine the innocence and complicity of the precocious children and the stunted adults who collaborated in these transgressions, and it was precisely these ambiguities that were emphasised in the media's obsessive coverage of these events. Similar ambiguities were also involved in the rise and fall of PeeWee Herman (the comical stunted manchild who rose to television stardom by hosting a Saturday morning kids show with subversive transgenerational and homoerotic appeal but then got 'caught' masturbating in an X-rated movie theatre) as well as in the discourse surrounding Madonna, that weather vane of popular culture. These stars have created personae that conflate the precocious child with the stunted adult – a conflation that disavows sexuality in these infantilised men (PeeWee, Michael, and even Woody) while intensifying it in the waifish woman (be it Madonna or Amy Fisher). Thus, if the manchild proves sexual or the childwoman plays innocent, the power of their representations is destabilised, a dynamic which triggers volatile emotional reversals in the transgenerational audiences they address.

Consider, for example, a recent *McCall's* article titled, 'How to Protect Your Kids from Madonna', in which Ron Taffel (a New York family therapist and the magazine's 'parenting columnist') perceptively describes Madonna's transgenerational address and then sternly warns parents against its dangers.

> Unfortunately, with her mass-market approach Madonna also blurs the boundaries between parents and children. Think about it. When was the last time parents and kids shared the same sex symbol? But that's what has happened. As 150,000 copies of *Sex* were sold to *adults* in the first day, Madonna's message was being delivered to our *kids* through MTV, videos and CDs. This unprecedented mass marketing has two effects: First, it puts children and parents in the same soup. In this way Madonna reflects and contributes to the blurring of the hierarchy children need to feel secure. Second, it guarantees that parents will be unable to act like parents – to monitor and supervise what kids are exposed to.[4]

In order to counter these alleged dangers, Dr Taffel grossly exaggerates the generational differences between Madonna and her young fans.

> Madonna's (and her publishers') intentional challenge to parental authority . . . comes out of another era, in which oppressive religious and familial mores made *some* children feel powerless and bad. But it doesn't fit today's upside-down world. Today's children have trouble not because they are oppressed and stifled by a rigid environment – just the opposite: they're let loose too soon, out on their own too early.

So convinced is Taffel of the immutable power of generational difference that he concludes that Madonna's transgenerational address will ultimately lead to 'her own demise': 'The more adults latch on to her, the less interested kids will be. *They* understand the need for differences between parents and children.' Yet the Clinton campaign and a wide segment of pop culture apparently do not agree with this analysis, for their discourse demonstrates that the exaggerations of generational conflation *and* difference go hand in hand.

### Home Alone at the Movies

No films demonstrate these combined dynamics of generational war and transgenerational address more powerfully than *Home Alone* and its sequel, *Home Alone 2: Lost in New York*. Both films are action-adventure movies that display a formidable mastery of stunts or special effect – a genre whose fantasy of empowerment appeals both to precocious children like Culkin and to powerless childlike adults who are threatened by unemployment in a global market rapidly being restructured by new technologies. Usually identified with George Lucas and Steven Spielberg, this transgenerational supergenre has generated Hollywood's biggest box-office successes over the past decade. *Home Alone*'s cumulative domestic grosses for 1990 and 1991 reached nearly $300 million, almost equalling *Batman*'s record for 1989. In 1992, *Home Alone 2* was second only to *Batman Returns*; by April 1993, it pulled ahead (grossing over $172 million, as opposed to the $162.8 million earned by *Batman Returns*).[5]

Despite these impressive box-office figures, according to a recent story in the *Los Angeles Times* called 'Honey, They Shrunk the Movie Audience', there has been a disturbing 12 per cent drop in admissions for American moviegoers between the ages of 12 to 29 over the past two years, which has led to a continuing overall decline in the number of tickets sold (964 million in 1992 as compared with the all-time high of 1.2 billion in 1984). Presumably lured away by videogames, VCR's, and cable television, 'the young moviegoer, who typically goes to the movies 12 times a year, is no longer the largest segment of the audience. That age group has been surpassed by a baby-boom-generation moviegoer, age 25 to 50, who typically goes to the movies only four times a year.'[6] *Variety*'s market analyst Art Murphy claims the prognosis is dire: 'It's absolutely dangerous for the continued health of the theatrical business if the under-25 audience is not lured back. . . . This is the weak link of almost 100 years of younger people continually replenishing and driving the film business.' Since this under-25 age group has managed to keep the American box-office thriving through the 1980s (in contrast to the sharp decline experienced virtually everywhere else in the world) and since entertainment media are currently America's second leading export, this decline could have serious global consequences.

On the other hand, this situation exposes the tremendous power of youth culture, for it can have a decisive effect not only on the American presidential election but also on the global economy and the balance of trade. Hence Hartley's perception about American television's strategy of 'paedocratising' audiences can easily be extended to American movies, particularly in the world market where the advantages of displacing ethnic, linguistic and cultural difference are far higher and where MTV is already helping to produce a global youth culture whose members are still avid consumers of Hollywood products. The more optimistic industry leaders are now reconceptualising American movie theatres as merely a 'test market' for worldwide multimedia distribution. As Jack Valenti, President of the American Motion Picture Association, puts it, American theatrical exhibition is now a 'platform' to other markets that now include 'about 3 billion persons watching the very movies that first appeared in the cinema.' Yet if American youngsters are turning away from movie theatres, can global youth culture be far behind? In any event, there is a strong incentive for the US film industry to 'lure' kids back to movie theatres.

David Fox reports that most Hollywood studios are now coping with this decline in theatre attendance by relying primarily on transgenerational address, that is, 'to make broader appealing films with stars that appeal to multiple age groups.' This refers not only to global superstars like Arnold Schwarzenegger, Sylvester Stallone and Harrison Ford (who are associated with fast-paced action and violent spectacle) but also more surprisingly to children's cult heroes from other media like Teenage Mutant Ninja Turtles (who first rose to prominence in comic books, action figures, and video games)[7] and Super Mario Brothers (from Nintendo's video games and television series) and even to a young unknown like Macaulay Culkin (who experienced an overnight rise to stardom in *Home Alone*). What helps give both sets of stars their transgenerational appeal is their ability to combine violence and humour – a tradition that has its filmic roots in American silent comedy and cartoon farce and that is absolutely central to the *Home Alone* movies.[8]

The *Home Alone* films have essentially the same David/Goliath plot: young Kevin McAllister (Macaulay Culkin) is accidentally separated from his large family during the Christmas holidays and through wit, courage and bricolage transforms common household items and electronic toys into formidable weapons that enable him to defend his suburban home (or a luxurious New York toy store) from two invading burglars. In both films his initial separation is triggered by a power failure (brought on by an electrical storm or a battery recharge). As a means of phallic empowerment, the abandoned boy uses his Talkboy tape-recorder and joystick to appropriate the soundtrack of a gangster movie on a VCR and to record his uncle's castrating threats from the shower so that he can simulate the murderous Voice-of-the-Father in his own oedipal scenarios. In both adventures, the only family member he truly misses is his mother.

On the one hand, the *Home Alone* films are children's domestic farce or live-action loony toons, genres that assure audiences of a happy ending and the victory of its precocious superstar over his dim-witted adult adversaries. The villains' behaviour is bumbling enough to be comical and to disavow the painful consequences of the violence, as in any Road Runner or Bugs Bunny cartoon. On the other hand, the plot also evokes violent vigilante movies that are popular with adult males and that frequently star Clint Eastwood, Chuck Norris or Bruce Willis. Moreover, the narrative structure features repetitive bouts of accelerating violence that are commonly found in video games. This strange combination turns *Home Alone* into a third-grader's *Die Hard* or a second-grader's *Straw Dogs* – a transgenerational hybrid that enables kiddy spectators to grow into the more mature action genre and their parents to enjoy a non-saccharine children's film with a cutting edge.

As if young Kevin's main bout with the burglars were not enough, the film's transgenerational address is further accentuated by several other generational skirmishes of the oedipal variety, none of which is focused on the boy's actual father. In fact, in *Home Alone 2* Kevin gets on the wrong plane because he mistakes someone else for his dad. In the first film, these displacements include Kevin's conflicts with his bullying older brother and his nasty uncle, and a subplot involving a lonely old neighbour and his estranged son, whom Kevin helps to reconcile. The sequel adds a running battle with a snooty concierge (played by Tim Curry), whom Kevin humiliates by using his pirated patriarchal tapes to position him as a voyeuristic homosexual 'pervert'. As in the Clinton campaign, most threatening conflicts are displaced onto the generation war.

Despite this one homophobic flourish, the primary displacements in the *Home Alone* films are conflicts of class and ethnicity – between the charmed well-to-do middle-class Anglo family and the ethnic criminal have-nots.[9] Although the ethnicity of the burglars is not emphasised, Harry is played by Joe Pesci, who is usually cast as an Italian-American gangster, and (playing against the 'shrewd Jew' stereotype) Daniel Stern is the moronic Marv, who wishes himself happy Chanuka as he steals the Christmas Eve takings from the toy store. Moreover, at the low point of the McAllisters' Christmas vacation the family crowds around a TV set in a tacky motel room on a rainy morning in a hispanicised Florida, watching *It's a Wonderful Life* dubbed in Spanish. Meanwhile the fair-haired Kevin wallows in luxury at the New York Plaza with his dad's credit card. These latent conflicts of class and ethnicity help explain part of the film's appeal to yuppie parents who may feel powerless against urban crime and guilty over raising latchkey kids. Adult viewers can identify both with young Kevin as he bests the bigger, darker, dumber, poorer bad guys and with the distracted yet loving, affluent parents who are relieved to discover that their youngest child can survive on his own – even in a dangerous decaying city like New York. Thus they are encouraged not to worry about the 'other guy' – whether it's the under-class or the next generation.

As if to acknowledge the class discourse that was suppressed from the first film, in *Home Alone 2* the lonely old neighbour is replaced by a pigeon lady in Central Park. Yet, since her homelessness is attributed to a broken heart rather than to social conditions, Kevin ends up giving her his friendship rather than food, shelter or money. As if to provide more evidence of the film's social consciousness, the money that Kevin saves at the toy store is destined for sick kids at Children's Hospital, who may not be poor but who are still needy. Yet ironically, it is Kevin and his affluent family who receive the biggest donations – a complimentary suite at the Plaza and a truckload of extravagant Christmas gifts sent by the rich old owner of the toy shop.

Kevin is much more confident in the sequel, for he takes great pleasure both in his luxurious homelessness and in the repeat bout with the bandits which proved so profitable in *Home Alone 1*. In fact, he lures them to his uncle's house, which (like the basic plot) is under reconstruction, a ploy designed to accelerate the violence. Thus the sequel is still a displaced generational fantasy in which a precocious rich kid (who will probably grow up to be Kevin Costner) beats up low-life infantilised burglars.

The fantasy dimension was highlighted by an actual case in a Chicago suburb, where David and Sharon Schoo were prosecuted and convicted for having left their 9 and 4-year-old daughters 'home alone' at Christmas while *they* enjoyed an eight-day vacation in Acapulco. A cover story in the *National Enquirer* ends by quoting the 9-year old: 'The movie *Home Alone* makes it seem like fun for little kids to be left alone by their parents. But I know it's not fun at all – it's a nightmare'.[11]

More recently, similar accusations have been made in the popular press against Macaulay Culkin's real-life family by his former nanny Kimberley Frank. A cover story in the *Globe* titled 'Tragic Mac's Home Alone – & Terrified!' also exaggerates both the similarities with and differences from the movie. On the one hand, it claims: 'It's absolutely amazing that the cute kid who's made so many millions in the *Home Alone* movies is actually left home alone quite often in real life'.[12] Yet, on the other hand, Mac's response is portrayed as being just the opposite from Kevin's for, instead of fighting back against his 'monstrous' dad, Mac goes 'wild with fear'. There's also the suggestion that part of the reason the 'raging drunken dad' is so abusive is that he cannot accept the generational reversal in the family's economic situation: 'he likes to play the big shot, throwing his money around . . . [but] everyone knows it's money Mac has earned.' Thus we are led to believe he recuperates his patriarchal authority through physical abuse. As if to strengthen this implication, the nanny brings in as moral authority the voice of Michael Jackson, reporting that when she answered his phone call to Mac, he told her, 'You sound like a really nice person. I know they need someone there to take care of things.' Thus before his own scandal tarnished his image, Michael functioned as a pop *deus ex machina*, for it was well known that he and his siblings had suffered similar abuses from their father and that he had subsequently become the world's most popular advocate for children's rights – a mission that was prominently featured in his performance at Clinton's inauguration-eve ball where he allegedly met Macaulay Culkin.

Clearly the abuses within the Schoo and Culkin families would never have received extensive media coverage if not for the popularity of the *Home Alone* movies. Like the Michael Jackson, Woody Allen and Amy Fisher cases and Dr Taffel's stern warnings against Madonna, they call attention to the dramatic contradictions between the fantasy conflation of generations being portrayed in texts like *Home Alone* and the actual anxiety and deep moral rifts being generated by the increasingly ambiguous boundaries between children and adults. Such anxieties have been most intense in the popular discourses around latch-key kids and child molestation, issues that raise troubling questions like 'Who's Old Enough to Stay Home All Alone?'[13] particularly in an age of working mothers and inadequate child care; or what is the proper age of sexual consent, particularly since it varies so widely in different nations and decades?

**Nickelodeon – The Children's Network**

The pairing of generational war and transgenerational address is even more pronounced on Nickelodeon, the successful national cable station owned by MTV which promotes itself as 'the children's network'. Most of Nickelodeon's schedule is devoted to syndicated reruns of classical television series from the 1950s and 60s, which are presented in a new parodic setting for a new generation of viewers and also (as *American Demographics* puts it) for 'baby boomers who still carry fond memories of their childhood indulgences . . . [and who] want to recapture the feelings of comfort and security they had as children'.[14] According to Marshall Cohen, MTV's senior vice-president for research, 'It's really two different networks. During the day, Nickelodeon is aimed at kids. After 8 p.m., we become "Nick at Nite – Programming for the TV Generation".'[15]

Yet these borders are permeable, for (at the time of writing) Nick's weekday mornings start at 6 a.m. with *Mr Wizard's World* and *Danger Mouse*, classics with nostalgic appeal, and close in the wee hours (from 5 to 6 a.m.) with *Mr Ed* and *Dick Van Dyke*. Moreover, in 1992 Nick started scheduling some of their children's shows on Saturday night prime-time (what they call 'Snick').[16] In fact, many of Nick's shows are aired in several different time zones, as if implying they can or should be read differently by different generations. Thus just as MTV exposed the commercial nature of all American television by obscuring the boundaries between commercials and regular programmes,[17] Nickelodeon exposes the generational dynamics that dominate (what Hartley calls) 'the paedocratic regime' of American commercial broadcasting – an exaggeration of generational conflict that actually functions in the marketplace as transgenerational address.

Nick's strategy seems designed to tap the dramatic increase in the 'kid's market' – which, according to *Zillions* magazine (a children's version of *Consumer Reports*), now has $8 billion a year to spend – and the simultaneous decline in children's Saturday morning viewing, the traditional way of targeting it. Between 1986 and 1991 Arbitron reports a 15 per cent decline, and Nielsen confirms this trend for the period 1990–91, showing a 13 per cent decrease in Saturday morning viewing for children aged 2 to 11.[18] According to Simmons Market Research Bureau, 29 per cent of children in this age bracket 'watch TV before dinner' as compared with 24 per cent who watch on Saturday morning. Yet since 'children spend the most time watching prime-time TV', Simmons concludes, they 'are an audience worth targeting . . . but reaching them with television commercials is rapidly growing more expensive and less efficient.'[19]

While some advertisers are turning to children's magazines (many of which are modelled on adult classics like *Sports Illustrated* or on popular TV shows like *Sesame Street Magazine*, Fox's *Kids' Club* and *Nickelodeon*),[20] others use TV with a transgenerational address that assures kids that *they* are the privileged target – even though these same shows and products can also be enjoyed in a different way by older consumers. Though this strategy is central to Nickelodeon, it is also being used increasingly on other networks.

On 13 February 1993, Fox Broadcasting pulled ahead of the other major networks (CBS, NBC and ABC) in the Saturday morning time zone with *X-men*, an animated adventure series based on one of Marvel's most successful comic books. This show appealed not only to kids between 2 and 11, but also to teenage boys and even to adult fans of the original comics. Yet the Saturday morning time-slot showed kiddies that they were still the primary target. According to Daniel Cerone, Fox's success was 'inevitable' precisely because of their generational strategy, which differs sharply from that of the other networks and (I would add) closely follows the Nickelodeon model.

> Unlike the other networks, Fox lets kids toon out six days a week with blocks of *Beetlejuice!*, *Tiny Toon Adventures* and *Batman: The Animated Series*, among others, on weekday mornings and afternoons – during which the network can plug its Saturday morning lineup. The other networks and their affiliates generally aim for adults on weekdays with network news programs in the morning and soap operas and syndicated talks shows during the afternoon.[21]

Thus, as Cerone observes, the other major networks can promote their children's shows only on Saturday mornings. This applies not only to NBC (which has dropped its Saturday morning cartoons and turned to live-action shows aimed at teens) and to ABC (which lost its popular Disney series), but also to CBS (whose successful children's series, such as *The Little Mermaid, Garfield and Friends* and *Teenage Mutant Ninja Turtles* are ghettoised within the Saturday morning time zone). In contrast to CBS, which 'rose to No. 1 in prime time primarily with sophisticated adult series,'[22] Fox scored its greatest success with *The Simpsons*, a prime-time animated series with enormous transgenerational appeal, and with *The Mighty Morphin Power Rangers*, a daytime live-action series (aired daily both mornings and afternoons) whose young multicultural shape-shifting heroes have overtaken the Teenage Mutant Ninja Turtles in cult status and promotional tie-ins within the lucrative children's market. According to Judy Price, vice-president of children's programme and daytime specials for CBS, this transgenerational approach gives Fox a tremendous edge over CBS with young viewers: 'Fox has the best of all worlds. It's a kid-friendly network to begin with, with a prime-time schedule that's very youth-oriented.'[23] Yet even CBS is beginning to emulate this transgenerational strategy. For example, after the 30 January episode of their animated *Back to the Future* series broadcast on Saturday morning at 10, the station ran a promotion for its surprisingly popular prime-time family show, *Dr Quinn, Medicine Woman*, that ended with the tag line, 'And kids, you can let your parents watch, too!'

This line evokes some of Nickelodeon's best station promos, which go much further than those for any other network in exaggerating generational difference. One warns children not to let their parents watch Nick because adults are untrustworthy; they wear deodorant and ties, they shave under their arms, they watch the news and do other disgusting things frequently depicted in television commercials. Another amusing promotional spot for Nick's syndication of old series shows a silhouette of a parent and child with clasped hands over an image on a TV set, with the tag line: 'Watch Nickelodeon together, because if you don't tell your children about television's heritage, someone else will.' Thus television history is represented as a 'dirty secret' like sex, one that controls reproduction – of the culture, if not the species. This promo has it both ways, for it parodies the generation gap as well as transgenerational togetherness.

Nick's generational discourse reminds viewers how frequently kids appropriate adult conventions (or vice versa) while insisting that *their* version is different and superior. These dynamics are particularly strong in the cereal commercials aired on Nickelodeon just before the 1992 election. For example, one showed a young blond kid imitating Clinton by campaigning in front of a sign reading 'Greg for President', yet what he was promising was to keep Trix cereal 'just for kids'. In an Applejack ad, a 10-year-old boy is shown eating a bowl of cereal with his friends while his mother complains that it doesn't have any apples. After lip synching one of her lines, he complains, 'Parents . . . they just don't get it!' In a commercial for Frosted Flakes, we see a yuppy executive in an expensive suit obsessively eating cereal before hearing the tag line 'the adult cereal with the taste that never grew up'. While one might find these same commercials on other stations, on Nickelodeon they call attention to the generational strategy of the whole network as well as to the medium and culture.[24]

The same dynamic works in the syndicated reruns. Take, for example, the 'Aesop & Son' cartoon segment within *Bullwinkle's Mooserama Show*, which is usually framed by a conversation between father and son. In one episode the father complains that Mother Goose stole all his stories and thus forced him to turn to fables. Despite this father/son bonding against the mother, the two generations compete over who can come up with the best moral for the patriarchal tale. Although the story is taken from the past, it is adapted for a new generation which produces a fresh, improved reading. This is precisely the structure of how Nickelodeon treats its syndicated series and how Clinton ran his campaign.

Nick's original shows use similar dynamics, for most of them are merely children's versions of popular adult genres – quiz shows like *Nick Arcade*, *Family Double Dare* and *Wild and Crazy Kids*; teenage soaps like *Hey Dude*;

in the show, Ford told Ellerbee that these children should urge their parents to vote; she responded by asking him, 'When you were ten years old, Mr President, what did you want to be?' When one little girl asked Ford why children can't vote, he replied: 'Eighteen seems to be the dividing line in this country, between being a child or an adult.' Taking this comment as a cue to remind viewers of the station's functional difference, Ellerbee remarked, 'Kids can't vote but here at Nickelodeon, kids' opinions count!' Another young girl told Ford that she wanted to be President. After asking her age, he assured her: 'By the time you're thirty-five, there will have already been a woman President in this country.' Thus even a direct question about gender was translated back into generational terms. Issues of race and class were simply never mentioned.

What I find fascinating about this show is not only that the generational discourse displaces all other issues but also that it is marked by the same contradictions I have been exploring throughout this essay. While the structure of the show works toward conflation (demonstrating that children are just as interested in the political process as adults and therefore their votes should be counted), the specific comments of the speakers, especially those of an old patriarch like President Ford, reaffirm and even exaggerate the traditional boundaries between generations.

I do not mean to imply that generational issues are trivial. Rather, in this essay I have argued that *when used as a site of displacement*, this emphasis on generational conflict in popular culture can have at least three unfortunate social effects that are closely interrelated. First, it leads to a marketing

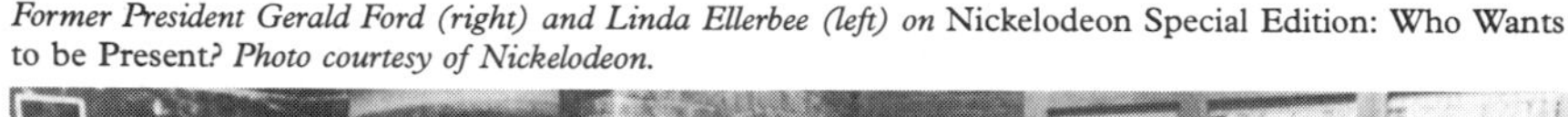

*Former President Gerald Ford (right) and Linda Ellerbee (left) on* Nickelodeon Special Edition: Who Wants to be Present? *Photo courtesy of Nickelodeon.*

strategy that masquerades as a moral or political issue. Second, it suggests that generational conflict is our most crucial social problem, one that lies at the core of, and therefore has priority over, other disturbing concerns (such as crime, drugs, the dysfunctional family, and the national deficit) whose economic and political complexities are far more difficult to address. Third, it distracts our attention away from other important conflicts of class, race, ethnicity, gender, and sexual orientation and thereby justifies the continued exclusive focus on the white middle-class patriarchal family with heterosexual tastes. It is this family that is currently being reproduced not only in movies like *Home Alone* and on television stations like Nickelodeon, but also in presidential politics.

NOTES

1. Marsha Kinder, 'Back to the Future in the 80s with Fathers & Sons, Supermen & PeeWees, Gorillas & Toons', *Film Quarterly*, vol. 42 no. 4, Summer 1989, pp. 2–11.
2. I first heard the term 'fiscal child abuse' on *Adam Smith's Journal*, which was broadcast on KCET, the PBS station in Los Angeles, on 1 November 1992.
3. John Hartley, 'Invisible Fictions: Television, Audiences, Paedocracy, Pleasure', in Gary Burns and Robert J. Thompson (eds.), *Television Studies: Textual Analysis*, (New York: Praeger, 1989), pp. 223–43.
4. Ron Taffel, 'How to Protect Your Kids from Madonna', *McCall's*, January 1993, p. 100.
5. *Daily Variety*, 12 April 1993, p. 10. Yet *Home Alone 2* was now second to Disney's *Aladdin* (which took in close to $197 million). An instant Disney classic based on an old oedipal tale, this new adaptation of *Aladdin* used the familiar voice of Robin Williams (another pop conflation of the precocious child and stunted adult who came fresh from his performance as Spielberg's Peter Pan) for the postmodernist genie, who was essential to the film's transgenerational appeal.
6. David J. Fox, 'Honey, They Shrunk the Movie Audience', *Los Angeles Times*, Calendar, 8 June 1993, section F, p. 1.
7. For an analysis of the successful supersystem constructed around Teenage Mutant Ninja Turtles, see chapter 4 of my book *Playing with Power in Movies, Television, and Video Games: From Muppet Babies to Teenage Mutant Ninja Turtles* (Berkeley, Los Angeles and Oxford: University of California Press, 1991).
8. A recent *TV Guide* cover story called 'Arnold, My Hero' (in the journal's special 'Summer Parents' Guide to Children's Entertainment') praised Schwarzenegger, along with Teenage Mutant Ninja Turtles and X-men, as wonderful role models for children because they use their muscle and mutant powers 'to fight for healthy causes'. The article touted Schwarzenegger's film, *Last Action Hero*, for showing that 'the violence in action movies belongs on the screen and not on the playground.' While admitting that Arnold's R-rated films like *Terminator, Predator* and *Total Recall* are 'not exactly kiddie fare', the article claims that 'much of the school-age population managed to see them anyway.' But we are told not to worry, for: 'Amazingly, what kids copied wasn't the violence, but the cartoonish quips: "Hasta la vista, baby" and "I'll be back!" Maybe that's Arnold's secret: He's the cross between a superhero and Garfield the cat.' Janice Kaplan, 'Arnold, My Hero', *TV Guide*, Summer 1993, p. 13. It's difficult to imagine parents being reassured by this article, particularly since no sources are cited other than Arnold himself.
9. This displacement of race and class on to the generational discourse is even

stronger in Universal's successful *Home Alone* spin-off, *Cop and a Half*, which opened in April 1993 and took in over six million in its first weekend (making it the top grossing film of the week, ahead of Disney's *Adventures of Huck Finn*, which opened the same weekend). The protagonist is a cute, eight-year-old African-American latch-key kid who is obsessed with being a cop. He has mastered the profession by watching television, especially the black and white cop team on *Miami Vice*. Thus, when the boy trades evidence about a dope ring for a place on the force, he chooses as his partner and surrogate father not the nice black officer but the more aggressive white cop played by Burt Reynolds. Conveniently for the film-makers, the kid lives with his grandmother, a strong, loving, desexualised nurse who raises no romantic complications with Reynolds. Avoiding these troubling racial dynamics, the film focuses instead on the generational conflict, which prevails both in the representation of the comical villain (a bumbling narcissist who loves to sing corny pop songs from the 1950s) and in the schoolyard scene that evokes the loudest cheers from young spectators. In this action sequence a group of racially mixed first and second graders of both genders not only beats up adult dope dealers but also gets revenge against the school's upper grade white bullies.

10. We can find a similar acceleration of violence in the 1993 movie version of *Dennis the Menace*, particularly in contrast to the live-action television series (which is now in syndication on Nickelodeon) as well as the animated series and the comic strip. Produced by John Hughes (who was also the producer of the *Home Alone* movies), this film seems designed to test the marketability of the generational war *without* the star power of Macaulay Culkin.
11. David Wright and Reginald Fitz, 'Real-Life "Home Alone" Kids Tell Their Own Story', *National Enquirer*, 19 January 1993, p. 8.
12. *Globe*, vol. 40 no. 21, 25 May 1993, pp. 6–7.
13. Gordon Monson, 'Who's Old Enough to Stay Home All Alone?', *Los Angeles Times*, 13 January 1993, section E, p. 1.
14. Brad Edmondson, 'Grown-Ups Just Want to Be Kids', *American Demographics*, vol. 9 no. 5, May 1987, p. 22.
15. Quoted in 'Grown-Ups Just Want to Be Kids', p. 22. According to this same article, in 1987 39 per cent of Nick's nighttime audience was in the 25–34 age bracket, 13 per cent between 12 and 24, 22 per cent between 35 and 49, and 26 per cent 50 or older. Moreover, 79 per cent of these adult viewers were homeowners, with 73 per cent making more than $20,000 per year.
16. For a discussion of this change in scheduling strategy, see Rich Brown, 'Saturday Night's All Right for Nickelodeon', *Broadcasting*, vol. 122 no. 21, 18 May 1992, p. 25. At the time of writing the 'Snick' line-up includes: *Clarissa Explains It All* (a female *Wonder Years*), *Round House* (a teenage version of *Saturday Night Live* or *In Living Color*), *Ren and Stimpy* (the most successful of their new Nicktoons), and *Are You Afraid of the Dark?* (a teenage version of *Tales from the Crypt* or *The Twilight Zone*).
17. For an elaboration of this issue, see my essay 'Music Video and the Spectator: Television, Ideology, and Dreams', *Film Quarterly*, vol. 38 no. 1, Fall 1984, pp. 2–15.
18. S. K. List, 'The Right Place to Find Children', *American Demographics*, vol. 14 no. 2, February 1992, pp. 46–7.
19. Ibid., p. 44.
20. For a discussion of the use of magazines to reach the children's market, see 'The Right Place to Find Children'. The most elaborate magazine-television marketing combination may have been developed by the Fox Broadcasting Company. According to Daniel Cerone, 'The Fox Children's Network, the umbrella organization under which all of Fox's children's programming falls,

runs a Fox Kids Club, which it says has swollen to in excess of 5 million card-carrying members. With Fox acting as a national "headquarters", spending $1.2 million a quarter to publish and mail fan magazines packed with Fox children's programming tidbits, Fox affiliate stations serve as local "chapters", holding community activities, meetings, and contests for the young viewers.' '*X-Men* vs. the Gang of Three: Animated Series Has Helped Fox Challenge the Other Networks on Saturday Mornings', *Los Angeles Times*, 20 February 1993, Calendar Section, section F, p. 1.

21. Ibid., p. 6.
22. Ibid., p. 6.
23. Quoted in ibid.
24. This transgenerational strategy is central to the popular success of network series like *Doogie Hauser, M.D.* (where a precocious doctor gives a unique adolescent perspective on a mature profession) and *The Wonder Years* (where a literary voice-over provides sustained adult commentary on adolescence).
25. As if in compensation for this promiscuous address, print ads tend to target a specific generation. For example, an ad in the *Los Angeles TV Times* emphasised the time slot as much as the show: 'Hey kid, don't miss Nickelodeon's Sunday animation treat. Tune in for non-stop action and side-splitting laughs on the *REN & STIMPY SHOW* each Sunday morning on Nickelodeon. *SUNDAYS AT 11AM.*' *Los Angeles TV Times*, 10–16 January 1993, p. 17.
26. While the *Ren and Stimpy* series consistently parodies consumerism (particularly in the hilarious commercials for logs), recent episodes have also mocked the inability of empowered adults to perceive differences between generations and species despite their claims to superior judgment. For example, in 'The Big Baby Scam' a hungry Ren and Stimpy pay off two nasty Baby Herman types so that they can take over their roles as infant twin brothers in a comfortable human household where, except for the praise won by Stimpy's prolific scatological production, their functional differences fail to be noticed by the doting mother or macho father, even in a three-generational family bath.
27. Linda Ellerbee is currently being celebrated in the popular press as the courageous TV personality who overcame a bad bout with alcoholism (at the Betty Ford Clinic) and a double mastectomy for breast cancer. She made her dramatic comeback via *Nick News* (which is produced by her small independent company, Lucky Duck Productions), particularly with a special called 'Conversation with Magic'. In a format similar to the one used with President Ford, she and a group of kids discussed the HIV virus with the basketball star, Magic Johnson. Not only did this show win the prestigious Cable ACE Award for the best News Special or Series, but it was taped only four days after Ellerbee had left hospital following her surgery. As she put it, 'A year ago, Nickelodeon didn't even have a news show, and now we beat out CNN for the big prize. And isn't it neat I'm still here to accept it?' Quoted by Claudia Dreifus, '. . . And I Lived!' *TV Guide*, 22 May 1993, p. 12.

# UNSHRINKING THE KIDS

## *Children's Cinema and the Family Film*

CARY BAZALGETTE AND TERRY STAPLES

> I was six when I was allowed to go with my mother to a cinema in Stockholm to see the film of *Black Beauty.* I remember one scene where a man wearing a cap comes into view from the right side of the frame climbing up a ladder and discovers that the straw on the threshing floor is burning. I was extremely excited, but I wasn't afraid because I already knew, from the book, that the horse would be saved. Even today, nearly seventy years later, I can see this scene very clearly before me.
>
> Ingmar Bergman, 1992.[1]

Cinema's relatively short career as a dominant cultural form has left it with a curiously ambivalent status. It is still, if only intermittently, castigated for its alleged power to deprave and corrupt; but on the whole, public anxieties about the effects of representations of sex and violence have shifted to television and video. Cinema now has museums and libraries and university departments devoted to it; there is an imposing body of theory about the ways in which it may be analysed and interpreted; space is devoted to it in serious journals; sponsors provide large sums of money to preserve 'classic films' almost as readily as they do to support performances of opera or ballet. On the other hand, cinema is not part of the school curriculum. Cinemagoing, at least in Britain and the USA, is not seen as an essential part of a child's cultural upbringing in the same way as visits to theatres or galleries are. Should it be?

In this chapter we explore the idea of cinema for children. This term can mean simply the exhibition of films for a general audience containing some children; it can also mean the dedicated production of films for children. By 'children' we mean people under the age of about twelve. We briefly survey a range of both exhibition and production at different times and in different countries; and then focus on films from two of the countries in which the concept of specialised production for children is relatively well-established. By analysing two films – one Danish, one Iranian – we exemplify this concept at work.

A common response to the notion of cinema for children, especially in the UK and the USA, is to doubt that it is worth bothering about, when video, computers, megadrives and soon, no doubt, other home-based screen technologies can provide a huge range of moving-image entertainment accessible to children. However, children certainly still do go to the cinema: recent surveys indicate that over 80 per cent of children in the UK under fourteen have at least some experience of it.[2] Making a journey specially to see a film; seeing a large, high-quality image and hearing a powerful soundtrack, perhaps on several speakers; watching in a darkened room as part of an audience, most of whom are strangers; living one continuous story for 100 minutes or more: all these are features of the cinemagoing experience that render it markedly different from watching videos or television at home.

We are not arguing in favour of the cinema experience as against domestic viewing; each has factors in its favour. But one is not a substitute for the other. Video offers the chance to view and re-view favourite or frightening episodes of a story, to buzz through the boring bits, to study effects, stunts and gags, to watch with friends and to talk and exclaim, comment and subvert, while the story goes on. Cinema is different. Among its antecedents is the magic lantern; its buildings have been called dream-houses. It is a medium whose audiences may be rapt or spellbound. Such intensity of experience is not guaranteed, but there is no doubt that cinema can be memorable in a different way from video and television.

If it is accepted that cinemagoing can be worthwhile and interesting for children, what kinds of experience should it, or might it, provide? To some the answer is self-evident: appropriate films already exist, exemplified most powerfully in the work of Disney, Spielberg and film-makers associated with them. Disney in particular would have choked with horror at the suggestion that his films were aimed at children, but the fact is that when children go to a cinema what they are most likely to see is a film from the Disberg stables. In recent years these would include not only *Hook* and *An American Tail* (directed, and produced, respectively, by Spielberg), *Beauty and the Beast* and *Honey, I Shrunk the Kids* (from Disney), but also the *Home Alone* films, *The Muppet Christmas Carol* and *Free Willy*, whose production teams have links with Spielberg's Amblin Entertainment or with Disney. A glance around the audience at one of these screenings will, however, bear out the marketing assumptions made by the producers: that these films offer something for everyone.

The idea that the child audience does not need to be catered for separately has not always been predominant, even in Britain and the USA. On both sides of the Atlantic the idea of a specialised cinema for children began to take firm hold in the 1930s, after the introduction of sound. Many talking pictures were quickly seen as too verbose, which made children in the audience restless; or too adult and immoral in theme. Alarm bells began to ring. Will Hays, President of the Motion Picture Producers and

Distributors Association of America, and author of its first Production Code on screen morality, said: 'We must have towards that sacred thing, the mind of a child, toward that clean and virgin thing, that unmarked slate – we must have toward that the same responsibility, the same care about the impressions made upon it, that the best clergyman, the most inspired teacher of youth would have.'[3]

Thus in the United States, Britain and elsewhere the practice of separate exhibition of selected, recommended films, usually on Saturday mornings or early afternoons, began to spread. It was driven by a sense of social responsibility, abetted by financial considerations. Charging a dime a head in the US, and twopence in Britain, managers were able to get an audience into the theatre at a time when it would otherwise be idle. Another commercial factor was the calculation that these matinee screenings would reduce the number of half-price children keeping out full-price adults at evening shows.

The obvious corollary to separate exhibition was specialised production, but this had no such profit inducement and was more rarely proposed. In London in 1936, reflecting on a national conference on the 'problem' of children and cinema, an editorial in *Sight and Sound* looked forward to a situation when it would be possible 'to evolve methods which might in time lead to the provision of children's films and children's cinemas, just as there are children's books and children's libraries'.[4] Outside the USSR this was then a fairly lonely voice, even though tentative; but ten years later, under the sunny smile of private philanthropy, the seed flourished in Britain and was soon transplanted.[5] In some parts of the world it still blooms, now with state support, and is responsible for, among others, the films we go on to discuss in this chapter: *Mig og Mama Mia* and *Khaneh-je Doost Kojast?*

In the United States, however, this seed soon shrivelled: the notion of specialised production for such a small audience – at most 8 per cent of the moviegoing population, according to Hays[6] – was just bad business. It was presumably with relief that producers read trade reports such as this in the *Motion Picture Herald*: 'A survey of juvenile attendance conducted by a Fox West Coast Theatres division manager is being cited as evidence in support of the conclusion that it is no longer necessary to produce pictures especially for junior audiences. On the contrary, according to the executive's interpretation, children are as grown up in their film tastes as a practical majority of adult theatregoers.'[7]

Low-price matinee screenings of such titles as *Abraham Lincoln*, *By Rocket to the Moon* and *Zoo in Budapest*[8] carried on in the US for many years after that, but were to some extent subverted by the vigorous development of a new genre, the 'family film'. The industry had perceived that its best way of surviving the Depression and at the time deferring to the Hays Code was through films that would attract adults and children together, at regular prices. (Clearly, animated features are part of the 'family film' phenomenon, but in this chapter we concentrate on live-action features.)

The differences between the family film (essentially American) and what we shall call the 'children's film' (essentially, but no longer exclusively, European) began then, and begin now, with casting. In their search for an 'all-American' boy to play the part of Tom Sawyer in the 1937 *Adventures of Tom Sawyer*, producer David Selznick and director Norman Taurog were explicit about their criteria. Out of the 25,000 who were looked at, over 60 per cent were ruled out on the grounds of 'size and general appearance'. The remainder underwent closer physical inspection and were rejected if they had any of the following 'defects': misshapen teeth; a short upper lip; eyes too close together; hairline too low; poor posture; a stammer, or an accent 'not typical of American youth'; ears too large; oddly shaped nose; weak chin; swarthy skin.[9] This left only a few hundred in the running. In other words, only about 3 per cent of American boys looked sufficiently 'American' to play an American boy for family film purposes. The quest finally produced Tommy Kelly, a Bronx schoolboy, described by one adult critic after seeing his Tom Sawyer as 'a pretty little fellow, with curly hair, sunny eyes and a slightly petulant lower lip which is rather attractive'.[10] It is clear from numerous accounts of such 'searches' for new child stars (which are also of course publicity stunts) that the child actors in family films had to offer not only national and ethnic identification to the child audience but sexual appeal to the adult audience as well. This aspect of their star qualities is, unsurprisingly, rarely noted; a celebrated exception being Graham Greene's description of Shirley Temple as a 'complete totsy' whose 'dimpled depravity' and 'well-shaped and desirable little body' was clearly calculated to appeal to middle-aged men.[11] And although it was undoubtedly the same criteria that brought forth Macaulay Culkin, similar remarks in these abuse-conscious days would seem even more outrageous.

By contrast, the children's film movement in Europe has always held that the child protagonists in a children's film should *not* be desirable moppets. Rather, they should be 'ordinary types of children . . . not the "sweet" little girls and waif-like little boys that enthral adult film-goers'.[12] This was not simply a matter of economics or even anti-Americanness. It was a positive belief that children in the audience could only properly identify with children on the screen if they were recognisably from the same world as themselves. This involves not only casting, of course, but also such areas as lighting, photography and editing; we discuss these in more detail later.

The difference in approach to casting goes beyond the selection of the child protagonists. There are also the adults to consider. In a family movie, there normally have to be well-known adult stars to help bring in the audience, from Walter Brennan's Muff Potter in *Tom Sawyer*, through Julie Andrews and Dick van Dyke in *Mary Poppins*, to Robin Williams in *Hook* and *Aladdin*. Naturally, the producer wants to get full value out of an expensive star, so the part has to be a meaty one, with commensurate production values. The focus therefore tends to be on the problems of coping with kids. Such problems, big or small, are often presented in adult terms and in ways that are inaccessible to children. This is not just a matter of script and plot content; it also involves *mise-en-scène* and editing. In

*Home Alone 2*, Kevin (Macaulay Culkin) is told by his father to fetch his tie from the bathroom. Kevin replies, in close-up, that he can't because 'Uncle Frank is taking a shower in there and he says if I walked in there and saw him naked I'd grow up never feeling like a real man' – cut to reaction shot of parental consternation – 'whatever that means.' On a broader scale, the central theme of *Hook* is the redemption of the adult Peter (Robin Williams) as a 'real father', expressed through scenes and visual metaphors that offer a great deal more to the adult males in the audience than to the children. In short, the overall viewpoint of a family film is summed up by the title *Honey, I Shrunk the Kids*, whereas in a children's film it would be *Sis, Dad Shrunk Us*.

Children's films can be defined as offering mainly or entirely a child's point of view. They deal with the interests, fears, misapprehensions and concerns of children in their own terms. They foreground the problems of coping with adults, or of coping without them. In the British *Hue and Cry* (1946) there are parents and choirmasters around, but they are of no account: the only adults who matter to the boys are the crooks whom they are hotly pursuing. In the Dutch *My Father Lives in Rio* (1989), Liesje's father, in prison for smuggling, is not many miles away from her. However, Liesje believes her mother's lie that he is working in Rio and secretly plans to fly out to see him. In the Germany–Turkmenistan co-production *Karakum* (1994), winner at the 1994 Berlin Kinderfilmfestival, two boys from different cultures are stranded together in the Karakum desert: they have to learn how to communicate with each other as well as construct a sand-yacht together.

The consequence of these differences is that whereas the family film can be packaged as a commercial proposition because of the size and wealth of the intended audience, not only in the country of origin but also abroad, the children's film almost invariably looks on paper like a complete non-starter, confined within its national boundaries. On occasion, when it can be chopped up into instalments or recast as a series, a children's department within a television company might put up some money. But if it aims at cinema exhibition, the only way a children's film can be made is through public subsidy. Even with such a subsidy, a children's film is always low-budget compared to a family film, and this has become part of its aesthetic.

Arguments in favour of family films have always stressed their 'universality' of appeal, although from a mixture of motives. Ideologies of 'childhood' stress that children are all the same, and are all the same the world over. There are certain themes and character types that are, it is assumed, 'guaranteed' to appeal to children. This idea is not exclusive to right-wing or romantic notions about the purity and innocence of childhood; the idea that children can transcend or ignore national, ethnic and religious boundaries has an obvious appeal to anyone wanting to prove that such boundaries are unnatural constructs. But whatever its ideological bent, the 'universal appeal' theme coincides happily with the needs of the American distributor seeking wider markets.

That children's cinema – and cinema generally – should be so thoroughly dominated by American companies seems perfectly natural in the United States, as one would expect. That it also seems perfectly natural in many other countries is the outcome of a cinematic cultural imperialism that has been energetically promoted throughout the twentieth century. This hegemony is found in its most comfortable form in Britain, where it hardly ever occurs to anyone to remark that almost all the films we see are foreign. Most of us in the UK just 'know' that most films are American and we have learned to ignore or assimilate their linguistic and cultural differences. Of course, there are specific reasons that have accentuated this situation; particularly the fact that, after the advent of sound, American cinema appeared less class-bound to British audiences than the drawing-room sets and cut-glass accents of much indigenous product.

In many other countries, resistance to the hegemonic threat of American cinema is expressed through state subsidy for indigenous production. Where this is established, films for children are often seen as an essential element of such production. It is assumed that national film industries must catch their audience young.

Subsidy, whether in the form of direct grants or fiscal inducements, is now frequently cited as the way in which indigenous cultural forms may survive the kind of imperialism exercised by the USA. For child audiences, it may be the only way. Within Europe, national cultures are not the only beneficiaries here; subsidised cross-border distribution may serve to offer children a wider range of cinema experiences by providing films from other cultures. Of course subsidy cannot by itself guarantee high quality, any more than the market can; it is just as subject to notions of 'worthiness', 'suitability' and ideological correctness. But the argument we are making is that children's films nevertheless do constitute a valid, distinctive, sometimes innovative and challenging form of cinema, which is just as much worth fostering as any other.

Two countries, among many, that believe it is important to make children's films are Denmark and Iran. Because there is such a small home market, Danish films cannot hope for a massive return, so virtually all of them are subsidised. Of the public money budgeted for this purpose, 25 per cent is reserved exclusively each year for the development and production of children's films. It means that in Denmark there are about three new feature films for children made every year, based on scripts approved by the state-funded Danish Film Institute.

In Iran there is no equivalent percentage obligation, but films for children are regularly made by the Institute for the Intellectual Development of Children and Young Adults, a body funded by the Ministry of Education. The Institute was originally set up in 1965 to develop specialist book libraries for children. Later, it began to create children's painting workshops and theatre schools in different parts of the country, and to produce short films for children. Before the revolution, there were six or seven film-makers working at the Institute; most of these have now left to work in Western Europe or the USA, but Abbas Kiarostami, whose work is now quite well-known in some countries outside Iran, particularly France, has remained and has been joined by others. They now make features as well as shorts.

In the late 1980s, these systems of support produced, among other films, Kiarostami's 1988 feature *Khaneh-je Doost Kojast?/Where is My Friend's House?* in Iran, and Erik Clausen's 1989 *Mig og Mama Mia/Me and Mama Mia* in Denmark. *Where is My Friend's House?* received adult critical acclaim and prizes not only in Iran but around the world; it also had a reasonable, limited run in Teheran and major cities. In Paris it played for four months during 1991 and 1992; it also had a provincial run in France and was made available for schools screenings. The Institute expected it not to reach the widest domestic audience until its television screening. *Me and Mama Mia*, on the other hand, performed very well at the domestic box office, was noticed at festivals, and soon went into dubbed distribution in five other European countries with the help of loans from the European Film Distribution Office.

It is perhaps predictable from their institutional and financial origins that these two films share a low-budget, realist aesthetic. Crowd scenes, special effects, big sets, even sweeping pans and travelling shots, are rare. The numbers of speaking parts and locations are limited. Both directors developed the child actors' performances through improvisation. They both also happen to draw upon myths within their own cultural traditions: *Me and Mama Mia* uses the myth of the flying horse Pegasus who can bring back souls from the dead, and *Where is My Friend's House?* the literary symbolism of trees and flowers. But apart from this they are markedly different.

*Me and Mama Mia* is more readily recognisable as a children's film, dealing as it does with the standard fare of an absent parent and the story of how parent and child (in this case, father and 11-year-old daughter) come to terms with the mother's death. Were it not for the language difference one can almost imagine it being shown by the BBC. But not quite. The film's most startling difference from British and American product is contained in its frankness about sex. The child Rikke overhears a drunken neighbour telling her father Poul that 'a man like you needs a woman next to him in bed – nothing can beat that.' Rikke – and the audience – finds out that Rikke's father Poul is more than just good friends with Rikke's nice teacher Charlotte when Rikke goes into the living room late at night and discovers Poul and Charlotte naked together on the sofa. 'Was that a private PTA meeting?' she angrily asks her father later. 'It won't get me better grades, you know.' 'It's been a long time,' her father tells her. 'I have a life too.'

*Me and Mama Mia* is not, however, just another Scandinavian let's-be-frank-with-the-kids piece of improving drama. Rikke's own way of finding solace after her mother's death is to fall in love with a horse. Again, we may think we are on familiar territory, typical of children's fiction, especially fiction for girls, but this is no rural idyll. The horse is won from a cereal packet competition, and Rikke lives with her father in an upstairs flat in a poor and run-down area of Copenhagen. The film's preoccupation is not with galloping across fields, but with what happens when you bring a horse into the living room; the boredom of seeing to the straw, feed and water every day; and whether you can keep a horsebox secure on a vacant lot in the middle of the city. The film is not unlike an Ealing comedy in its respect for the poignancy, as well as the comic potential, of ordinary folk's aspirations and fantasies.

It opens with a fantasy scene: a horse and a child in sunlit fields in slow motion; a smiling couple waving. But a freeze-frame on the horse cropping the grass reveals it as simply the photo on the cereal packet at which Rikke gazes while she eats her breakfast in the dim, cluttered urban kitchen, absent-mindedly acknowledging her father's instructions to wash the dishes and get the shopping on the way home. Rikke is blonde and slim, but there her likeness to the family film heroine ends: she wears glasses, not as a cosmetic gesture to 'ordinariness' but because the actor Christina Haagensen's visual impairment is immediately evident in her distinctive squint. Haagensen's performance is central to the film and one of its chief pleasures. She is by turns gormless, hot-tempered, sniggering, tearful, and has a fine line in 'fed-up' expressions. But in this film her performance is not used to build her as a star or to hammer home dramatic points.

In fact there are few heavily meaningful moments in *Me and Mama Mia*: there is no major dramatic conflict or portentous distinction between good and bad. In this the film again presents a contrast with most Anglo-American product 'for children'. The assumed audience is clearly not built on a deficit model of childhood where 'getting the point' and 'following the story' are supposed to be difficult and therefore everything must be spelt out at length and several times.

The first Rikke hears about having won the pony is when the cereal company has it delivered to her street in a horsebox; it so happens that the neighbourhood tramp, Ludwig, is around at the time and it is he who takes charge of the situation and leads the pony into the courtyard of the flats – 'I grew up with horses,' he says. Because Poul, while watching football on TV, had impatiently fobbed off Rikke's nagging about having a horse with ironic asides about keeping it in the kitchen and letting it sit on the sofa, Rikke commands Ludwig to lead the pony upstairs and install it in the living room. Poul is completely unaware that there was a real possibility of acquiring a horse, which allows for a fine comic scene when he arrives home to find it scrunching apples from the sofa and nuzzling into the fridge, while Ludwig contentedly butters the loaf for a quick snack and wipes his fingers in his hair. An angry scene in the courtyard follows: 'I know, "you must ask daddy first",' screams Rikke. 'All the other kids ask their mum, but I haven't got one!' The neighbours listen with interest and the factory-owner next door offers an upstairs storeroom, hay and access by the freight elevator. Poul is defeated.

Nothing that follows is particularly unexpected. The pony is named 'Tarzan'; Ludwig helps Rikke and her friend Bettina build a paddock in a vacant lot behind the flats and finds an old horsebox for Tarzan to live in; they and their friends learn to ride and the pony becomes a feature of the neighbourhood. Other characters are drawn in: Helmuth, the disabled but randy old watchmaker who lives downstairs; the nice teacher Charlotte who's concerned about Rikke's 'lies' – 'Sorry I'm late but I had to feed my pony' – until she finds out from Poul that they have become truth. It is she who suggests a visit to a suburban riding school, where posh kids in breeches and riding helmets ride big horses over jumps. Rikke has a go, wearing the watchmaker's crash helmet, and does well until she falls off at the double jump. Bruised and disconsolate, she's talking to Tarzan by herself when she notices another girl watching her. 'Go and stare somewhere else,' Rikke snaps, and mounts Tarzan for another ride. But Tarzan bolts: the other girl punches one of the posh kids into a ditch, snatches her pony and gallops off to rescue Rikke. It turns out that she is Tarzan's previous owner: when her father lost his job they sold the pony, then called 'Mama Mia', to the cereal company. That night, two roaming drunks open the horsebox and let Tarzan/Mama Mia out. Ludwig and Helmuth set off in pursuit on Helmuth's invalid tricycle, and it is in the course of this emergency that Rikke finds Charlotte and Poul on the sofa. The pony is tracked down, but Rikke is having to confront the fact that the desires of others can conflict with her own: from Charlotte taking the place of her mother to her friends' preference for football and skating rather than mucking out the stable. And when the girl from the riding school appears on her bike, it is clear that the pony prefers to be with her. The narrative resolution is swift and without dialogue. We see Rikke and her new friend taking turns to ride the pony in a country field; then suddenly in long shot Helmuth and Ludwig are setting off home together on the tricycle and we see Poul, and Rikke and Charlotte with their arms around each other, walking away over the horizon.

This narrative structure contains many of the same elements as an American-style family film. The pony is the catalyst that enables Rikke to come to terms with her mother's death, and to understand more about human relationships, about responsibility and the nature of ownership; above all, it brings about the reconstitution of the conventional nuclear family, the lack of which is stressed throughout. There are other similarities. Erik Clausen, the film's writer and director, plays Helmuth: he and Leif Sylvester Petersen, who plays Ludwig, are well known in Denmark as a comic double-act. Poul and Charlotte are also played by well-known actors, Michael Falch and Tammi Øst, and the film has a theme song by a popular Danish group. The opportunities are thus there for serving adult pleasures and offering an adult point of view, but they are largely refused; the adult roles, despite being important to the plot, are played down.

This is achieved through the film's photographic, editorial and performance styles, which are markedly different from those of the family film. Rikke and the other children are consistently shot from low-angle camera positions, often lower than their own head height. This is maintained even in dialogue scenes where alternating point-of-view shots would be expected in classical continuity editing. For example, in the angry courtyard exchange, we see Poul from Rikke's point of view, but we see Rikke

*Not a 'sweet little girl': Christina Haugensen in* Me and Mama Mia. *Photo courtesy of Danish Film Institute.*

from a point to the side of Poul and at about the height of his elbow. This contrasts sharply with, say, *Home Alone 2* where exchanges between Macaulay Culkin and adults alternate between the child's and the adult's point of view in dialogue scenes to emphasise Culkin's diminutive size and consequently his precocious pertness.

Reaction shots too are handled differently in *Me and Mama Mia*. The commonest use of a reaction shot in American cinema is to show a facial expression changing, and thus to emphasise a narrative point. Such shots are frequently edited to a slow beat, particularly in the family film, encouraging the audience to savour the performance and perhaps to laugh. The more dramatically significant the moment, the more reaction shots will be used, allowing time for all the implications to sink in (both to the characters and the audience). Clausen's cutting style in *Me and Mama Mia* is far more elliptical. Take, for example, the key moment when Rikke discovers that she has won the pony: this is achieved in just eight brief mid- and close-shots as she sees the horsebox and walks towards the pony with an almost disbelieving smile. Rikke's change of expression is not emphasised; in fact at one point she turns her head to smile away from the camera; and there are no cutaways to bystanders or the friends with whom Rikke has been playing a moment before. The emotional charge of the sequence is heightened only by brilliant lighting behind the pony's head, which both outlines its mane and floods into Rikke's face, and by a few bars of the theme tune which stop abruptly as soon as she comes face to face with the pony.

The growth of the relationship between Poul and Charlotte is sketched in with similar economy. In their first conversation, when Charlotte calls at the flat (one of the very few scenes not shown from Rikke's point of view), her acceptance of a beer instead of a second coffee is significant in narrative terms but is shown in the same kind of mid-shot as the rest of the sequence. In a later scene, when Charlotte walks towards the group of neighbours gathered at the pony's paddock, there are three reverse-angle mid-shots in which Poul can be seen gazing awkwardly towards her. Then at the riding school we surmise that Rikke is aware of something going on by seeing a very brief glimpse, in a crowded long shot, of Poul's hand on Charlotte's shoulder, followed by a reverse shot in which Rikke says to Bettina, 'Look, there's dad drinking beer again', implying that he's more interested in his own, adult pursuits than in her. In other words the audience is assumed to be able to glimpse these things as they happen and to make the necessary connections.

Music is also used sparingly, and for emotion rather than drama: key sequences, such as the search for the pony over the rail tracks at night, use only natural sound. The main 'non-diegetic' use of music is the theme song itself which accompanies Rikke's first gallop with the pony down a city avenue, and is repeated in just a few other similarly exhilarating scenes. Thus, although *Me and Mama Mia* is not action-packed, the story moves along at a cracking pace and the film is only eighty-five minutes long.

*Where is My Friend's House?* is very different, and as a proposition for exhibition to child audiences, problematic. This is not because it is 'disturbing' in content but because its style is so radically different, not only from the established forms of the family film, but also from the variations offered in *Me and Mama Mia*. And if that film's plot is simple, the Iranian film's is austerely prosaic. One day 8-year-old Ahmad takes home his friend's school exercise book, as well as his own, by mistake. He knows that his friend, Mohammad Reza, won't be able to do his homework acceptably without it and will therefore be expelled; the problem is that he doesn't know where Mohammad Reza lives. The major part of the film is taken up with Ahmad's search for his friend's house. He doesn't find it. The resolution of the problem takes up a mere ten minutes at the end of the film.

The reason this little tale lasts eighty-three minutes on the screen is that a great deal of it is told in real time. For example, we don't just see Ahmad leave his own house and then arrive somewhere else in the next shot, as happens in conventional continuity editing. We see him run down the street, up a path, up every zigzag of a track crossing a bare hillside, along a ridge, through a wood, and up the hill to the next village, Poshteh. When he has to return to his own village, Koker, we see the same sequence in reverse. And yet again, when he makes a second attempt to search Poshteh, we see the same journey for a third time. The realist conventions of time and space that we have learned are bent, if not broken. For an audience prepared to accept this entirely different time-scale, it becomes possible also to accept the intensity and suspense of the narrative on its own terms. We – not only the foreign audience but also the predominantly city-bred middle-class Iranian audience – are presented with a different world here. This is a tough rural society in which children are burdened with responsibilities and no excuses are accepted. Eight-year-old Ahmad has to mind the baby, fetch and carry for his mother, get his homework done, go out to buy bread, listen respectfully to boring old men. At the same time he bears the moral responsibility of knowing that Mohammad Reza's life will be ruined if he doesn't get the book back to him. The film's central theme is the harshness of adult-child relationships, in which the brutal imposition of endless obligations is redeemed only by children's mutual support and comradeship.

It may seem odd, in relation to our earlier comments about the family film, that Kiarostami does not see this as a film specifically for children. 'We try to make films *about* children rather than *for* children, which seems to me more serious, more interesting and more important. It allows more understanding to develop between adults – particularly parents – and children.' He cites an occasion when a 50-year-old intellectual stormed out of a screening of *Where is My Friend's House?*, protesting at its inappropriateness for a child audience, while a 4-year-old girl at the same screening had already seen it three times and 'understood it very well'.[13] This proves, he says, that classification of films by age group never takes account of individual interpretation. He admits that audiences consisting entirely of children get impatient with the film, wanting more action and excitement, but asserts that the same children, watching with their own families, perhaps on television, like it very much: the film becomes a catalyst for communication within the family.

Kiarostami's predominant concern through his twenty-year career as a film-maker has been with the nature of Iranian society and problems within it. In a 1992 interview he implies that his interests pose problems for his choice of subject-matter: 'With the tacit agreement of the censors, there is now a sort of self-censorship among film-makers.'[14] But by addressing the world of childhood he is able to explore problems which are nevertheless, in his view, fundamental within Iran. Homework is a recurrent theme in his films, a preoccupation which may seem bizarre to Western audiences, but he argues that 'as in all countries of the world, we stop children from playing and make them do this work in an obsessive manner. In the Third World, the problem is more serious than in the West. Parents and teachers pass their frustrations on to these poor children.'[15] In *Where is My Friend's House?*, homework and other adult-imposed tasks are the pivot upon which turn misunderstandings and antagonism between adults and children.

In a remarkable extended scene early on, the film's themes are unsparingly laid out. It takes place in the courtyard of Ahmad's family house. A formally composed long shot and leisurely pans establish the physical set-up: Ahmad and his parents and baby brother live downstairs; upstairs 'Granny' and 'Ali' (we're not told the exact relationship) are in rooms that give on to a wooden balcony running the length of the house.

Ahmad's mother is washing clothes at the pump in the courtyard and hanging them on lines stretched across the yard; his baby brother lies in a hammock stretched between the posts that support the balcony. Coming home from school, Ahmad sets out his homework books on a low rug-covered platform under the balcony, but he is instantly subjected to a barrage of demands from his mother: 'Get a nappy – no, a dry one, hang up the wet one again; get boiled water from Granny; put two lumps of sugar in it; do your homework; give him the bottle; rock him a little; do your homework, then play; rock the baby; do your work; quick, get me the washbasin.' Granny's contribution to these instructions consists of what one suspects to be a well-worn theme (ignored by Ahmad) about why he doesn't take his shoes off to go upstairs; she does, so why can't he?

It is while attempting to combine these duties with tackling his homework that Ahmad discovers that he has got Mohammad Reza's exercise book as well as his own. Since the opening scene of the film has shown the teacher reducing Mohammad Reza to tears because he keeps on losing his book and doing his homework on loose paper, we are prepared for the moment when, in silent long shot, we see Ahmad shuffling the two books to and fro, studying their covers and suddenly sitting up aghast: we are left to guess what has happened. In fact, Kiarostami has revealed in an interview that the actor, Babak Ahmadpoor – chosen for the part from the children of the village where the film was shot – had simply been asked to solve some mental arithmetic problems while this scene was being shot; the preferred reading is created entirely from the context.[16] The next part of the scene, however, which is performed through dialogue, directly conveys the failure of communication between adult and child. Since the mother is washing clothes, she is squatting by the washbowl and Ahmad speaks to her from a standing position; the subsequent shot/reverse shot sequence from their two points of view thus reverses the usual disposition of speakers in an adult-child dialogue. The cross-purposes of the dialogue are banal but relentless:

AHMAD: Look, I took his notebook by mistake, they're both alike.
MOTHER: So what?
AHMAD: I must give it back.
MOTHER: You'll give it tomorrow.
AHMAD: Tomorrow the teacher will throw him out of school.
MOTHER: Serve him right, he has to be expelled.
AHMAD: I took it by mistake.
MOTHER: Why didn't you pay attention?

Nothing in the performances, *mise-en-scène* or editing encourages the audience to take sides in this dialogue: Ahmad is anxious and baffled, but the mother looks up at him equally baffled, and preoccupied with other problems. All the film's dialogue is shot in this low-key way. In a later scene, when Ahmad returns from his first trip to Poshteh, he runs into his grandfather who's smoking with cronies outside a village house. Showing off to his friends, the grandfather insists that Ahmad must stop whatever he is doing and fetch his cigarettes from the house. This is one of two points when Ahmad actually quits a scene. The camera stays with the old man as he reveals that he has the cigarettes after all; he was ordering Ahmad about just to show that he could, and for the child's moral good. There follows a long disquisition on the value of his own father's habit of giving him a penny once a week and beating him once a fortnight: 'He sometimes forgot the penny, but he never forgot the beating.' No one judges this outrageous attitude and no retribution is visited upon the tedious old tyrant; in fact we never see him again.

Much of the film is thus in an apparently documentary style, appearing to eavesdrop on inconsequential conversations and observe people going about their daily work; and most of the praise heaped upon it has commented on its naturalism. But this quality is contained within a rigorously structured framework. Kiarostami's choices of locations and sounds consistently stress Ahmad's bewildered isolation. Poshteh seems like a ghost village as Ahmad runs up and down its deserted alleys and staircases beset by noises: dogs bark, cats mew, voices chatter in the distance but hardly a soul is to be seen. Each encounter – an old man bent double under a huge load of brushwood, a sick old woman with a cloth across her mouth, an old man inexplicably chucking rocks out of a doorway – introduces complications rather than solutions. Which Nematzadeh family does Mohammad Reza belong to? Does he live in Mazevar, Khanevar, Kashegar or Assemar? By the blacksmith's or over the sheep-pen? Maybe the Nematzadeh family know the Hemmati family who live up some stairs behind a blue door. And so it goes on.

*Not a 'waif-like little boy': Babak Ahmadpoor as Ahmad in* Where is My Friend's House? *Photo courtesy of Farabi Cinema Foundation.*

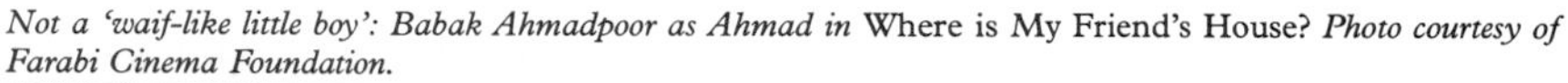

this problem is the negative way in which 'suitability for children' is regularly defined. Thanks to the right-wing lobbies who tend to set agendas here, suitability is arrived at through the deletion of factors such as violence, sex and bad language; what is left when these are removed is supposed to be fit for children to see and hear. From this the perception has grown up that children's fare is essentially anodyne and harmless, self-evidently unfit for the expression of real creative talent. Thus the hypocrisy of our society's much-vaunted concern for children and the sanctity of childhood is exposed. If we really cared about children as much as our political rhetoric says we do, then we would be voting funds to ensure that the films children see do not all emerge from the same low-risk, high-yield philosophy.

NOTES

1. Ingmar Bergman, quoted in 'The First Film Scene I Remember', in *Felix 92*, European Film Academy, 1992.
2. Cinema and Video Industry Research Association table in Tina McFarling, 'Cinema 1990–91 Exhibition', in David Leafe (ed.), *Film and Television Handbook* (London: British Film Institute, 1992), p. 39.
3. Speech by Will H. Hays in 1922, quoted in Mrs Charles E. Merriam, 'Report of the Chairman of the Better Films Committee of the National Congress of Mothers and Parent-Teacher Associations', reprinted in Lamar T. Berman (ed.), *Selected Articles on Censorship of the Theater and Moving Pictures* (New York: H. W. Wilson Company, 1931), p. 205.
4. Editorial, *Sight and Sound*, vol. 5 no. 18, Summer 1936.
5. See Mary Field, *Good Company* (London: Longmans Green & Co., 1952), p. 2.
6. Will H. Hays, 'Motion Pictures and Their Censors', *Review of Reviews*, April 1927, reprinted in Berman, *Selected Articles on Censorship*, p. 84.
7. *Motion Picture Herald*, 8 February 1936, p. 41.
8. Ibid., p. 40.
9. Studio press handout for *Tom Sawyer*, 1937.
10. Review of *Tom Sawyer*, *Evening News*, 11 May 1938.
11. Graham Greene, review of *Wee Little Winkie* in *Night and Day*, 27 October 1937.
12. Field, *Good Company*, p. 87.
13. Abbas Kiarostami, interview with Michel Ciment in 'Dossier du Cinéma Iranien', *Positif*, no. 368, October 1991, p. 76 (our translation).
14. 'Entretien avec Abbas Kiarostami, l'Humaniste', *Revue du Cinéma*, no. 478, January 1992, p. 20 (our translation).
15. Abbas Kiarostami, ibid.
16. Abbas Kiarostami, 'Dossier du Cinéma Iranien', p. 78.
17. Farah Nayeri, 'Iranian Cinema: What Happened in Between', *Sight and Sound*, vol. 3 no. 12, December 1993, p. 27.

# ONCE UPON A TIME BEYOND DISNEY

## *Contemporary Fairy-tale Films for Children*

JACK ZIPES

Without question, Walt Disney set the standards for feature-length fairy-tale films in the world of cinema. After his early beginnings during the 1920s in Kansas City, where he and Ub Iwerks made several shorts such as *Puss in Boots*, *Little Red Riding Hood*, and *The Bremen Town Musicians*, Disney moved to Hollywood and began perfecting the techniques of animation, organising his studio along the lines of efficient modern factories, and experimenting with storylines that would appeal to large audiences of all age groups and social classes. By 1934 he was finally ready to produce the film that would institutionalise the fairy-tale genre in the cinema industry in a manner that was just as revolutionary as the collecting and editing of the Brothers Grimm was for the print industry in the nineteenth century: *Snow White and the Seven Dwarfs* (1937) was the first animated feature in history based on a fairy tale and made in colour with music. Moreover, as a mass-market commodity with the trademark 'Disney' it was created with such technological and artistic skill that the Disney Studios have been able to retain a market stranglehold on fairy-tale films up to the present. Consequently, any film-maker who has endeavoured to adapt a fairy tale for the screen, whether through animation or other means, has had to measure up to the Disney standard and try to go beyond it.

But just what is the Disney standard, or rather the Disney standardised fairy tale? Since all Disney fairy-tale films are alike, from *Snow White* of 1937 to *Aladdin* of 1992, it may be more appropriate to talk about standardisation and not about standards.

In fact, the success of the Disney fairy tale from 1937 to the present is not due to Disney's uncanny ability to retell nineteenth-century fairy tales with originality and uniqueness, but due to his intuitive genius that made use of the latest technological developments in the cinema to celebrate mechanical reproduction in animation and to glorify a particular American perspective regarding individualism and male prowess. In short, Disney 'taylorised' the extraordinary talents organised in his studios to represent himself as the prototype American hero who cleans up the world in the name of goodness and justice. Embodied as the stalwart prince in all his fairy-tale films, Disney himself became the product of technical animation controlled by corporate powers that communicated a single message: what was good in the name of Disney was good for the rest of the world.

By 1937 everything was in place for Disney to convey and reinforce this message tirelessly in all the animated fairy-tale films and other cinematic products of his studios. In fact, already in 1934 the American magazine *Fortune* was able to state with remarkable perspicacity that 'in Disney's studio a twentieth-century miracle is achieved: by a system as truly of the machine age as Henry Ford's plant at Dearborn, true art is produced. Hereafter we shall examine that system and see how it resembles and how it differs from the automatic simplicity of an assembly line.'[1] Though the *Fortune* article maintained that the final products of the Disney studio were artfully manufactured, it also demonstrated that the films were made not for the sake of exploring the story as an art form, or for the sake of educating children and stimulating their imaginations, but for the sake of promoting the label marked Disney. There was very little difference then as now between a Disney plate, watch, T-shirt, cap, or amusement park filled with other commodities and rides and the fairy tales that he adapted for film and book publication. The copyrighted label was what counted most. Disney's signature designating ownership over the fairy-tale films was part of his 'modern' endeavour to re-create an ancient mythic cult through mechanical reproduction. However, what is perhaps most striking about Disney's fairy-tale films, unlike his other inventions and commodities, is that he avowedly sought to make the characters and background as lifelike as possible; and the more he did this, the more his versions of the classic fairy tales became lifeless.

Indeed, he did the opposite of what fairy tales generally do, for they illustrate how people and things can be magically restored to life, while he transformed himself from a living being into a brand name that became synonymous with what Nietzsche called 'the eternal return of the *same*'. In Disney's case it is the eternal return of the same kind of youth. There is something peculiarly American about this striving to remain forever young and blissful in Disney's fairy-tale films that perhaps accounts for their appeal. However, youth and bliss are packaged continually in the same manner so that the end effect is homogeneity depicted in perfect synchronisation.

All the Disney fairy-tale films focus on synchronisation, one-dimensionality and uniformity for the purpose of maintaining the brand name Disney as champion of entertainment. If we were to study each one of the studio's fairy-tale films from *Snow White* to *Aladdin*, we would discover the following similar features.

1. Each of the films is a musical that imitates the standard Hollywood musical of the 1930s. Special attention is paid to catchy lyrics and tunes, background music, and sound effects that either heighten or break the action so that the characters can reveal their innermost thoughts. For

instance, Snow White sings about wishing for a prince, while Beauty announces that she wants to break out of her provincial town and find the love of her life. As Richard Schickel has remarked:

> There is also a structural rigidity about the Disney animated features that has grown increasingly obvious as the years have passed. The editing principles applied to *Snow White* were those of the conventionally well-made commercial film of the time. There was nothing particularly daring about the way it was put together; its merit was based on other skills. In general, a scene would open with an establishing or master shot, then proceed to an intermediate shot, then to close-ups of the various participants, with conventional cut-aways to various details of scenery or decor as needed. Confusing flashbacks or dream sequences were avoided, and special effects were introduced in such a way that every child was aware that something out of the ordinary was about to happen.[2]

2. The sequential arrangement of the frames with clear breaks between each scene follows essentially the same plot: the disenfranchised or oppressed heroine *must* be rescued by a daring prince. Heterosexual happiness and marriage are always the ultimate goals of the story. There is no character development since all figures must be recognisable as character types that remain unchanged throughout the film. Good cannot become evil, nor can evil become good. The world is viewed in Manichean terms as a dichotomy. Only the good will inherit the earth.

3. Since the plot is always the same, the incidental characters and their antics play a larger role in the film version of the story. They are always funny, adorable, infantile and mischievous. They are the dwarfs and animals in *Snow White*; the mice and fairy godmothers in *Cinderella*; the household utensils in *Beauty and the Beast*; the genie and animals in *Aladdin*. Their slapstick humour and marvellous feats place the technical wonders of the film on display and prevent the fairy tale from becoming boring. Since nothing new is told or explored in the story, there is always a danger that it will indeed become boring.

4. What passes as new is the introduction of innovative camera work, improved colour, greater synchronisation, livelier music and lyrics, and unique drawings of exotic characters. Yet this 'newness' reinforces the nostalgia for eternal youth and a well-ordered, clean world in which evil is always recognisable and good takes the form of a male hero, who is as dependable as the phallic principles that originally stamped the medium of animation at the beginning of the twentieth century.[3]

5. Disney's films were never intended solely for children but to captivate the 'child' in the viewers. If one can discern in the films an attitude toward children, it is that they are to be swept away as objects by the delightful and erotic images. This sweeping away is an envelopment that involves loss of identity. That is, children as viewers are to lose themselves in oedipal wishes that are depicted on the screen. The process of viewing involves infantilisation as each frame regulates the drives and wishes of the viewer

according to rigid sexist and racist notions that emanate from the nineteenth century and are recalled in the film with nostalgia.

Since Disney never really wanted to explore the narrative depths of the fairy tale through cinema but wanted to celebrate the technics of animation itself and to figure prominently as the power behind these technics, he left a space open to other film-makers, who have sought to go beyond Disney in re-creating fairy tales for the screen with varying success. They range from Jean Cocteau to Jim Henson, and they have used realistic means and animation to focus more on changing the tale than re-establishing its antiquated view of the world. Since there have been hundreds of fairy-tale films produced for both children and adults since 1937, it would be extremely difficult to discuss all the experiments that have sought to transcend the standardised Disney film. Therefore, I want to focus on some of the more recent endeavours of such film-makers as Jim Henson, Shelly Duvall and Tom Davenport, who have tried to produce 'high-quality' fairy-tale films for young viewers. Indeed, these film-makers, all marked by Disney, have different attitudes toward children as viewers, and instead of using the film medium to infantilise them, they have produced films that challenge children and seek to make them think and act for themselves. Their success cannot be measured by their breaking the Disney stranglehold of the fairy-tale film because no studio can really challenge the corporate power that the Disney studios have over the means of distribution and market for fairy-tale films. Even the Henson Studios had to accept this reality after Jim Henson died in 1991.[4] However, their success can truly be measured by the ingenious manner in which they use innovative narrative strategies to deviate from the 'Disney standards'.

### Jim Henson

Until his sudden death in 1991, Jim Henson and his associates appeared to be the greatest challenge to the Disney studios in developing animated and live shows for children that not only captured their pocket books but managed to stimulate their minds as well. More daring and stimulating than the Disney films, the productions of Henson Associates covered a wide variety of topics and continually tapped the technical possibilities of puppetry, animation and acting to challenge the creative and critical capabilities of young viewers, whether it was through *Sesame Street*, telecast on American Public Television from 1969 to 1981, *The Muppet Show*, which ran on American television from 1976 to 1981, the films *The Muppet Movie* (1979) and *The Great Muppet Caper* (1981), or the television production of *The Storyteller* (1987).

In the area of fairy-tale films, Henson experimented in different ways by parodying the classical and Disney tradition through his Muppet characters and by addressing serious concerns of history, folklore and narration in his brief series *The Storyteller*. I want to discuss three examples of his work to demonstrate how the Henson films have subverted the standards of Disney fairy-tale films to break the infantilisation, narrative strategies of closure and exaltation of homogeneity conveyed by the Disney products.

*The Frog Prince*, directed and produced by Henson,[5] was telecast by CBS on 11 May 1971 and was later made into a videotape for distribution in North America. It is notable for its irreverent attitude toward the Grimms' version of *The Frog King* and is a critical transformation of the classical beast/bridegroom narrative that basically celebrates male authority. The Muppet film is told tongue-in-cheek from Kermit the Frog's perspective, and with the exception of live actors as the prince and princess all the roles are played by bizarre puppets who remain puppets. That is, the story is fantasy with no pretensions to being lifelike or having characters who act like real people, even though a frog-puppet is transformed into a human being in the end.

The new story as fantasy reads as follows. Kermit, sitting by a pond, recalls an incident in which he encountered a tiny frog, a stranger named Robin, who tells him and the other frogs at the pond that he is an enchanted prince, bewitched by an evil motley witch and her sidekick, a dumb ogre called Sweetums. None of the frogs, including Kermit, believe him as he sings 'They call me Robin the brave, and history will one day rave. I'm noble and brave . . .' Since Robin is such a runt of a frog, they all think his story is just a fairy tale, but Kermit soon realises that he is telling the truth when he sees that Robin cannot swim.

Now the only way that Robin can become human again is to be kissed by a princess who lives in a nearby castle. However, Kermit tells him that there is little chance of this because Princess Milora has also been bewitched and can only speak backwards. When she comes to the pond she accidentally loses her golden ball, and Robin promises to retrieve it if she takes him to the castle and befriends him. Since he promises not to cause any trouble, she gladly agrees, and Robin miraculously gets the ball. Once at the castle, where Kermit continues his narration, we learn that the princess was cursed by her Aunt Tamanella, who is none other than the witch who had changed Robin and had tricked the stupid king into believing that she is his long-lost sister. Tamanella's eyes are on the king's throne, and she seeks to be crowned queen instead of Princess Milora. To make sure she will succeed without interference, she captures Robin and gives him to Sweetums the ogre to eat. However, Kermit helps Robin escape, and along with the other frogs of the pond they intercede at the coronation of Tamanella and smash the ball on the handle of the witch's cane. She loses her powers, is transformed into a bird, and flies off. The princess, who has regained her ability to speak directly, thanks her friends for their help and gives Robin a kiss. Of course, he is transformed into a prince, and the spectators sing a song of joy to celebrate the coronation of the princess. At the end, we are returned to the pond, where Kermit sits on the ledge of the well and tells the viewers that he still sees the prince and princess a lot. They appear on the scene with a baby, and Kermit adds that he feels proud to have a baby named after him.

This cinematic spoof of the Grimms' fairy tale is filled with humorous songs such as the lullaby song for the ogre: 'Go to sleep, you stupid brute. Lay your ugly head on your wretched bed. Close your eyes and go to

*'Keeping him on his toes': John Hurt as the Storyteller. Photo courtesy of Jim Henson Productions Ltd.*

different that each film demands detailed discussion. I shall here deal with just one of the films, *Hans My Hedgehog*, to demonstrate how unique the Henson productions are.

The most popular version of *Hans My Hedgehog* is to be found in the Grimms' collection. It is based on the beast/bridegroom type of folktale in which a young woman is obliged to sacrificc herself because her father has made a promise to a monster. The most well-known tale of this kind is *Beauty and the Beast*, and the plot generally makes an equation of beauty = passivity = femininity, whereas ugliness is due to some curse in need of salvation. The girl is supposed to sacrifice herself for the welfare of her father or parents, and she is generally rewarded for being docile and virtuous.

In the Henson/Minghella version, various themes beyond the necessity for feminine sacrifice are explored. With regard to the 'monster', there is the hedgehog's personal struggle to overcome his bestial shape and form his own whole identity, the conflict with his father that leads to his mother's death, the betrayal by the princess and the suffering he endures because of his split personality. With regard to the princess, the question of sincerity and loyalty becomes germane. She is depicted as strong and valiant. When asked by the hedgehog whether she finds him very ugly, she responds, 'Not so ugly as going back on a promise'. Here she is referring to her father's promise, and we are introduced to another aspect of ugliness and beauty. Beauty is connected to loyalty, honesty and respect, and later the princess feels ugly when she goes back on her promise to the hedgehog not to reveal that he sheds his skin at night and is a handsome man. Swayed by her mother's false advice, the princess drives the hedgehog away, and she wears out three pairs of iron shoes on a long quest to find him. In the end, she must struggle with him so that he can regain his human form, and the tale ends with a second wedding, the storyteller concluding, 'This time the feasting went on for forty days and forty nights and I myself was there to tell the best story there is to tell, a story that begins in hello and ends in goodbye, and for a gift they gave me a shoe worn to nothing. And here it is.'

As the storyteller holds the shoe up, the dog shakes his head sceptically, bringing the film to a close – but not really to a close, for the story is questioned and may indeed have another version. In fact, at one point during the narration the dog interrupts, insisting that the storyteller was telling the story wrong. The dog shifts the narration according to his viewpoint, until the storyteller picks up the threads and builds a role for himself within the narrative so that he is both inside and outside the narration. Throughout the film the narrative perspective keeps shifting through the interchange of the storyteller and the dog, and through the artistic use of the camera, lighting and sets. The initial fireplace scene is the hearth of the stories, and out of the fire in darkness the story is unravelled through the silhouettes of puppets behind a sheet, the painted figures on a cracked antique plate, and finally the rural cottage in which the hedgehog is born. Live characters interact with puppets and fantastic creatures without a line drawn between reality and fantasy. The action moves from sets that imitate real homes and castles to canvas paintings of imaginary woods and hills. The surrealism of the images is heightened by slanted frames and camera shots taken from below. The cinematic portrayal of the storyteller's tale is fabulous and filled with surprises so that the viewer is encouraged to expand his/her knowledge of storytelling and manner of looking at images. Even – or especially – if one is familiar with the Grimms' version of this beast/bridegroom tale, the film offers new insights into the traditional scheme, exploring new artistic forms for conveying the themes of this particular tale.

All the films in the *Storyteller* series are creative experiments with classical tales, puppetry, cinematic techniques, painting and music that reveal the potential of the film through television and video to recapture communal aspects of storytelling. In homes in front of a small screen viewers see the storyteller engaged actively with a listener who interrupts, questions, mocks, laughs and sighs while the story is told and enacted. There is a bond formed between storyteller and listener and viewer, and the sharing of the story becomes a unique experience that does not call for identification or envelopment of the viewer.

**Shelley Duvall's Faerie Tale Theatre**

In an article that recorded the success of Shelley Duvall as a TV producer, *Forbes* magazine reported:

> In 1982 the pay television network Showtime, desperate for original programs to help it compete with both HBO and network TV, finally commissioned three *Faerie Tale Theatre* shows. Like most struggling business people, the first thing Duvall did was ask some of her friends – in this case Hollywood stars – for help, thereby bypassing the traditional channels of agents, managers and studios. Shrewdly targeting stars with children, Duvall asked for their help in creating quality television for kids.[9]

One has to question the use of 'quality' in this article and whether the fairy-tale films were actually done for 'kids'. From 1984 to 1987, when *Faerie Tale Theatre* sold into syndication, Duvall produced twenty-six episodes, each 50 minutes long, featuring Klaus Kinski and Susan Sarandon in *Beauty and the Beast,* Dick Shawn, Art Carney and Alan Arkin in *The Emperor's New Clothes,* Eve Arden and Jean Stapleton in *Cinderella,* Ben Vereen and Gregory Hines in *Puss in Boots,* Lee Remick in *The Snow Queen,* Elizabeth McGovern, Vincent Price and Vanessa Redgrave in *Snow White,* Liza Minnelli and Tom Conti in *The Princess and the Pea,* Robin Williams and Terri Garr in *The Frog Prince,* to name just a few of the star-studded productions.

Obviously, with actors like Redgrave, Remick, Williams and direction by Eric Idle, Roger Vadim and Duvall herself, the films had a certain professional quality, but the emphasis in most of them was on the stars' ability to do *tour de force* performances rather than to re-create the classical fairy tales in an innovative manner. Spectacle, amusement for the sake of the actors' obvious enjoyment and for amusement's sake, simplistic renarrating of the traditional plots that are merely touched up with ornaments – these are some of the conventional 'quality' features of *Faerie Tale Theatre.* And yet, amid the glitter and pomp of the series, there are some stimulating films. Duvall's policy was one of laissez-faire, so that there are many different cinematic styles and interpretations of the fairy tales.

For example, the productions of *Red Riding Hood* and *Beauty and the Beast,* directed by Roger Vadim, are indicative of the retrogressive quality of the entire series. Though Malcolm McDowell is amusing in his role of the bungling wolf, the portrayal of Red Riding Hood and her relationship to her father is so infantile, so blatantly oedipal, that the story is reduced to a tract denouncing female gullibility and celebrating male power. The setting and the characterisation are one-dimensional, no better than the kind of cheap storybook version one can buy in a supermarket. *Beauty and the Beast* is not much better. Vadim offers a slavish imitation of Jean Cocteau's *La Belle et la Bête,* but without its sophistication, and there is no endeavour to re-create the storyline or add to the characterisation as the Disney studios did in the animated version of *Beauty and the Beast.*

Everything is predictable, and it is difficult to comprehend why Beauty would want to sacrifice herself for her father or the beast, despite Klaus Kinski's fine acting.

In contrast to these stale imitations of the classical fairy tales, Eric Idle's production of *The Frog Prince* is a superb adaptation because of its hilarious parody and unusual artistic use of puppets and masks. In Idle's script, the story opens with a curse placed on a baby prince by an old crone, who was not invited to his christening because the forgetful queen did not think she would fit in well in the courtly society. Of course, the queen and king are aghast to find their son turned into a frog, but there is nothing they can do about it. Many years pass, and we are introduced to another royal household in which an extremely vain princess terrorises the servants and her parents. Wonderfully played by Terri Garr, this princess is so excessively haughty that she is ridiculous – even the servants make fun of her. Once she loses her golden ball, given to her by 'an adolescent prince with

*Terri Garr and Robin Williams in Faerie Tale Theater's* The Frog Prince.
*Photo courtesy of Pandora International Entertainment Group.*

homicidal tendencies', she strikes a deal with a talking frog, played by Robin Williams, who speaks the voice of an adroit green puppet.

Of course, the princess breaks her promise and calls the frog a sucker. When the frog pursues her, he is almost cooked by a French chef but saved by the king, who is afraid of disorder and revolution and thus wants his daughter to keep her promise. The frog turns out to be a charmer at the king's feast; he dances, sings, tells jokes and does a Shakespeare routine. When the princess retires for the evening, she is compelled to take him with her. Then, to her surprise, he defends her with sword in hand against an ugly insect. She finally softens and rewards him with a kiss. All at once the frog turns into a naked prince, covered only by a towel. Attracted to each other, the princess and the prince begin kissing again to see how the charm works. But then the king arrives, and refuses to believe that the prince was once a frog. So the prince is thrown into prison, and the princess sent to a strict boarding school. Later the old crone, who had started everything, appears to the king in a golden ball and reveals the truth, and the king pardons the prince and arranges for a marriage. The crone promises that will be the end of her frog tricks, but there is a great deal of doubt whether this will occur.

Similar to the Muppet version of *The Frog Prince*, this film subverts the traditional storyline to stimulate the viewer to question the old fairy-tale lines. The language is American slang, and there are numerous sexual innuendos that charge the film with exciting and comical erotic play. Most of the characters undergo change in the course of the story, and the puppetry, music and sets are designed to enhance the humour of the narration. The cinematic portrayal of the monarchy and court life is clearly critical of the pomposity of royalty and the arbitrary use of power. In the process the beast/bridegroom tale is no longer about the self-sacrifice of a woman who is obliged to save a bestial man, but about vanity and hypocrisy and the power of humour to expose false consciousness.

There are other films in the *Faerie Tale Theatre* series, such as *The Three Little Pigs* and *Jack and the Beanstalk*, that are innovative adaptations of classic fairy tales and other fairy-tale films. However, without a clear educational or philosophical policy with regard to children, the films are hit-or-miss commodities that may or may not contribute to the creative and critical awareness of young viewers.

**Tom Davenport**

If there is little 'systematic' thought determining the philosophical and production policies of Duvall's *Faerie Tale Theatre*, the reverse may be said of Tom Davenport's remarkable adaptations of the Grimms' fairy tales for young audiences. An independent film-maker, Davenport has carefully elaborated his ideas about exploring fairy tales and folk traditions in films since 1975, and in a recent article he discusses how his new three-part film series about fairy-tale adaptations are intended to develop the creative potential of his young viewers:

*Kelly Mancini and Mitchell Riggs in* Ashpet: An American Cinderella. *Photo courtesy of Davenport Films.*

> Because film and television have become the primary bearers of myth and storytelling (and consequently the charter for social action in our country), understanding how to make film and video will empower people who may otherwise feel helpless and manipulated by media. Some teachers are already accepting video reports from students who are eager to explore the power of camcorder, VCR, and computer. Once people begin to understand how the film and television are made, they will fear it less and respect it more.[10]

Indeed, Davenport's current work in fairy-tale adaptation for the screen shows a steady progression in innovative experimentation and a concern for educating children about fairy tales and film.

Relying mainly on grants from the National Endowment for the Arts, the Public Broadcasting System and other foundations to further his explorative work, Davenport has collaborated with actors, technicians, storytellers and writers to bring out essential psychological and social features of the Grimms' tales in his films and printed versions that are directly related to folklore. He has not modernised the tales in a slick, sensationalist manner. Rather he has historicised them and shifted the focus carefully by giving them American settings from the seventeenth century to the present.[11] By introducing American characters and events in American history, he has shown how such qualities as patience, cunning and courage have helped his protagonists overcome poverty, prejudice and hardship during wars, famine and economic depression. Davenport is interested in how people survive oppression, particularly how they survive with pride and a sense of their own dignity. Through his films he conveys these 'fairy tales of survival' to give young viewers a sense of hope, especially at a time in American history when violence, poverty and degradation appear to minimise their hope for a better future.

The first three films, *Hansel and Gretel* (1975), *Rapunzel* (1979) and *The Frog King* (1980), which Davenport co-produced with his wife Mimi, were all set in the South and Appalachia and are period pieces. Most of the shooting was done on location, with close attention paid to typical customs, architecture, landscape and dialects. The difficulty with these films, however, is that Davenport relies too closely on the plots of the Grimms' tales. For instance, while *The Frog King* is a faithful rendition of ante-bellum life in the South, it is also has some racist and sexist implications in its depiction of the servants and the princess. In his early work Davenport had not yet learned to use folklore and history critically so that more liberating alternatives to oppressive situations could be explored.

However, since the production of *Jack and the Dentist's Daughter* (1983), an adaptation of an Appalachian folktale with black characters, one of the only fairy-tale films ever produced with minority people as protagonists, Davenport has made great strides in his original use of the fairy tale and film to enhance viewers' understanding of storytelling, politics and creativity. One of his best endeavours is his 1990 film, *Ashpet: An American Cinderella*. This cinematic version is about a young white woman named Lily, who learns to reclaim her rights and heritage through the help of a wise black woman whose sense of history and knowledge of oppression empowers the 'enslaved' Lily to pursue her dreams. The action takes place in the rural South during the early years of World War II, when people were forced to separate because of the military draft. But Lily manages to find the strength to overcome isolation and exploitation by piecing together a sense of her own story that her stepmother and stepsisters had taken from her. Consequently, Davenport's Cinderella story is no longer history in a traditional male sense, that is, no longer the Grimms' story or a simple rags-to-riches story. Nor is it a didactic feminist interpretation of *Cinderella*. Instead, Davenport turns it into an American tale about conflicts within a matrilineal heritage in the South, narrated from beginning to end by a well-known black storyteller, Louise Anderson, who plays the role of Dark Sally, the magical conjure-woman and fairy godmother. The focus of the film becomes Dark Sally, as it shows how her storytelling can lead a young woman to recover a sense of her history and give her the strength to assert herself.

The fairy tale as historical document/history as fairy tale: these are two premises which Davenport works from in all his films. Since his training was in documentary film-making, it is not by chance that all his films have a unique reportage quality, as though they were newsreels of the past. Davenport works closely with historians, folklorists, artists, storytellers and actors to develop a sense of historical authenticity that does not undermine the magic of the fairy tales. Paradoxically, the fantastic occurrences in the film have more impact because of their historical foundation.

In addition to using history and the fairy tale to shed light on social developments and the nature of storytelling, Davenport has published newsletters about each film that are made available to schools. These newsletters are pedagogical tools intended to help the teacher and students explore and understand the film in its present context and to go beyond it.[12] In this manner, Davenport himself has learned from the responses to his films and tries to incorporate what he has learned into each new production.[13]

## Conclusion

As the work of Henson, Duvall and Davenport reveals, film-makers have indeed gone beyond Disney in the adaptation of fairy tales for the screen,[14] and one could point to other interesting fairy-tale films such as Rob Reiner's *The Princess Bride* (1987), Ralph Bakshi's *The Wizards* (1977), Wolfgang Petersen's *The Never Ending Story* (1984) or TV series productions such as *The Fractured Fairy Tales* (1961–4).[15] Indeed, in one of the more pointed and hilarious cartoons, *Sleeping Beauty*, the handsome prince is a caricature of Walt Disney, and when he discovers Sleeping Beauty, he withholds his magic kiss and builds an amusement park around her called Sleeping Beautyland to make money. The evil fairy wants a cut of the profits, and Walt the Prince tries various ways to have her eliminated. Disney never wanted to share or to have anyone try to go beyond him, but this fractured fairy tale exposes him and demonstrates through its clever humour and animation that there are ways to transcend Disney.

Keeping things in perspective, we must remember that Disney was in fact a pioneer in that he pointed out the great possibilities animation and film had for the effective expansion of the fairy-tale genre into the age of mechanical reproduction. However, instead of fully realising those possibilities, he became too absorbed in their commodification after establishing the fairy-tale film as art form.

Just what is the potential of the fairy-tale film as art form and ideological expression, already realised in part in the works I have discussed? How can fairy-tale films further the autonomy of young viewers and stimulate their creative and critical faculties?

Children are exposed to the social design of 'reality' from the moment they are born. Adult versions of 'reality' are imposed upon children to ensure that they are positioned physically, socially and culturally to experience their own growth and life around them in specified ways. 'Reality' is held up to them as empirically verifiable and an inexorable force. Fairy tales have always balanced and subverted this process and offered the possibility of seeing reality as an illusion. It is as children become aware of the artifices and machinations in their lives that they gain the sense of alternatives for making their own lives more meaningful and pleasurable. It is thus through the cinematic adaptations of fairy tales that reality can be displayed as artificiality, so that children can gain a sense of assembling and reassembling the frames of their lives for themselves.

Going beyond Disney is therefore the realisation that fairy tales do not begin and stop with Disney, but that one can make one's own life resemble a fairy tale that transcends antiquated notions of patriarchy and racism. To paraphrase the German romantic writer Novalis – 'Menschwerden ist eine Kunst' – learning how to become a compassionate human being involves learning to live life as an artist and to realise fairy-tale dreams as narratives of our own making.

NOTES

1. 'The Big Bad Wolf', *Fortune*, November 1934, p. 88.
2. *The Disney Version: The Life, Times, Art and Commerce of Walt Disney* (New York: Simon and Schuster, 1968) p. 206.
3. Cf. Donald Crafton, *Before Mickey: The Animated Film 1898–1928* (Cambridge, MA: MIT Press, 1982), pp. 1–33. With regard to Disney, Crafton states: 'Perhaps the aspect that most set Disney's series apart from his competitors' was the overtly libidinous (but presumably naive) content of the humor. Present audiences cannot help but be impressed by the extent to which phallic imagery informs the majority of gags.' (p. 294).
4. See Andrea Rothman, 'The Henson Kids Carry On', *Business Weekly*, 4 February 1991, pp. 72–3. Before he died, Henson was negotiating a $150 million deal for the Disney Studios to purchase Henson Productions. It was eventually blocked by Michael Eisner of Disney for undisclosed reasons, which in my opinion may be a blessing in disguise for Henson Productions. Buenavista now handle Henson's distribution, however.
5. Jerry Juhl wrote the screenplay. The princess was played by Trudy Young, the prince by Gordon Thomson. The film was co-produced by Henson Associates and VTR Productions (Canada).
6. This ending may also be a hidden reference to the well-known lines in *Annie Hall* by Woody Allen: 'You know, even as a kid I always went for the wrong women. When my mother took me to see *Snow White*, everyone fell in love with Snow White; I immediately fell for the Wicked Queen.'
7. See the book based on the TV series, Anthony Minghella, *Jim Henson's 'The Storyteller'*, illus. Darcy May (New York: Knopf, 1991).
8. 'Miss Piggy Went to Market and $150 Million Came Home', interview with Jim Henson, *American Film*, no. XV, November 1989, p. 20.
9. 'The Shelley and Ted Show', *Forbes*, 5 February 1990, p. 174.
10. 'Making Grimm Movies', *From the Brothers Grimm*, vol. 5 no. 1, 1993. See also Tom Davenport, 'Some Personal Notes on Adapting Folk-Fairy Tales to Film', *Children's Literature*, no. 9, 1981, pp. 107–15.
11. See Anthony L. Manna, 'The Americanization of the Brothers Grimm, or Tom Davenport's Film Adaptations of German Folktales', *Children's Literature Quarterly*, no. 13, Fall 1988, pp. 142–54.
12. The newsletter is called *From the Brothers Grimm* and is published by Davenport Films in Delaplane, Virginia. Each issue generally focuses on one of Davenport's films. For instance, volume 3, issue 1 of 1990 featured a discussion of *Cinderella* and *Ashpet*.

13. At present, Davenport is at work adapting *Snow White* for the screen. He has taken a Kentucky folk tale, 'The Step Child That Was Treated Mighty Bad', collected by Marie Campbell, and has set the story in the Shenandoah Valley at the beginning of World War I.
14. There are also numerous fairy-tale films that continue to reflect the standardised mediocrity of the Disney productions and ideology. For instance, the Cannon Group produced a series of films in 1987–8 – *The Emperor's New Clothes, Hansel and Gretel, Rumpelstiltskin, Sleeping Beauty, Snow White* and *Red Riding Hood* – that have dubious value. Operating with stars (Amy Irving, Sid Caesar, Diana Rigg, Isabella Rossellini among others) as Shelley Duvall did, the executive producers Menahem Golan and Yoram Globus managed to make fairy tales look stale on the screen. A reviewer for *Variety* commented: 'Will Cannon's Movie-tales sell tickets? Maybe, but only if the kiddies and their parents want to watch thoroughly unsophisticated but very straightforward storytelling with only the slightest inkling of modern technical production values' (27 May 1987, p. 16).
15. *The Fractured Fairy Tales* were narrated by Edward Everett Horton and were part of the American TV series *Rocky and His Friends* and *The Bullwinkle Show*. This series is currently being reproduced for the American TV channel Nickelodeon as *The Adventures of Rocky and Bullwinkle*.

BIBLIOGRAPHY

Caron Lowins, Evelyne, 'Il était mille fois, il sera encore . . .', *La Revue du Cinéma*, no. 401, 1985, pp. 43–8.

Cholodenko, Alan (ed.), *The Illusion of Life: Essays on Animation* (Sydney: Power Publications in Association with the Australian Film Commission, 1991).

Davenport, Tom and Gary Carden, *From the Brothers Grimm: A Contemporary Retelling of American Folktales and Classic Stories* (Fort Atkinson, Wisconsin: Highsmith Press, 1992).

Finch, Christopher, *Of Muppets and Men* (New York: Alfred A. Knopf, 1981).

'How to Help Your Kids Get the Most from TV', *TV Guide*, no. 39, 2–8 March 1991, pp. 5–9.

Hutchings, David, 'Enchantress Shelley Duvall Creates a Magic Garden in her Faerie Tale Theatre for TV', *People Weekly*, no. 20, 12 September 1983, pp. 58–60.

Kantrowitz, Barbara, 'Fractured Fairy Tales', *Newsweek*, 18 July 1988, p. 64.

Lenburg, Jeff, *The Encyclopedia of Animated Cartoons* (New York: Facts on File, 1991).

Loevy, Diana, 'Inside the House That Henson Built', *Channels*, no. 8, March 1988, pp. 52–3.

Lulow, Kalia, 'Fractured Fairy Tales', *Connoisseur*, no. 214, November 1984, pp. 54–5.

Magid, Ron, '*Labyrinth* and *Legend*, Big Screen Fairy Tales', *American Cinematographer*, no. 67, August 1986, pp. 65–70.

Owen, David, 'Looking Out for Kermit', *New Yorker*, 16 August 1993, pp. 30–43.

Smoodin, Eric Loren, *Animating Culture: Hollywood Cartoons from the Sound Era* (New Brunswick, NJ: Rutgers University Press, 1993).

Stilson, Janet, 'Mother Goose Rock 'n Rhyme', *TV Guide*, no. 39, 12–18 January 1991, p. 12.

Stilson, Janet, 'Shelley Duvall; The Fairy Godmother of Children's TV', *TV Guide*, no. 39, 2–8 March 1991, pp. 23–7.

Woolery, George W., *Children's Television, the First Thirty-Five Years, 1946–1981* (Metuchen, NJ: Scarecrow Press, 1983–5).
Woolery, George W., *Animated TV Specials: The Complete Directory to the First Twenty-Five Years, 1962–1987* (Metuchen, NJ: Scarecrow Press, 1989).

# TURTLE POWER

## *Illusion and Imagination in Children's Play*[1]

CATHY URWIN

Recent discussions of film and television for children have focused on the possible effects of violence and the extent to which these mirror an increase in violence in society as a whole and/or changing attitudes towards it. Rather less attention is given to how children cope with the anxiety associated with social change itself, and to the role of imagination in creating notions of continuing identity and self-efficacy.

The subtitle of this chapter intends a contrast between the use of imagination as a means through which children can work through loss, disappointment and the implications of vulnerability, and the power of illusion described by Freud in *Civilisation and its Discontents*.[2] Here Freud describes a tendency to create cultural ideals to support the human wish for happiness, security and unbroken continuity, or being at-oneness, as opposed, for example, to struggling with limitation and the irrecoverability of the past.

My aim is not to arbitrate between these two kinds of psychological functions. Rather I want to explore the tension between them by focusing on the *Teenage Mutant Ninja Turtles*/*Teenage Mutant Hero Turtles*, hugely popular among children from four to ten years old in the late 1980s. The craze was distinctive for its explicit concern with costs and gains associated with technological and scientific advance and the break-up of an old world order. Though there is a clear resonance between fear of social change and the Turtles' themes, my central argument is that the huge popularity of the Turtles depends on ways in which the fiction supports unconscious phantasies and mental operations for managing or defending against primitive and universal anxieties.

After outlining the general content of Turtle mythology, and the marketing drive which supported it, the chapter draws on psychoanalysis to develop a framework which highlights these anxieties. Finally, this framework is used to analyse Virgin Films' highly successful production *Teenage Mutant Ninja Turtles*, the interest being in whether it supports an attitude to change which is developmental in the sense described above, or one more concerned to reproduce more of the same.

Firstly, who are the Turtles?

**Turtle mythology**

In their most usual representation, the Turtles are four cartoon characters named after Renaissance artists: Donatello, Leonardo, Michelangelo and Raphael. They live in the sewers of backstreet New York with their mentor Splinter, a wise old rat of Japanese extraction. They have shells, scaly skins and only three digits on hands and feet. They also have humanoid characteristics. They joke, they talk, they differ from each other in some respects; they have adventures, fears and enthusiasms. Above all, they love eating pizza, the fast food takeaway.

Though these are clearly cheerful characters, the Turtles do not represent a simple anthropomorphism of friendly animals. This is no Little Grey Rabbit. The Turtles, like Splinter, are mutants, produced through a spillage of mutagenic or radioactive drugs into the sewers. Though how the spillage occurred is never entirely clear, a central notion is of a bad/mad scientist whose past greed and irresponsibility has turned the outside world into a dangerous place, perilously close to destruction through carelessness, wastage and evil self-interest. This evil is personified in the character of Shredder, a long-standing rival of Splinter's, who also derives from Japanese culture. Obtaining some control over the mutagenic substance, Shredder has become transformed into a vicious creature who surrounds himself with mutated slaves, whom he brutalises in the name of demonstrating the superiority of his destructive power.

By contrast the Turtles are committed to ridding the world of Shredder and his corrupted machines, and must conceal themselves for protection. They wear masks, cultivate invisibility of movement, make forays into the outside world in secret and, as budding karate experts, use violence to secure good ends. In every cartoon story the viewer is invited to believe that the Turtles face defeat as enormous remote-controlled machines threaten to mow them down or to overflow the sewers. Ultimately, however, good triumphs and the Turtles live to fight another day, while the humiliated Shredder swears, 'You wait, Turtles – the next time!'

As Dr Miles Harris, a psychiatrist writing on the appeal of the craze, has observed, the story is highly moral, if not moralistic.[3] In many ways it repeats the structure of much comic book fiction and romance screened for children: for example, the story of Robin Hood or Popeye's battles with bully-boy Bluto. But in addition there is clearly a particular topicality in the nature of the anxieties which the stories explicitly represent. Effects of pollution, genetic engineering and the implications of nuclear power are contingent upon the scientific advances of the twentieth century. They raise anxieties which ultimately concern the continuation of the human race.

Perhaps surprisingly there has been little public discussion of the positive or negative implications of exposing children to these issues. Instead, media

*Top and Bottom: Ninja Turtles bubblegum cards, courtesy of Mirage Studios.*

coverage has largely centred on professional and parental concern over effects of violence, some of the speculation drawing on research discussed in other chapters in this volume. Here it is important to note that the Teenage Hero Turtles are actually a toned down version of the Ninja Turtles, which originated in an American martial arts comic strip noted for its focus on violent excitement rather than on cerebral aspects of martial arts. However, creating a distinction between adult and child viewing did not assuage parental anxieties entirely, particularly as a mounting concern over more videos and associated products raised questions about children's suggestibility and the nature of the grip of these videos on children's attention.

The marketing of the Turtles was a hugely successful operation, boosting sales of a surprisingly wide range of products, from pizza and children's toys to plastic plates, clothes and popular literature. But marketing drives do not operate on blank slates, nor do they explain children's fascination. Interestingly, one of the few research studies on children's perceptions suggests that, whatever it is based on, the appeal does not depend on children believing that Turtles are real. Children interviewed by Martin Barrett and his colleagues were particularly clear that the Turtles were not real, in spite of, or because of, the fact that at this time Turtles were 'favourites' for identifying with imaginatively in their play, to support them in dealing with their own conflicts.[4]

This kind of identification raises questions about the relation between fiction and the internal world of the child. As Valerie Walkerdine has argued in her study of girls' relation to schoolgirl comics, to understand the pull of fiction and its psychological implications it is necessary to consider how material viewed or read may tap into desires, conflicts and anxieties; that is, how it supports the work of phantasy.[5]

## Psychoanalytic perspectives on fiction for children

Within psychoanalysis it has become customary to distinguish between 'fantasy', which refers to stories, daydreams and other fiction with a plot or structure of which we are consciously aware, and 'phantasy', which accompanies engagement with fiction but largely consists of unconscious processes. These processes are partially biologically given and partially originate in infancy and early childhood. Comprised of primitive drives, early memories and images, they are ultimately concerned with the reduction of tension, the perpetuation of pleasure or satisfaction, and the regulation of, or defence against, anxiety.

As is well known, Freud stressed the value of phantasy in regulating our instinctual lives and identified dreams as crucial to its expression in adults.[6] The fictional line conceals, but nonetheless supports, the working through of anxieties, desires and conflicts through processes of symbol formation, displacement and other forms of substitution. Paradoxically, the dream-work allows individuals greater freedom to think and act autonomously in relation to external demands. Freud also argued that the creation of symbols depends crucially on the work of mourning and the ability to let go eventually, thus playing a big role in moving forward.[7]

In small children, comparable processes operate through play. For example, a child may, in pretend play, actively repeat an unpleasant experience, like a visit to the dentist. In bringing about an alternative ending or reversing a passive experience into one initiated by the self, the child masters the anxiety associated with the original event over which he or she had little control.[8] At the same time, the active creation of symbols introduces a distance which enhances the distinction between internal and external aspects of the event. This itself increases an awareness of mental experience and the possibilities for reflecting on alternative realities.

Dreaming and playing are active processes on the part of the subject. Nevertheless, the work of phantasy requires objects or vehicles for substitution and displacement. These could be provided by the thematic and iconographic content of drama, films, stories and other forms of fiction. One would anticipate, for example, parallels between processes operating when children use play to express desire or master anxiety and what may be working at an unconscious level when they are absorbed in an unfolding story or a film. One would also anticipate that, to hold attention and to be experienced as psychologically convincing, the fictional work must be consistent with ways in which unconscious processes operate.

This kind of application of psychoanalytic thinking emphasises the viewers' engagement and may be contrasted with psychoanalytic analyses which focus on meanings produced through the text. Arguably it is a method instigated by Freud himself, who first introduced the theory of the Oedipus complex, central to psychoanalysis, by referring to plays recognisable as classic tragedies, such as *Oedipus Rex* and *Hamlet*. Freud argued that these works do not achieve their power to move by creating effects *de novo*, but through ways in which they touch desires, anxieties and feelings we already hold. That is, it is because we have wished to control and possess parents and to triumph over siblings, and have been tormented by guilt in consequence, that this literature holds our attention and enriches us, through making internal experience in some way comprehensible.[9]

On children's fiction, one of the best known analyses in this tradition is Bruno Bettelheim's *Uses of Enchantment*.[10] Struck by how very disturbed children could gain reassurance from fairy stories, despite their ghoulish content, Bettelheim analysed stories from a wide range of cultures. He identified several universal themes. These include Oedipal themes and the arrival of new siblings, as in 'The Three Bears', and the problem of separating from parents and of finding yourself alone or in the society of other children. 'Hansel and Gretel', for example, the 'Babes in the Wood', set themselves up as a little couple to parent each other as they escape the effects of the father's poverty and the stepmother's cruelty. Other common themes involve greed, envy and cunning, and in particular the problem of retaining belief in parents' goodness in their absence despite the potential to be deceived or seduced by appearances. This is illustrated in the temptations of the gingerbread house in 'Hansel and

Gretel' and in the extraordinary power of the beautiful but ultimately destructive 'Snow Queen'. There are issues to do with adults' power over children, which may be dealt with by a reversal as children slay the dragons or giants at an age when their own sense of size may oscillate wildly, like Alice's in *Alice in Wonderland*. Finally, there are issues of time, life, death, individual history and the history of the world, which both changes and repeats itself. This recycling is now built into the fairy story genre through the opening words 'Once upon a time . . .' Introducing an imaginary narrator and establishing a temporal distance between the present and the events recalled, the fairy tale, as it were, refers to another world.

Arguably, this distancing device protects young readers from being overwhelmed by horrific content. But many classic fairy tales originated in folklore, where they were shared between adults and children and where the meanings were connected to social realities and the social systems of the community. This link to culture is retained implicitly, just as themes of conquest and court are implicit in the rules of chess, as the psychologist Vygotsky has argued.[11]

Nevertheless, given the unchanging format and the universal themes, it is easy to miss the salience of links to social structure in explaining the appeal of fiction to young children. This is well brought out by Margaret and Michael Rustin in a more recent analysis of children's fiction, *Narratives of Love and Loss*.[12] Like Bettelheim, the Rustins highlight the commonality of themes of separation and reunion, crises of conscience, and the problem of believing that anything good can be achieved again. But in addition, they point out that much literature aimed at children between the ages of five and ten requires children to explore or take up an attitude towards a social world. It presents images of how societies work, what binds groups together, what constitutes social order and social isolation, as is evident, for instance, even in Noddy's relation to the other inhabitants of Toy Town.

The Rustins argue that children can be particularly interested in these issues at an age when they are not only separating from parents but are taking a place in group culture. Though in our society this generally occurs with starting primary school, the Rustins observe that the shift is also in line with Freud's observations on the problem of being alone which comes with the dissolution of the Oedipus complex from the age of about five.[13] Further they suggest that this struggle to establish a sense of an inner identity, or a unique personal self, is often concealed from parents; children's fiction can provide 'metaphors or containers for typical life experiences of its readers', at both conscious and unconscious levels.[14]

## Infantile Anxieties and the Turn to Turtles

Both Bettelheim's and the Rustins' accounts raise issues directly applicable to the Turtles, particularly the separation between adult and child worlds and the transformation from powerlessness to powerfulness: in the absence of grown-ups, the heroic Turtles take on the future of the world. The manifest content is dominated by contemporary social themes. These may be particularly apposite areas for identifying allegiances, adopting moral positions, and expressing a capacity for concern and social responsibility. However, at this point, the applicability of previous accounts ceases. Closer inspection suggests that the Turtles raise psychic dilemmas seldom identified or rarely discussed in analyses of children's fiction.

From the outset, the Turtles present a view of a world ridden with catastrophe. It is not just a question of 'leaving home'. 'Parents' in the Turtles world are not just absent or even dead; they have fundamentally failed, principally through having already committed the unpardonable crime of calling into question the very possibility of continuing the species. The themes for the Turtle stories which are uppermost, therefore, are not those of separation and reunion but those of surviving and holding together in a world in which any hopefulness is ever accessible to attack. This fundamentally paranoid world view is linked to anxieties which are very primitive, of falling apart or falling for ever, of being 'shredded' or torn to pieces.

These anxieties may be reminiscent of those experienced by tiny infants in distress, when there is some capacity to grasp the significance of external events but as yet limited ability to effect changes in the outside world. They have been well described by Melanie Klein[15] in her account of the 'paranoid-schizoid' position in which, according to Klein, even young babies can deal with the anxiety of being overwhelmed by hunger or cold by 'projecting' the source of pain outside the self into an object, prototypically the mother or mother's breast. The infant can then defend itself against feared retaliation by 'splitting' or separating off what has now become a 'bad object' from the 'good object' which provides lifegiving food, comfort and love. Another early defence is 'projective identification', in which parts of the self are projected into the object with which the infant subsequently identifies, either to control an object felt to be dangerous or to prolong a positive experience.

In this way, by keeping good and bad firmly apart, or by regulating the distance between them, the infant gains some control over internal experience. However, this results in a partial world view which does not remain the only one as, typically from the middle of the first year, the infant begins to grapple with the idea of whole people, and that to be a person is to be good and bad. This inaugurates what Klein calls the 'depressive position', which brings a different quality to anxiety. The individual's experience is less of being persecuted than of grief, ambivalence and inadequacy as concern for the object displaces preoccupation with imminent threats to the self.[16]

Of course, these feelings can be as difficult to deal with as persecutory ones. They imply a degree of separateness between oneself and others. For the infant, an awareness of separateness will also bring a recognition that the mother may have relationships with somebody else. This inaugurates the Oedipus complex in its pregenital aspects, observable in overt displays of jealousy, attention-seeking and sleep disturbances as in phantasy the infant attacks the parents or attempts to split them apart to deal with the anxiety of being displaced. But since this is related to a greater awareness of love and dependency, the infant may also experience extreme distress and guilt, Klein identifying a primitive and highly savage superego or conscience originating in infancy and early childhood.

Ultimately, working through the depressive position requires the work of mourning and, in phantasy, repair work of various kinds through which the infant restores the parents' generative capacity. Prototypically, in imagination, allowing parents space for themselves also allows room for a new baby. Paradoxically the creative act of letting go frees infants to be actively curious about external events, to think and play imaginatively. The depressive position is thus the seat of change. However, it is important to stress that although described as having a developmental logic, the distinction between the two phases is never worked through completely. Even adults are thrown back into the paranoid-schizoid position at times of crisis, oscillating back and forth under conditions of internal and/or external stress.

Since Klein, more recent work has focused on this oscillation, providing a fuller account of differential anxieties and qualities of thought which go along with them. Donald Meltzer, for example, has shown how, under excessive paranoid anxiety, cruel alliances can be set up within the self which impede the development of object-centred relationships.[17] Following Herbert Rosenfeld, he has described an essentially narcissistic organisation in which parts of the self are distributed to form something like a psychic gang presided over by a particularly harsh and cruel superego.[18] Taking its strength from the degree of terror to which a tiny infant can be exposed, this is associated with a highly rigid, tyrannical form of justice which insists on 'an eye for an eye'. Since it is dominated by paranoid anxiety, it inevitably knows the presence of badness all too well. Prejudice is justified as the safest option and quality displaces quantity in criteria of human value; quality, after all, implies an investment or commitment to an individual person rather than to a repository of parts.

This mistrusting and highly pessimistic form of knowing can be contrasted with what, following the poet John Keats, the psychoanalyst Wilfred Bion described as 'negative capability': the ability to be in or remain in a situation of doubt and uncertainty 'without reaching after facts and reason'.[19] This ability is associated with the capacity to retain trust in the goodness of one's objects in their absence.

Bion's own work added a further dimension to Klein's account of the move from paranoid-schizoid to depressive positions. This is the necessity for a protective mental space for holding, processing and meditating on otherwise unthinkable infantile anxieties which Bion referred to as 'containment'. Bion concluded that in infancy this was normally provided by the mother/caretaker, who more or less consciously receives the infant's projections, primitive communications and feelings roused in her and tries to make sense of them, eventually finding some way of feeding back the experience in a form which is manageable and meaningful. For Bion, this provides the baby with a primitive experience of being understood. It is the basis of a sense of personal identity which precedes any notion of identity that comes from having a status conferred by society. It is also integral to the development of thought. An identification with a mother capable of thinking in this way, receiving and transforming anxiety, and a subsequent introjection, provides the origins of mind as a space within the self. By contrast, if this process fails because of factors in the infant, the environment or both, the infant is left at the mercy of a 'nameless dread'. What becomes installed in the infant psyche is an object actively hostile to the communication of emotional experience. This contributes to the severity of the persecutory superego described above.

A similar process has been described by Esther Bick.[20] In a paper particularly pertinent to the Turtles, 'The Experience of the Skin in Early Object Relations', Bick argues that a tiny infant depends initially on an external object to provide a fulcrum around which a personal centre can be established, giving a sense of a body boundary. This object must be powerful enough to hold the infant's attention. It might be light from the eyes, the mother's voice, or the nipple in the mouth.

Like Bion, Bick proposed that an identification with this holding function is crucial to the notion of internal and external spaces. Failures in this function may affect both subsequent learning and personality development. Impairments range from the common teething rashes of early infancy to the difficulties in conceptualising a third dimension characteristic of autistic children. In between are examples of children needing extra protection in negotiating separations. In going to their first parties or starting school, some children will refuse to take off their coats. This is a temporary need for an extra layer which should, however, be contrasted with what Bick describes as a 'second skin'. Akin to Winnicott's descriptions of a 'false self',[21] this is felt to be *part* of the child. It represents an identification with an object brought in initially to compensate when parental holding was lacking. Unfortunately, this impedes the child's opportunities for relating effectively with other people, and for dealing flexibly with the experience of change.

Similarly, where protective camouflage is linked not to a temporary need but to a psychic alliance against discovering one's need for others, the stresses of change produce an escalation of problems. As external trappings cease to serve their functions, the fear of fragmentation is heightened. This exacerbates the tendency to adopt omnipotent defences, to locate the problem on the surface. This in turn fuels the compulsion to seek a thicker skin, better armour, and we become identified with nothing but our clothes.

**An Application to Teenage Mutant Ninja Turtles**

The Turtles appeal directly to the phantasy of a protective armour, a perfect camouflage against the fear of falling apart in the face of catastrophic anxiety, a camouflage neatly paralleled in adult fiction in *Robocop* and *The Terminator*.[22] For children, the iconography raises questions about the extent to which the Turtles offer scope for creative adaptation to problems of change. Where what is offered is essentially pseudo-containment, reinforcing narcissistic and omnipotent processes, the Turtles provide evasive solutions; they operate psychically in what I have earlier described as an area of illusion. On the other hand, within the mythology there is an acknowledgment both of vulnerability and dependency and of the need to stand against corruption and contamination. This suggests a pressure to create alternatives which might demand an act of imagination.

These contrastive processes are observable in Turtles cartoons, but the tension between them is particularly clear in *Teenage Mutant Ninja Turtles*, a full-length feature film. This uses human actors rather than animation. It provides a stronger narrative structure, and takes advantage of greater scope for tying the story to specific socio-historical events.

This intention is made clear in the opening sequence, which presents a world upside down, as litter-strewn New York City is terrorised by a gang of child thieves. Disillusioned with parents, their hypocrisy and the failure of the 'old order', in their vulnerability the children have been seduced by the evil Shredder. Shredder encapsulates the terror of fragmentation, and is an exemplary representation of the cruel superego. Aptly ruling with an iron claw, Shredder asserts a subversive logic based on the Law of Talion and the exploitation of envy. This insists on the desirability of aping achievements of the adult world through a triumphant celebration of corruption, greed and denigration. Dressed as little courtesans and gangsters, the children behave like victims of political indoctrination. They cannot make decisions. Without their leader they can only gibber or repeat his rhetoric.

Dependency is also an issue for the Turtles, though in a different way. At the outset they are equally in need of contact with their master Splinter, but they reflect another aspect of the catastrophic change. They live in the sewers, let drop or expelled as outcasts. Nevertheless, their names conjure rebirth and, as in the cartoons, their armour protects something hopeful, if vulnerable, partly from the dangers of a hostile and intrusive outside world, but also from their own impatience and other frustrations of youth. This pull between impetuosity and limitation is well captured in an early scene. Planning an adventurous exploit, they are momentarily checked by contemplating what would happen if there were no Splinter, if he died and they were alone. 'Have you ever thought . . .?' The subject is rapidly changed.

As in many fairy stories, the separation of the Turtles from this protective if vulnerable parental figure is crucial to promoting the psychological shifts advanced in the film. This depends on the introduction of a maternal object, in part provided by the arrival of a glamorous television journalist, April O'Neill, who takes upon herself the investigation of the juvenile crime wave holding the city to ransom. Unsurprisingly, these heroics involve dangerous stuff. A violent battle ensues, in which the Turtle Raphael is injured trying to rescue April from Shredder's henchmen. By this time the Turtles have been joined by a Robin Hood-like thief of principle, a 'dropout' in the older order, now spurred to action. Together they flee the city, taking refuge in a house in the country. This represents for April both a recognition of loss and a return to happier times. To the adult viewer, it conjures images of the heyday of the 1960s.

The shift in location provides a convenient resting place for containing anxiety, collecting thoughts, and the development of something like a domestic scene. With this containment, the film begins to show psychological shifts akin to a move from paranoid-schizoid to depressive functioning. The Turtles show their concern for Raphael's health. They grieve over what the violence has brought about and the bleak prospects for the future. Splinter has been taken prisoner by Shredder and his crew, and may be dead.

One response to this fear of loss is a retreat into paranoid-schizoid defences. Leonardo and Michelangelo complain belligerently, or muck about being deliberately useless to avoid feeling helpless. By contrast, Donatello alone sticks to the requirements of mental work. He struggles to practise the meditative art his master taught him, to collect his mind. He appears to sit for days, then announces, 'Splinter is alive, it is time to go back.' The other Turtles attempt to console, expressing their own doubt: 'We all think he is alive.' Donatello asserts, 'I don't think, I know!' This belief in the absent object's survival is based on an internal experience, reflecting the good object's resilience. In the film it mobilises the little band's return. Psychically, it implies some working through of the depressive position and, with it, the arrival of Oedipal themes, as April and the good thief combatively begin to sort out the cost of trusting each other.

Once the possibility of some kind of loving alliance in the present has been reinstated, the narrative reveals the original crime which perverted the city. This was not simply an Oedipal conflict between father and son, but a rivalrous conflict between two symbolic brothers, Shredder and Splinter in their human incarnation, over the love of a woman. Shredder, the loser, in his jealous hatred murders the woman, attempting to kill Splinter at the same time. This reflects a psychically disastrous configuration, a phantasy in which one member of the couple is bent on destroying the other. Prototypically, it is brought about through the infant's jealous attacks on the parent couple, who the infant fears will be only too ready to generate new babies to render him or her displaced. The tragedy is that, in the process, the infant also destroys the life-giving parents who are desperately needed to secure the future.

The drama of the Turtles hinges on this cusp. With a murderous and retaliatory father in psychic reality, the child in such situations depends on establishing a protective and life-giving paternal object; a loving father or equivalent is essential. In the film, this reassurance is secured as a boy captured by Shredder struggles against Shredder's power and makes it across to the Turtles' side. Charged with the task of guarding the prisoner Splinter, who has been left to die, the boy begins to confront the horror of what he is involved in. Splinter hears the boy's story and accepts his rage against his father, acknowledging and hearing out the uniqueness of his grievances. But he also insists compassionately that all fathers love their sons. This reinstates both the possibility of good parents and a non-punitive orientation and the possibility of some kind of effective communication of experience between generations.

Although he is initially sceptical and defensive, the boy eventually lets Splinter go. Consistent with this internal reparative movement, Shredder's external hold over his little gang begins to collapse. The children emerge sheepishly from the underworld to tell the police about the warehouses where the stolen goods are to be found. The boy's father greets his son in relief. He has been 'so worried, Danny'; 'Call me Dan,' the boy insists. Recognising limitation in himself, the father accepts this upstaging. This allows that development may have taken place within the separation and acknowledges the boy's wish that independence can be achieved without loss of respect.

Implicitly the film now raises the question, where from here? Is it a question of emerging from a nightmare, or of establishing some new order? Up to this point the film has been dramatically intense and attention-absorbing; it has psychological validity. However, in the closing sequences this dramatic tension is lost. In part, this may reflect box-office requirements to produce a happy, if sentimental, ending which conforms to conventions on what is desirable for young viewers. Principally, however, the loss of dramatic tension is brought about through a psychological collapse which introduces violence as a reactive or defensive flight from the anxiety created by uncertainty at the point of change.

Through restitution and repair, and the recovery of hope, the possibilities for the future are wide open in the closing scenes of the film. The reworking of a co-operative link between parents and children and the new alliance between April and her partner offer hope for the next generation. But actual outcomes are not knowable in advance. Doubt, pessimism and negative reactions easily spring from such uncertainty. Consistent with the way good objects are tested in psychic reality, Shredder predictably returns. The Turtles become embroiled in battle. They are in danger of being beaten.

At this point one possibility would be to sustain the uncertainty with a reaffirmation of lost values, of remorse and forgiveness, which have recently been regained. Another would have been to expose the tragic consequence of human fickleness. Here, the solution is to resurrect what I have called the illusion of the heroic ideal, as a rejuvenated Splinter is brought in, to unite with the Turtles and take on the fight. Shredder is now overthrown by superior might.

This kind of solution, of course, is a highly familiar one. Here, as a device to end the film, the 'triumphant' conclusion in fact represents an omnipotent and manic flight from the level of internal conviction touched by the Turtles earlier in the film, when Shredder's hold over the gang was severed and the irrelevance of his propaganda exposed. A rapid splitting of the paternal function represents a retreat from the demands of the depressive position, to produce a hero and a devil as inextricably opposed. Since the power of one is tied to the hold of the other, the opposition is irreconcilable. In the short term this can create excitement, but ultimately it leaves a gaping hole. With this is generated an appetite for more of the same: after all, a Shredder is always there. Thus, in the manic solution, the film removes its support for the imaginative struggle as a necessary component of working through, and at the same time sets the stage for a repeat performance, and the appearance of *Teenage Mutant Ninja Turtles 2*.

**Conclusion**

By the beginning of the 1990s, *Teenage Mutant Ninja Turtles* had become one of the most commercially successful films of all time, rapidly spawning *Teenage Mutant Ninja Turtles 2* and *3*. I have argued that the success of the film and the craze which first supported it may have depended on a particular conjunction of socio-political events which gave the manifest content particular salience. But I have also argued that the pull of the thematic material depended crucially on the interlacing of topical content with universal sources of anxiety and defences against it. These include omnipotent phantasies for controlling the future. The child as hero emerges as a kind of compromise which does not entirely succeed in transforming the deeper anxiety that the jealous and envious attacks of infancy may have destroyed the generative parents for ever.

As the tenacity of the craze may suggest, the Turtles' story has qualities which could justify its status as a myth particularly apposite to our times; that is, it is a way of depicting social and psychological truth in the service of understanding. Here, dilemmas to be comprehended include accepting both the limits of control and responsibility for the future through the last decade of the twentieth century. Equally revealing, however, may be limitations in the Turtles' film itself for what it suggests about the difficulty of sustaining creative thought or psychic growth. Dramatically failing just at the point of facing a future essentially unknowable, it produces a retrogressive outcome which reinforces omnipotent triumph and a pseudo-appetite for the familiar formula.

Of course, it may not be the place of popular fiction to create contexts for comprehending the nature of fear when it is ill-managed by adults, and when consumerist pressures rapidly step in to fill and perpetuate the ideological vacuum. Indeed, one of the positive aspects of the Turtles and similar figures for children of today may be to foster a cheerful cynicism. Drop them before they drop you and move on to the next thing. In this way, children may themselves discover the power and illusion of the temporary craze. The down side, however, is that the repetitive recycling rests on a compulsive power which can actually produce children as 'consumers of crap'. Further, the dangers of an easy slippage into violent excitement in the face of uncertainty may be less the promotion of violent behaviour than the reinforcement of non-thinking, passive and ultimately highly pessimistic views of people's ability actively to effect the process of change.

fantasy, vest rolled up to signify breasts where there are none, belly exposed, dancing across the frame of the TV screen, the mirror or the window.

Of course, television is also boring. Sometimes it's a source of anxiety and distress. There are, nevertheless, an increasing number of daytime or early evening programmes broadcast in the mainstream of British television to provide the opportunities which I have described here. *Top of the Pops*[1] continues on BBC1, *The Chart Show* on ITV and, generally at weekends, there are music items interspersed with cartoons and talk in the blocks of programming that explicitly address children. Other occasions to dance come from video replays of such films as *The Little Mermaid* or, to a lesser extent, *Beauty and the Beast*. In these films the narrative impetus is always interrupted by occasions which, in a more specifically textual sense, make room to dance. In what I want to examine in this chapter, it is a variety of instances of TV dance which have attracted my attention. I want to argue that, for young girls, the dance repertoire cuts across a range of television and video material, some of it addressed to very young children but much also engaging an older audience of adolescents and beyond. There is no strictly circumscribed corpus here, no delimited body of texts precisely aligned with safely demarcated age phases. Madonna, Michael Jackson and 2 Unlimited mingle, in this repertoire, with the nostalgic choreography of *Beauty and the Beast* or the exuberant 'Under the Sea' from *The Little Mermaid*.

There is a broader argument to be made, though largely represented here through the particular case study, about the terms in which the 'culture of childhood' is understood. Too often, perhaps, the phrase is used to suggest something bounded and, in particular, distinct from the cultures of youth or adolescence. Without dissolving differences between six and sixteen-year-olds, I want to suggest that there are continuities across the customary divisions of age and that, in particular, young children constantly engage with and, in the mode of play, enact identifications associated with the sexuality of adolescence and early adulthood.

In making such an argument for the view that there is no clear insulation of childhood from adolescence, it is possible to draw upon perspectives which stress the power of the media. The power to define and reconstitute identities is seen as an effect of both the invasive proliferation of media texts and the often strategic combination of multiple modes of address within a single text. Thus there may be a case for saying that because of the pervasive character of television and, in Britain, of domestic video use, boundaries between childhood and youth have been eroded very rapidly. A version of this argument, as a lament, has been advanced by Neil Postman.[2] Furthermore, Disney films, and many television programmes, contrive to address a broad audience conceived as including a diversity of age-groups, a spread of differently informed generations. Or, to advance in the same direction and with a more left political inflection, it can be argued that any weakening of the boundary between childhood and youth is symptomatic of a consumerism which has achieved cultural dominance through the expansion of advertising and the subservience of television and film production to the needs of marketing. Tom Engelhardt[3] and, more dispassionately, Stephen Kline,[4] offer arguments which are broadly of this kind.

Engelhardt's review of deregulated children's television in 'Reagan's 80s', and his frequently despairing fascination with its market-driven energy, comes to a thoughtful and unexpected conclusion: 'If kidvid is really a flat, repetitious, utterly predictable backwater of some other far more energetic world, why do kids incorporate it into their fantasy life and fantasy play, into their desires and dreams?'[5] Despite the vehemence with which he condemns the incursion of consumerism into the lives of children, he reveals the limits of his own problematic in this late recognition of the active pleasures which children find in television. But whatever recognition he gives to pleasure is also tinged with regret, as he notes that 'childhood' is itself an adult construction: 'Ideally we want to think of them as belonging to another race of beings . . . innocents open to the best we can possibly teach. We want to see them as different, more sensitive, somehow more human than ourselves.'[6] Against Engelhardt's pessimism, my own argument for questioning the separation of childhood from youth and adulthood intends to acknowledge the power which children realise through forms of engagement with television.

Stephen Kline's perspective is of importance here in that he gestures beyond texts themselves to argue that the imaginative play of children is being colonised by marketing strategies. In doing so he extends Engelhardt's argument, suggesting that the 'consumption ethos has become the vortex of children's culture'[7] and that 'when the television is off, the fantasy world lives on in the child's imagination, and is recreated regularly in their play . . . the fictional world generated in programming still defines the play of the child.'[8] But as with Engelhardt, such observations stand as a plausible hypothesis unsupported by evidence of what meanings children develop through their television-related play. In one respect Kline's argument about the power of consumerism also involves making a case for seeing an increasing separation of the culture of young children from that of adults. So if on the one hand consumerism diminishes differences between childhood and adulthood, on the other it can involve 'clear market segmentation', ' "ghetto" viewing, with only young children watching'.[9]

However, throughout Kline's argument runs the assumption that what audiences do with television is contained by, and corresponds exactly to, the terms on which it is offered, terms currently under the domination of powerful market strategies. Children's play is thus seen as imitating exactly what is presented within one type of programming rather than borrowing from and bringing together material from a diversity of sources. But even young children watch more than deregulated cartoons and, in the development of my argument, it is essential to stress the heterogeneity of children's experience of television and indeed of other media. Beyond this, but without diminishing the importance attached to the media in making available the material of narrative and play, I want to emphasise that play is never just imitation or assimilation but is enacted in particular social contexts and, emotionally, in terms which cannot be reduced to those allowed by texts alone. The scope and detail of the evidence I give here, though limited, does represent something more than my own speculative reading of texts and is informed by observation and discussion with young children. In this case, I talked to my own daughters and watched them watching television; at the time of writing they were six and ten years old.

**Mermaids**

The figure of the mermaid can unite a set of perhaps improbably associated images of female sexuality, current in a disparate array of popular texts addressed to a diverse audience. The meanings of *The Little Mermaid* are my first focus of attention, and such a choice is motivated both by its wide popularity and by the priorities of my 6-year-old daughter – 'Dad, this is what I like!' *The Little Mermaid* is a Disney transformation of a Hans Christian Andersen story. It is the Disney version and its contemporary intertextual associations which are of consequence here. It was the songs and particularly those that became the occasion for dancing which attracted my interest, though the narrative too has its special significance.

Despite the title, *The Little Mermaid*, Ariel, the heroine, is sixteen and in conflict with her father, a conflict which unfolds through confrontations and evasions little different from those replayed across a wide array of texts, including, for example, television soap operas. It is her transgressive curiosity about the world above the sea, in defiance of Tritan's insistence upon the division of one world from the other, which initiates the narrative. The resolution, with her marriage to above-world Eric, achieves a predictable movement from father to husband but, more unusually, it also depends on the acquisition of legs, sexually pertinent, and without which dancing might seem improbable. Among the human artefacts with which Ariel lines her 'room' are the figures of a couple dancing; these, along with all her other curiosities, are destroyed by Tritan in his anger at her having seen and 'fallen in love with' a human. But this motif recurs in her subsequent dance with Eric, and indeed in her ultimate attainment of adult human sexuality, on legs.

Ariel's song, reflecting on her fascination with the debris of human life which falls into her under-sea world, crucially motivates the narrative; as my 10-year-old daughter put it while watching *Beauty and the Beast*, there's always 'a long solo about what they want which is always different from what they've got'. Ariel's song sets out a series of binary oppositions and it is through these that her yearning is constructed. Her desire is animated by the distance between the treasured, but lifeless, objects in her cavern and the vibrant mobility of life on two legs shared by the people on land. The wish to be part of that world above, from which her physical form appears irrevocably to exclude her, is expressed in terms which divide her fishy attributes from those which might be associated with maturity and sexuality.

The gravity of the song, despite its often whimsical lyrics, defines her conflict with Tritan and her vulnerability to the sea-witch, Ursula, as an emotionally necessary dynamic. The song mixes a quasi-feminism, adolescent rebellion and childlike curiosity and could thus be read as employing multiple forms of address, attempting to engage an audience across a wide, if youthful, age range. More precisely, what appears to be present here is something of a paradox: the words of a 16-year-old girl keen to leave childhood behind and to move into an unknown world in a new and adult body, but contained in a narrative and a form clearly addressed to very young children. Those elementary binary pairs – feet:fins, dancing:swimming, sand:sea – and the privileging of the first term in each pair, suggest the desired movement from a watery indeterminacy to a more defined world in which actions may be more subject to will and purpose. If this replicates the risky passage from an amniotic sea, it also articulates adolescent sexual curiosity, though largely through metaphorical concealment: jumping and dancing and wandering mingle with a longing to be warm, to know the pleasure of fire and why it burns. Later, Ariel is bored by, and has disappeared before the end of, Sebastian's extraordinary celebration of life under the sea; like a moody teenager at a children's party, she's suddenly nowhere to be found.

The paradox is familiar. The popularity of Barbie dolls depends upon it. The presentation of narratives, and of toys, which dramatise growth into sexual maturity engages children's uncertainty about their own futures: what are they to become and how are they to live through the transformation from child into adult? Such future-oriented fantasies are fraught with tensions between dependence and autonomy, engaging the gulf between childhood subordination and the apparent power of adults. Ursula, a character exciting ambivalent fascination, takes Ariel into the dilemma:

> ARIEL: If I become human I'll never be with my father or sisters again . . .
> URSULA: That's right – but you'll have your man – life's full of tough choices, isn't it?

In thus foreshadowing the real difficulties which children, and particularly girls, will face, *The Little Mermaid* offers one version of the route to sexual maturity. Its romance is that of heterosexual coupling in marriage, and its moral lesson is that, in the achievement of romantic love, girls must preserve the grain of individual personality. The risk which Ariel takes is to agree to give up her voice in exchange for the legs that will enable her to be a partner to Eric. Ursula's persuasion, of the importance of 'body language' or of men's dislike of 'blabber', connects with Ariel's yearning for human form and the romantic credibility which legs will give her. But in surrendering her voice, she loses the means to animate herself through singing; in gaining access to a human female sexuality she is, in the same moment, deprived of the individual distinctiveness which the voice confers on the otherwise under-differentiated body. Moral and emotional prescriptions to guard the boundaries of the self, and to 'be oneself', are implicit in the risk which Ariel takes. She signs away her voice to the possession of Ursula and it is taken from her by a kind of oral rape, her body penetrated by hands reaching in to pluck it out. Ursula encloses the disembodied voice in a shell resting above her breasts, its sexual power thus contained and withheld in a form and a place clearly marking its significance. Without her voice, Ariel is unable to identify herself as the 'girl' with whom Eric is in love and she cannot distinguish herself from Ursula's strategic transformation into rival female form. Of course, in Disney, Ariel does not suffer the consequences of her mistake, but they are nevertheless prolonged and threatened by the various detours and frustrations of the narrative. The recovery of her voice, when the shell is broken, enables her to secure Eric and his agency in defeating Ursula and thus, simultaneously, establishing the basis of reconciliation which allows a harmonious resolution and her transfer from father to husband.

From an adult perspective, this narrative may seem just as dubiously pre-feminist as Barbie dolls, and both Tom Engelhardt and Stephen Kline make a case for alternative narratives to those offered by the US film and television industries in their subservience to market interests. Undoubtedly, other narratives of growth and transformation could be produced and made available to young children. However, given the massive popularity of *The Little Mermaid*, it is my priority to explore in what terms the figure of Ariel might be enjoyed by girls. There is much in the film which can be identified as a source of pleasure for children – the way in which they are positioned as always 'ahead of' Scuttle, the bewildered seagull, for example. But Ariel is likely to be regarded by adults as the central focus of identification for young girls and is therefore also the most probable object of hostile criticism. For this reason, and because the narrative momentum of the film is carried through actions assigned to her, it is important to examine the possible meanings she may have for those excluded from adult debates. I want to argue that Ariel – 'I'm sixteen years old. I'm not a child' – can perhaps be understood as a fantasy sexual self for young girls, a figure through which the relation between the self as experienced in the present, with the body of a small child, to the self as imagined and projected into the future, with the sexual body of a woman, can be played at, perhaps rehearsed, perhaps learned.

The relation between the present self and the self in play is essential to my argument. One way of understanding this relation can be derived from the work of Vygotsky. He argued, in *Thought and Language*,[10] that children can learn more effectively in company with others at a higher level of development than they can learn alone or with children at levels of development identical to their own. When other children, or adults, are not available, learning might be achieved through forms of play in which the child projects herself into the role of a more advanced other. In this case I want to say that the child imagines herself in the body of the more developed girl – Ariel, no less. In *Mind in Society*, Vygotsky comments on play:

> In short, play gives a child a new form of desires. It teaches her to desire by relating her desires to a fictitious 'I', to her role in the game and its

rules. In this way a child's greatest achievements are possible in play, achievements that tomorrow will become her basic level of real action and morality.[11]

. . . play creates a zone of proximal development of the child. In play a child always behaves beyond his average age, above his daily behaviour; in play it is as though he were a head taller than himself.[12]

Ariel's scenario is not to be a head taller but to have legs. With legs she can play at the human game: 'ready to stand/ready to know' . . . 'part of that world'. So in part Ariel projects herself, in imagination, into human shape; through Ursula's intervention she realises the game in more real terms. For those watching this narrative progress, the analogy with their own forms of play may be recognised but, equally, Ariel is herself a figure to be appropriated into a version of dance as play.

For young children, even perhaps for adolescents, dancing can be understood as having the urgency and intense importance of play. What I want to suggest is that children do not dance as themselves but that, often, they dance as an 'other': Michael Jackson or Madonna. Dance therefore involves playing at being someone older, more sexual, more accomplished, more knowing and, briefly, trying out the rules of the game in which they appear to act. Dancing to Madonna is about projecting the self into, taking the form of, her body. To achieve this seems to depend upon reorganising the child's body to mark out the place of breasts and the nakedness of the belly: really, to select and display the key elements of the Madonna-Ariel mermaid iconography. To complete the fictitious 'I', the reflected image in a mirror, a window or a television screen confirms the transformation, the ephemeral assumption of a sexual body. Though in terms of the *narrative* placing of binary oppositions in *The Little Mermaid* the fishy tail of the mermaid is counterposed to the sexuality of legs, in the broader cultural context, and in the visual display so prominent in the film, the descending V of her belly is a vital signifier of female sexuality. As is so often the case, it is possible to see it both ways.

2 Unlimited, with their 'No Limit' video, though not displaying female nakedness, certainly replay aspects of the iconography of sexuality which I have suggested here and which is taken up by young girls and reworked in their dancing. Arms raised above the head to display the breasts and belly, even if encased in mock armour or underwear, represent the crucial stance. As with Madonna, clothing is used to represent, in stylised form, what lies beneath. I asked my 6-year-old daughter about it and, the similarities seeming obvious to her, she suggested I add Sonia (the singer) and belly-dancers to the set. Perhaps, despite the patriarchal structure in which dancing is located, be it in *The Little Mermaid* or, more substantially, in *Dirty Dancing*, for girls there is a visible proof of bodily autonomy and self-control implicit in being seen to dance, to present a body enacting intention.

The practice of dancing, among girls, is present from an early age and does seem to evolve in a variety of contexts ranging from playgrounds[13] to the privacy of bedrooms. Some of what I have suggested in describing dance as a form of play is probably oriented towards more outward social contexts: preparing for playground re-enactments, learning to be looked at and to be in control of the body in movement and on display. But it is also about defining the self for the self through the detour of the other reconstructed as a fictitious 'I'. In this sense, it is about trying out various kinds of identity and the relation to the body that they might entail, as much as being a method of learning to monitor the public presentation of the self. Again, therefore, I want to stress that this practice of dance as play, and even the enjoyment of *The Little Mermaid*, is not peculiar to a culture of childhood but is rather to be understood as continuous with the phase we call youth or adolescence. Of course, depending upon positions in age phases, different texts will be engaged, different kinds of context become available for dancing; shifts in biology and in social and familial relations do take place. But, crucially, it needs to be recognised that young children are trying out the identities that pertain to adult life long before they get there.[14]

**Under the Sea and in the Living Room**

There are other ways in which dance figures in the viewing practices of young children. This further strand in my argument relates more to questions of domestic space and its regulation within families than to strategies of self-identification as such. However, even here the dance around the television is one through which another version of the self is explored in terms which go beyond those within which children tend to be confined.

Again, I can most usefully anchor my argument in *The Little Mermaid*, and particularly in the dance 'Under the Sea'. Sebastian, the crab and master of music, attempts a counter-argument to Ariel's determined preoccupation with the world above the sea. It is presented as song, brilliantly choreographed and drawing together elements of steel band and other Caribbean music. The song begins with an elaborately humorous reprise of Ariel's own yearning, but also moves immediately into an unambiguous, and celebratory, reassertion of life where it's wetter, under the sea. Music and dance down below are set against toiling in the sun above.

It is a fast-moving and witty lyric, worth some close listening, but here the detail of the song matters less than the way in which the sequence opens up a carnivalesque lunacy in the narrative. The song and dance sequence literally impedes the seemingly inexorable movement towards conflict between Ariel and Tritan and, in its lyric, refuses the desire which leads her to the surface and away from the party below. In doing so it points, unsuccessfully, to a state in which desire, a yearning to be elsewhere, is expelled from the immediacy of the present moment and the lush excess of a place apart from human work and need. But if, narratively, 'Under the Sea' fails, it nevertheless invites a different satisfaction from that given priority in the romantic scenario. So whereas the romantic elements, singing to the half-drowned Eric for example, are often rejected ('Oh, I hate her when she does this, I hate it!'), the exotic fishiness of Sebastian's carnival is likely to bring young viewers to their feet in jubilant mimicry. For example, while I watched with my younger daughter, she took off around the living room saying: 'This is when it goes . . . I just like to turn it up a bit, turn it up, so you can dance . . . [around three minutes of dancing followed] . . . Now I'm coming back to you.' The creation of a participatory space, by increasing the volume of sound and by 'taking the floor', is a repeated moment of assertion in which, at odds with the customary physical passivity of watching television and in denial of the ordered arrangement of living rooms, a more amorphous and kinetic pleasure is achieved.

The use of television as a means through which to negotiate, or even defy, parental regulations of domestic space may seem an improbable paradox if television is more usually regarded as anchoring the particular, and fixed, arrangement of living rooms. But in such moments as that offered by 'Under the Sea' or by *Top of the Pops* and *The Chart Show*, modes of engagement with television expand beyond either distracted attention or passive absorption to become a powerful means of redefining space on terms which children themselves elaborate. I am inclined, therefore, to see some ironic reversals in looking across the text to include its viewing audience: if Tritan, as angry father, invades and destroys Ariel's 'room', then young viewers, for whom claims to space of their own are an everyday matter of urgent contest, are among those most keen to grasp any chance to appropriate the more common, household, areas and imbue them with that much more of themselves.

## Conclusion

The argument I have outlined here, largely with reference to girls and the kinds of television they enjoy, is one that implies a need for research which looks in some detail at the everyday viewing practices of children and which might attend to their accounts of what it is that they enjoy in what they watch. In many ways the particular case presented here is informed by what young girls do and say in front of the TV, but it is still an account which speculates about them while claiming to be on their behalf. More of what children have to say, and more attention to their explanations of their own viewing, needs to be incorporated into studies like this one. But of course it is not at all easy to get at children's perspectives, and I think it just has to be acknowledged that this is an area in which being tentative is an obligation.

As I have argued, childhood is not an enclosed and separated phase in which the meaning of adult life does not figure. The enjoyment of dancing, both as a mode of fantasy in which a more sexual self is explored and as a means to occupy domestic space, suggests the power of children to shape everyday domestic life on terms which are not entirely governed by the adults with whom they live. It is possible to suggest that though parents do regulate the lives of their children, there is also a sense in which 'parents' are remade by those they 'bring up'. In looking more closely at what goes on around the TV, some hints of how this might be happening emerge and take a more definite form.

NOTES

Once again, thanks to my daughters Francesca and Fay for helping out with this.

1. Reference is made in the following discussion to *Top of the Pops*, broadcast by BBC1; *The Chart Show*, broadcast by ITV; *Beauty and the Beast* (Walt Disney Classics, 1993) and *The Little Mermaid* (Walt Disney Classics, 1990); and *Dirty Dancing* (Vestron Pictures, 1987).
2. Neil Postman, *The Disappearance of Childhood* (London: W. H. Allen, 1983).
3. Tom Engelhardt, 'The Shortcake Strategy', in Todd Gitlin (ed.), *Watching Television* (New York: Pantheon, 1986).
4. Stephen Kline, 'Limits to the Imagination: Marketing and Children's Culture', in I. Angus and S. Jhally (eds.), *Cultural Politics in Contemporary America* (New York: Routledge, 1989), pp. 299–316. For a further development of his argument, see Kline's 'The Empire of Play' in this volume.
5. Engelhardt, 'The Shortcake Strategy', p. 109.
6. Ibid., p. 110.
7. Kline, 'Limits to the Imagination', p. 311.
8. Ibid., p. 315.
9. Ibid., p. 313.
10. L. S. Vygotsky, *Thought and Language* (Cambridge, MA: MIT Press, 1962).
11. L. S. Vygotsky, *Mind in Society* (Cambridge, MA: Harvard University Press, 1978), p. 100.
12. Ibid., p. 102.
13. See David Reedy, *Pop, Playgrounds and Performances: The Inter-relationship of Children and Popular Culture* (unpublished MA dissertation, University of London Institute of Education, 1989). For discussions of dance in the lives of adolescents, see Angela McRobbie, 'Dance and Social Fantasy', in Angela McRobbie and Mica Nava (eds.), *Gender and Generation* (London: Macmillan, 1984), pp. 130–61, and, in revised form, Angela McRobbie, 'Dance Narratives and Fantasies of Achievement', in McRobbie, *Feminism and Youth Culture* (London: Macmillan, 1991), pp. 189–219.
14. See Chris Richards, 'Taking Sides? What young girls do with television', in David Buckingham (ed.), *Reading Audiences: Young People and the Media* (Manchester University Press, 1993). Marsha Kinder's *Playing with Power in Movies, Television and Video Games* (Berkeley: University of California Press, 1991), examines closely related issues.

# THE EMPIRE OF PLAY

## *Emergent Genres of Product-based Animations*

STEPHEN C. KLINE

Since the very first broadcasts, commercial children's television in North America has been besieged by critics. The problems with letting businessmen decide the fate of children's culture, they say, are abundantly evident not only in the banality and violence in the programming, but also in the growing commercialisation of the children's cultural industries, wherein artistically sophisticated, intellectually demanding and socially relevant programming finds it harder to compete for audiences with cheaply produced low-quality entertainment.[1] Critics are concerned that this entertainment bias of the market helps to cultivate, especially among heavy viewers, an unrealistic and gender-biased picture of society.[2]

The industry has responded to these arguments by suggesting that the real problem with 'kidvid' has always been underfunding. As Cy Schneider suggests, since children's television is a business like any other, the producers are reluctant to fund production of programmes when it is so difficult to make children's TV profitable. Producers have always had the same three concerns in children's TV, he says: 'Keep the costs down, the ratings up, and the regulators out.'[3] Arguing against the critics who see these programmes as banal, sexist and violent, Schneider asks why producers should be held accountable to the public by regulators for all the problems of modernity. Only by encouraging investors and shareholders to divert more money into production, he argues, will it be possible for better children's programmes to be made.

It is with these same economic arguments in mind that the US Federal Communication Commission (FCC) changed their regulatory stance in 1982, allowing more commercials every hour and casting aside their rather ineffective restrictions on programme content and marketing tie-ins. In a period when American public television production experienced cutbacks, deregulation opened children's television to whoever was willing to take the business risk of producing children's programmes.[4] Over eighty-five new animated TV series (with production costs of between 15 and 20 million dollars) have been produced in the last ten years, thanks to the licensing and toy merchandising interests who became involved in using '30-minute commercials' as the flagship of the promotion of toys, clothes and related leisure product lines. Spending on children's marketing promotions and advertising has shown a very healthy increase during the 1980s, with toy advertisers becoming the leading spenders ($350 million annually) in a $1 billion annual spending spree on product promotion which has helped inaugurate commercialised school television and the sale of advertising space within Nintendo games.

**Television and its Discontents**

Schneider concedes that marketing criteria now dominate the production of US children's television, which he calls 'little more than a creative outlet for toy and greeting card manufacturers'. Deregulation resulted in a kind of production environment where programming became 'dominated and commercially fuelled by the creations of the toy companies'. But Schneider doesn't believe this has been a bad thing because he finds that little has really changed in 'kidvid' beyond the increased funding and a few minor modifications in 'characterisation and story line'.[5] He suggests that the new generation of promotional animation may even be better because marketers have had to respond to the critics' and regulators' concerns by reducing the amount of violence depicted or by contextualising it in pro-social narratives. The stories, he argues, usually climax in one long battle or confrontation scene where the good guys triumph, rather than stringing together endless violent episodes of falling objects, crashes and accidents typical of traditional cartoons like *Roadrunner* or *Tom and Jerry*.

It is worth noting, too, that the narratives have also been written to take account of concerns about 'gratuitous' violence and 'impoverished' role models by situating these new heroes within a moral universe where good and evil are clearly defined and aligned with particular characters. For example, GI Joe fights for freedom; Ninja Turtles resist a megalomaniacal genius bent on world domination. This makes the heroes' violent acts defensive and justifiable by clearly drawn moral codes. Other series have even added a green hue to the struggles between good and evil (*Captain Planet, The Sun Tots*).[6] Still others like *He-man* began to employ a thirty-second tag-ending for the programme where a character draws out the moral lesson ('Never pet stray dogs').

Critics have also argued that television's role depictions are gender-biased.[7] As in prime-time TV, male characters are overrepresented, have higher occupational status, and are more commonly associated with power in children's programmes, although educational programmes which try to overcome these role portrayals and cartoons often make general role classification systems unworkable.[8] As David F. Poltrack, the senior CBS vice-president for research, concedes, 'children's television has always been male-dominated and remains so'; yet he argues that this male-orientation is based on pragmatic business judgments and has nothing to do with sexism on the part of network programmers.[9] Girls will watch shows with boy heroes, though not vice versa.

Noting these limitations, the marketers can point to several promotional series which feature powerful and resourceful female characters who can act on their own to solve problems, thus providing better role models for girls (She-ra, Jem, Wonder Woman). This new breed of female characters possesses many heroic elements found in the boys' action adventure format, including secret identities, muscular physiques, super-powers and an ability to defeat evil. Other promotional series appear to accommodate female cross-viewers by portraying a new type of female character as a member of the male-dominated action team (Cheetara in *Thundercats*, Cat Woman in *Batman*). Yet the critics wonder about the effect of these kinds of changes in female role portrayal – a question which ultimately depends upon how children judge, imitate, identify with and otherwise use these unrealistic characters in the formation of gender identity and knowledge.[10]

Are these programmes actually providing children with helpful female role models? The marketers have created more engaging animated female personae who model human-like behaviour, yet who as fantasy heroes are also unburdened by narrative plausibility, realism or representational authenticity. Studies have indicated that children's judgments of social realism vary with age and the content of the programme[11] and that the distinction between cartoons and live drama can be a major factor in how children respond to and interpret these stories.[12] Yet paradoxically, because these animated stories and characters bear little relationship to children's understanding of real-world behaviour, marketers will argue that children 'may not be as easily exploitable'[13] by animated characters and that the impacts of fantasy on their behaviour and attitudes is minimal because of reduced identification with and imitation of animated characters.

In summary, the marketers suggest that the new generation of animation enhances representational diversity while giving children improved pro-social fantasy which is unlikely to have any deleterious effects. Noting that children have increased their viewing of TV cartoons, Jib Fowles believes that deregulation has been in children's interest because it has given them more of what they want to watch and enjoy.[14] Many in the industry also claim that children watch these animations simply to have fun, and gain a much needed distraction from the stresses of daily life, finding fuel for the imagination in television's entertaining diversions. They ask us to believe that kids' TV is nothing but good entertainment provided free to kids.

### The Commercialisation Effect

Yet these defences of commercial programming have not mollified recent critics who maintain that what we mean by 'good' television must be defined in terms of the ways the medium contributes to children's socialisation needs. For this reason, recent critics take particular umbrage with deregulation because it marks the end of children's special protected status in the market and further erodes the idea that television should serve children's socialisation and education positively.[15]

tially the result of economic factors stemming from the US market. American companies have responded to global opportunities with an increasing tendency towards offshore production (most animation, clothing, printing and toy production is done in Asia), and there is a growing emphasis on global distribution through direct satellite broadcasts, cable and videocassette. New global distribution networks for toys, games and other cultural products (Disneyland, Nintendo, McDonald's, Toys 'R' Us etc.) are likely to consolidate the promotional strategy in the global market. Globalisation appears to be necessary to maintain profitability and is part of the continuing redefinition of post-modern cultural production which emphasises product design, deal-making and marketing over product improvement and manufacturing.[23]

It is clear that these new promotional programmes were not such a radical rupture in the traditions of children's television, because most of these programme formats were derived from 'tried and true' marketing successes.[24] For example, the success of *Star Wars* inspired a cluster of space empire sagas. Similarly, the amazing popularity of *Strawberry Shortcake* and *Smurfs* fuelled a host of ersatz folk communities. *Superman*, *Wonder Woman*, *A-Team*, *Batman* and *Star Wars* all existed in other media formats before finding their way into promotional TV. This gradual process of 'spinning off' past successes makes it very difficult to distinguish analytically the role that marketing considerations play in characterisation and storyline.

There is, however, evidence that the promotional purpose has some influence on the way series develop characters and plot lines. An excellent summary of how the marketing considerations squeeze creativity, plausibility and innovation out of a script for a character toy is provided by Stern and Schoenhaus in their account of the development of the animation series for the Dino-Riders toy.[25] Dino-Riders toys were originally conceived and designed as museum-accurate models based on children's fascination with dinosaurs. But as the back-story narrative was developed for the promotional animation series, important changes were made to the shape, colour and implied behaviour of the creatures.

In order to launch the line, writers perceived the need to mythologise the dinosaurs, giving them a grandly scaled origin tale by dividing them into good and bad species – one free and one subjugated. This ensured a basic conflict in every story which would capture boys' attention and give structure to their play. The subjugated dinosaurs were dominated by an evil extra-terrestrial, led by a classically brutal megalomaniac, while the free ones were in telepathic communication with their benevolent humanoid riders headed by a golden-haired hero. By the time the animation series was shown in 1988, it was indistinguishable from all the other animated action series, lacked humour and freshness, and found that in a market cluttered with Ninja Turtles and GI Joes the toys didn't sell well.

Among producers, very specific marketing considerations are taken into account in programme design, based upon positioning strategies (how the product is different from others in the market) and the need to gain instant character recognition. The objective is quickly to saturate the market and implant character identities within children's culture, so that children talk about them, want to play with them and can communicate their preferences to their parents.[26] Producers must do this, however, while achieving greater economies in the production process because these programmes are paid for by licensing arrangement pre-sales rather than the long-term residuals of venerable cartoons. The super-heroic personalities, equipment intrigues, team-based conflicts, and bifurcated moral universes all reflect 'tried and true' selling tactics formulated to increase the attractiveness, acceptance and selling potential of product lines.

To assess whether promotional television is different in terms of format and content, Eaton and Dominick performed a content analysis which contrasted toy-linked to non-toy linked cartoons. Results indicated that toy-linked programmes tended to use music as an integral part of plot, run promos for upcoming episodes, use robots as characters, contain more violent and anti-social acts, and be set in present-day America more often than non-toy linked programmes, although these trends are not that strong.[27] For example, in terms of overt merchandising and numbers of characters, they found few differences between these programmes. They also found very minor differences in programme complexity; overall their stories were more similar than different.

Yet in their study of promotional influences, Eaton and Dominick fail to take account of positioning and targeting strategies and their influence on programme style and form. For example, they consider *My Little Pony* and *G. I. Joe* as belonging in the toy-linked category, although the lead characters (female and male), narrative techniques and themes of these stories are very different because they feature very different toys for different market segments. To lump them together reduces the magnitude of the differences. Most striking is the authors' failure to find any differences in the sex role portrayals and characterisation between toy-based and non-toy based cartoons.

Evidence is strong that gender and age-based preferences are very well defined in the children's market, extending to both programmes viewed and toys desired.[28] According to age and gender, children's toy preferences are generally thought age/gender-undifferentiated in the 'magic years' (3 to 5 years old), followed by a more highly gendered early school experience (6 to 8 years old). Since toy preferences tend to be more gender and age-specific than programme preferences, marketers were forced to target audiences more carefully. Based on their marketing research, promotional advertisers advised that children should not be viewed as one audience: 'It is vital for marketers to understand the complexity of the children's market, which is not one market but three, with children's preferences and values showing major differences.'[29]

An analysis of favourite programmes and characters of 143 six to eight year-old Canadian children also showed that children's preferences clearly clustered around programme genres rather than particular programmes (see tables 1 and 2). The effects of gender and age targeting were clearly evident in a review of the eighty-five new series that have been shown on US TV. In our study of these series we found it made less sense to talk about toy-linked programmes in the abstract than about three distinctive new genres of animation, which can be called Action Teams, Female Heroes and Imaginary Companions.

## Action Teams

Most promotional programmes (60 per cent) bear a strong resemblance to the action-adventure narratives of movies and television. Gina Marchetti noted that action-adventure narratives eventually come to the point where the hero must resolve the dramatic conflict through physical confrontation: 'Within the action-adventure genre, narrative takes a back seat to spectacle. The emphasis is not on plot or characterization but on action, on the visual display of violence. . . . The main pleasure of the text revolves around spectacular fights, gun play, torture, and battles.'[30] Power struggles and combat define the main dramatic moments in these animations, targeted at boys, leading to the common accusation that these programmes promote 'war play'. The difference between the animations (which do not show blood and in which the villains generally live to fight again) and the films is largely that these programmes feature well-known boys' 'action toys' as lead characters.

The Action Teams formula adapts most elements from the action-adventure format, yet simplifies the narrative and characters for the target audience of boys between 5 and 9. Compared with the movies, the stories reduce the complex motivations of the characters, often replacing the misfit alpha-male, who acts as an isolated individual, with a superhero who is part of a structured team through which hero capacity is expressed as

TABLE 1
**FEMALE VIEWING PATTERNS OF PROMOTIONAL CARTOONS**

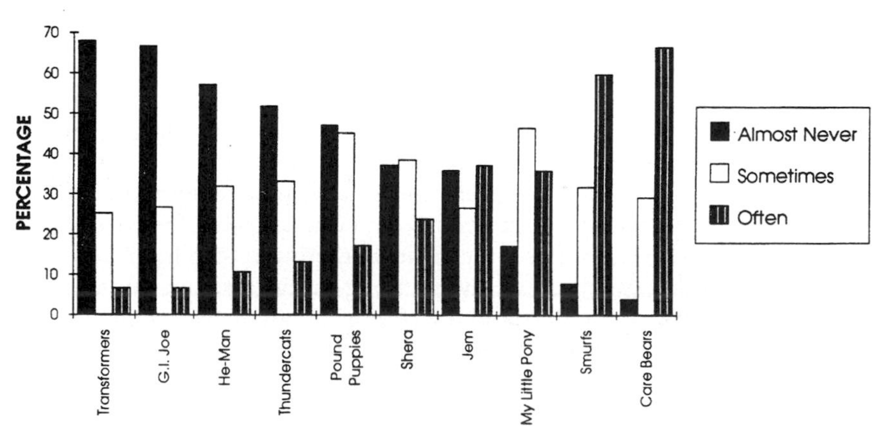

leadership among peers. These teams are always in mortal conflict with a rigid hierarchy led by a megalomaniac. The hero's character traits include a sense of adventure, bravery and audacity, so the plots hinge on action, quests and challenges rather than negotiation or compromise. After all, it is through great deeds that heroes become heroes – it is their mastery and their inborn skills that ensure triumphant struggles, successful quests of daring, rescues of the innocent, all of which demonstrate their nobility of spirit and legitimate dominion. Given the need to feed action play, it is not surprising that these stories also have a strong technical overlay which links particular weapons, vehicles and martial techniques with specific characters.

## Imaginary Companions

Maturational processes are an important issue in toy marketing because children's toy preferences and play styles change with age. Age segmentation has increasingly become a factor in children's promotional programming, and to sell the plush anthropomorphic characters of early childhood a unique type of programming had to be developed which attracted the pre-schooler. Following a narrative strategy laid down by *The Smurfs*, *Sesame Street*, *Teddy Ruxpin* and *Carebears*, these animations feature 'animal friend' characters typical of fairy tales, but their simplified and self-consciously pro-social storytelling resembles neither the earlier violent cartoons nor a real fairy story. These tales centre around the daily domestic lives of a gang of cuddly plush creatures who are sometimes portrayed as the 'imaginary companions' of children who may communicate with them (as in *Megan* or *My Little Pony*). They live in quasi-alternative communities where the characters experience the familiar domestic challenges of trickery, meanness and social ineptitude, and emotional states typical of sibling and family interaction. Their gentler conflicts, low-key confrontations and

TABLE 2
MALE VIEWING PATTERNS OF PROMOTIONAL CARTOONS

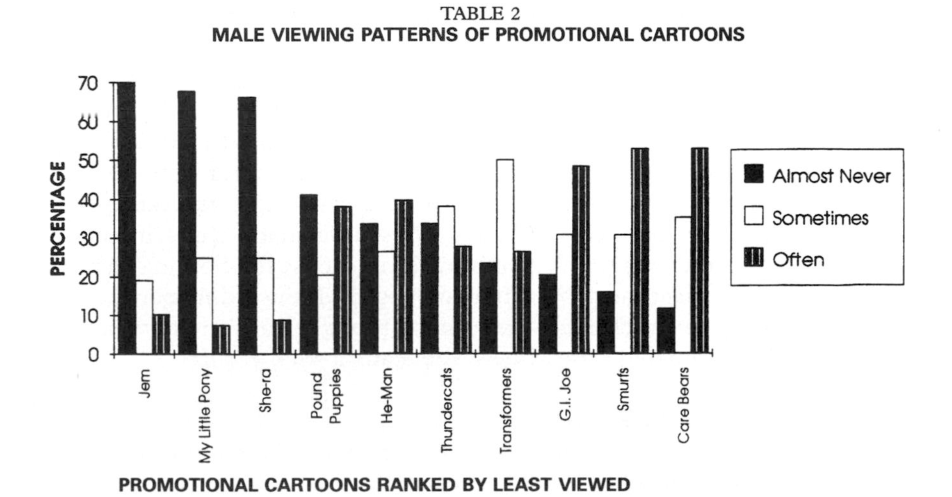

episodic storytelling are the hallmarks of a kind of animation considered appropriate and preferred by pre-schoolers. These programmes accounted for about 30 per cent of children's programmes.

Imaginary companions are defined by their simplicity of structure and language, which to many adults makes them unbearable to watch. For example, the Care Bears are distinguished only by the colour of the heart on their chests which is emblematic of their characteristic motivations and responses (Proud Heart, Tender Heart, Playful Heart and so on). Their verbal exchanges are childlike ('Ooooo. A small icky doggy, He, Haaaa', 'Oh, oh, it gives me the willies'). For example, a trickster introduces crab-apple pie to the Care Bear clan, causing them to become mean and nasty. Crafty old Gramms Bear discovers the cause of the non-niceness, and changes the crab-apple pie recipe, adding three parts sugar and a dose of love. Tender Heart had his feelings hurt when Gramms was under the mean spell. Gramms reassures him: 'People can change their behaviour, but my love and caring for my family will never change.'

Characters never learn from their experience, but rather come programmed with traits that pre-ordain them to experience particular challenges and overcome their circumstances in a particular way. Characters rarely act outside of their defined orientation (Papa Smurf is always wise, Tender Heart bear is always gentle and caring). Interactions are formulaic, predictable and often consist of cliché responses ('What do ya say, dudes?' 'Long time no see', 'Sight for sore eyes'). Moreover, the pastel illustration practices, coupled with limited dialogue, give this genre a look and feel that reflects economies in production.

### Female Heroes

As marketers discovered, the fact that girls will view boys-oriented action-adventure programmes does not induce them to buy those toys and accessories promoted in them. For this reason, about 10 per cent of the promotional animations specifically feature strong female leads in an action-drama format. These stories, clearly developed around the toys, assume promotional values stressing fashion and more complex social relations deemed appropriate for the older girl. Jem, for example, is both the lead singer with the Holograms and runs a home for orphaned girls. She-ra, although sister to He-man, goes through more extensive wardrobe changes and is more likely to consult, negotiate and use magical powers rather than her sword to solve problems. These stories have many shifts in setting (performances, festivals) which help provide an excuse for clothing changes and grooming motifs thought essential to the girls' fashion doll market. The fashion orientation was clearest when Mattel brought Barbie to television in the form of an animated series where she leads a rock group.

### A Study of Promotional Genres

Genre differences in the themes, character actions and emotions wereevident from a narrative analysis of 511 episodes drawn from the ten most viewed animated series of 1987. The events undertaken in each episode were recorded, using a typology of twenty-one codable actions. In these broad terms, there are no major differences between the genres because most cartoons are taken up with simple events and conversations. The most often registered action was 'purposeful', which is defined as simple everyday acts such as picking up a chair or driving a car (see Table 3). Yet some subtle distinctions between genres can be noted. For example, Imaginary Companions appeared to be the busiest in terms of these everyday actions, and more conversational, because their conflicts amount to arguments and squabbles rather than overt battles. Their low frequency of physical aggression might be accounted for by designers' realisation that parents are more concerned about violence in younger children's programmes. The internal life of the Female Heroes seemed to be much more important than that of the male Action Teams, as indicated by the use of soliloquy. As might be expected, combat and working with advanced technology were much more typical of the Action Teams heroes, while the technology used by Imaginary Companions was predominantly domestic.

TABLE 3

| Action Typology | Action Teams % | Female Hero % | Imaginary Companions % | Total % |
|---|---|---|---|---|
| Purposeful | 25 | 25 | 31 | 27 |
| Conversation | 9 | 9 | 13 | 10 |
| Soliloquy | 4 | 17 | 11 | 8 |
| Battling | 14 | 6 | 2 | 8 |
| Working with technology | 11 | 8 | 3 | 8 |

Of the episodes examined, 16 per cent provided no basis upon which to judge social or emotional content. Of the three genres, settings and action sequences which typically lack emotional content were most prevalent in Action Teams. The actual social and emotional relations expressed reflected slight differences of emphasis. Of the forty-three emotions coded[31] the seven most frequent (representing 38 per cent of the total) are presented in Table 4. Across the genres, with the exception of confidence, the emotions generally appeared to lack a positive dimension, although Imaginary Companions were rarely serious or sombre beings, yet were more likely to express frustration or impatience as befitted their immaturity. Anger, meanness and confidence are the most frequently expressed qualities of Action Teams and their enemies. A lack of confidence is noted in the Female Heroes stories.

TABLE 4

| Emotions Typology | Action Teams % | Female Hero % | Imaginary Companions % | Total % |
|---|---|---|---|---|
| Confident | 9 | 5 | 8 | 8 |
| Mean/Petty | 10 | 6 | 5 | 7 |
| Despair | 6 | 6 | 6 | 6 |
| Serious/Sombre | 8 | 7 | 1 | 5 |
| Frustrated/Impatient | 3 | 3 | 6 | 4 |
| Angry/Rage | 5 | 3 | 3 | 4 |
| Agitated/Anxious | 5 | 6 | 2 | 4 |

The three genres also differed in their thematic orientation. Of the thirty-eight possible themes the five most prevalent accounted for 40 per cent of the episodes coded (Table 5). An emphasis on technology, hierarchy and offensive action reflects a skew within the male-oriented Action Teams genre in which cosmic power struggles between good and evil frame the narrative. The less hierarchical communities of Imaginary Companions were focused on domestic problem-solving, while both the Action Teams and Female Heroes stories were set in situations where technology played an important role, often being the narrative focus (for example, someone steals the power crystals or the magical solution to the problem).

TABLE 5

| Theme Typology | Action Team % | Female Hero % | Imaginary Companions % | Total % |
|---|---|---|---|---|
| Problem Solving | 7 | 10 | 14 | 10 |
| Rely on Technology | 13 | 11 | 4 | 10 |
| Hierarchy | 13 | 5 | 2 | 8 |
| Offensive | 9 | 3 | 4 | 6 |
| Race Against Time | 5 | 5 | 7 | 6 |

**The Value of Narrative**

Any observer of contemporary children's television must realise that this medium has become the great storyteller of post-modern culture. Children's television pulsates non-stop with an endless round of quasi-mythic stories which fascinate children as audiences and consumers. Yet for too long the issues surrounding children's television have been framed in terms of what harm television does to kids – its potential to elicit violence and perpetuate stereotyped attitudes in children, rather than its potential to contribute to their lives.

Clearly children's television and films have become a very successful venue for promoting products. Sales of promotional and licensed goods have risen from 20 per cent of total toy sales (1977) to 65 per cent (1987) through featuring these character toys in TV programmes. At the same time, the market for toys and games has grown from 2.6 billion (1982) to 17 billion (1992) in the USA, based on this system of marketing which annually sows new personae into the fertile soil of children's imagination. Clearly one consequence of deregulating commercial TV has been the channelling of whatever production money was available into promotional animation. The children's culture boom has resulted in few new live-action dramas, educative programmes or serials, because such programmes are simply less conducive to tie-ins; thus those who would produce them find it harder to gain an adequate market share and so attract support from funders. This may be an important change if, as post-modern critics of 'kidvid' note, the young child who grows up in a fantastic simulacrum world of promotional television may fail to develop adequate points of reference for integrating their real day-to-day experiences.[32]

It is not just a matter of a rejection of the aesthetics of fantasy, or of kids confusing cartoons with reality. As research has shown, children as young as 4 recognise cartoons as purely 'make-believe' (a fantastic representation with little link to reality). Yet animation conveys its own paradoxical epistemological status. In his analysis of children's judgments of television, Hawkins saw fit to distinguish 'magic window reality' – an awareness of the constructed nature of TV – from 'social expectations reality' – whereby an event is viewed in relation to how it conforms to children's expectations of the world.[33] To illustrate this point, *The Simpsons* can be viewed as fantasy because its animation is 'constructed', but the behaviour of Bart may also be judged as realistic in the sense that he reacts and talks like a real kid. What is clearly needed is a better understanding of how children internalise and use the social knowledge conveyed in these cartoons.

Bettelheim says of fairy tales that 'For a story to truly hold the child's attention, it must entertain him and arouse his curiosity. But to enrich his life it must stimulate his imagination; help him to develop his intellect and to clarify his emotions; be attuned to his anxieties and aspirations; give full recognition to his difficulties, while at the same time suggesting solutions to the problems that perturb him.'[34] Similarly, Clarissa Estes declares that 'stories are medicine' because they are 'embedded with instructions which guide us about the complexities of life' and contain the ability 'to engender excitement, sadness, questions, longings, and understandings that spontaneously bring the archetype back to the surface'.[35] To their clinicians' eyes, stories enlighten, nurture, guide and shape a child's mental life, by coalescing those difficult-to-recognise aspects of our thoughts and feelings. This is a matter of not only telling the right stories, but telling them right so that they can have their effect. Stories can be blunted and maimed, truncated and sanitised to the point where they lose their healthy aspect and become mere distractions.

These authors speak of the profound psychological potential of stories.

The American commercialised television institution has privileged private profit without consideration of the cost to society of not using television to educate and to build a supportive fictional environment for children's maturation. Marketers are fully aware of the power of the story, yet what is missing is the desire to make good ones. With the aid of satellites, pay and cable TV, marketers around the world are discovering the potential of promotional media to engage children with their product lines and encourage them to want to play with particular toys and games. This detailed content analysis has helped illustrate the significance of targeting within this emerging matrix of children's crucial first stories.[36] Yet without an adequate appreciation of the importance of narrative and the psychological role of televised fantasy in children's well-being, appeals for a pro-social dimension in children's television are bound to fall on deaf ears.

NOTES

1. Aletha Huston-Stein, Sandra Fox, Douglas Greer, Bruce A. Watkins and Jane Whitaker, 'The Effects of TV Action and Violence on Children's Social Behaviour', *Journal of Genetic Psychology*, vol. 138, 1981, pp. 183–91. Also D. Kunkel and D. Roberts, 'Young minds and marketplace values: issues in children's television advertising', *Journal of Social Issues*, vol. 47 no. 1, 1991, pp. 57–61.
2. Neil Postman, *Amusing Ourselves to Death* (New York: Penguin, 1985).
3. Cy Schneider, *Children's Television: The Art, the Business and How it Works* (Chicago: NTC Business Books, 1987).
4. Edward Palmer, *Television and America's Children: A Case of Neglect* (New York: Oxford University Press, 1988).
5. Ibid.
6. 'New Kids Shows Marketed to Pass FCC Muster', *Broadcasting*, 28 January 1991, p. 27.
7. Nancy Signorielli, 'Television and Conceptions about Sex Roles: Maintaining Conventionality and the Status Quo', *Sex Roles*, vol. 21, 1989.
8. Kevin Durkin, 'Television and Sex Role Acquisition: III, Counter Stereotyping/ British', *Journal of Social Psychology*, vol. 24 no. 3, September 1985, pp. 211–22.
9. Bill Carter, 'Saturday Morning TV is a Boys' World', *Globe and Mail*, Toronto, 2 May 1991.
10. Michael Morgan, 'Television, Sex-Role Attitudes, and Sex-Role Behavior', *Journal of Early Adolescence*, vol. 7 no. 3, Fall 1987, pp. 269–82.
11. A. Dorr, P. Kovaric and C. Doubleday, 'Age and content influences on children's perceptions of the realism of television families', *Journal of Broadcasting and Electronic Media*, vol. 34 no. 4, 1980, pp. 377–97.
12. Chris Downs, 'Children's Judgements of Televised Events: The Real Versus Pretend Distinction', *Perceptual and Motor Skills*, vol. 70, 1990, pp. 779–82.
13. Stuart Van Auken and Subhash C. Lonial, 'Children's Perceptions of Characters: Human Versus Animals Assessing Implications for Children's Advertising', *Journal of Advertising*, vol. 14 no. 2, 1985, pp. 13–22.
14. Jib Fowles, *Why Viewers Watch, A Reappraisal of Television Effects* (Beverly Hills: Sage, 1992).
15. Huston-Stein, *et al.*, 'The Effects of TV Action and Violence on Children's Social Behaviour'; Kunkel and Roberts, 'Young minds and marketplace values'.
16. Tom Engelhardt, 'The *Strawberry Shortcake* Strategy', in T. Gitlin (ed.), *Watching Television* (New York: Pantheon Books, 1986).

17. David Fox, 'Disney gets 200 million wishes with Aladdin', *Vancouver Sun*, 23 April 1993, p. C8.
18. David Smith, 'Nintendo hitches magic carpet ride', *Vancouver Sun*, 4 November 1993, p. D1.
19. Stephen Kline, 'Toy Marketing and the Internationalization of Children's Television', forthcoming.
20. Stephen Kline, 'Let's Make a Deal: Merchandising in US-Kinderfernsehen', *Media Perspektiven*, no. 4, 1991.
21. Selina Guber and Jon Berry, *Marketing to and Through Kids* (New York: McGraw-Hill, 1990).
22. Stephen Kline 'Limits to the Imagination', in I. Angus and S. Jhally (eds.), *Cultural Politics in Contemporary America* (New York: Routledge, 1988).
23. Stephen Kline, 'Toy marketing and the internationalization of children's television'.
24. Tom Engelhardt, 'The primal screen', *Mother Jones*, vol. 16 no. 3, May-June 1991, p. 68(4).
25. Sydney Ladensohn-Stern and Ted Schoenhaus, *Toyland: The High Stakes Game of the Toy Industry* (Chicago: Contemporary Books, 1990).
26. Stephen Kline, 'Limits to the Imagination'.
27. B. C. Eaton and Joseph Dominick, 'Product-Related Programming and Children's TV: A Content Analysis', *Journalism Quarterly*, vol. 68 no. 1/2, Spring/Summer 1991.
28. Clive Vander Burgh and Heather Knoepfli, *Batman would only live in the United States* (Toronto: Ryerson, 1993).
29. Stephen Kline, *Out of the Garden: Children's Toys and Television in the Age of Marketing* (London: Verso, 1993), p. 251.
30. Gina Marchetti, 'Action-Adventure as Ideology', in Ian Angus and Sut Jhally (eds.), *Cultural Politics in Contemporary America* (New York: Routledge, 1988).
31. A content analysis study conducted by Stephen Kline in 1987 based on 511 episodes drawn from the ten most viewed animated series.
32. G. Ray Funkhouser and Eugene F. Shaw, 'How Synthetic Experience Shapes Social Reality', *Journal of Communication*, Spring 1990.
33. R. P. Hawkins, 'The Dimensional Structure of Children's Perceptions of Television Reality', *Communication Research*, vol. 4, 1977, pp. 299–320.
34. Bruno Bettelheim, *The Uses of Enchantment: the Meaning and Importance of Fairy Tales* (New York: Random House, 1976), p. 5.
35. Clarissa Pinkola Estes, *Women who Run with the Wolves: Myths and Stories of the Wild Woman Archetype* (New York: Ballantine, 1992).
36. Robert L. Schrag, 'Narrative Rationality and "First Stories": Pedagogical Implications for Children's Television', *Communication Education*, vol. 10, October 1991.

# TOY-BASED VIDEO FOR GIRLS

## *'My Little Pony'*

ELLEN SEITER

When in doubt, use boys.
Cy Schneider, *Children's Television*

US television producers, like most children's authors, cartoonists and movie-makers, have favoured male characters in action-packed adventures for boys. Male characters predominate because conventional wisdom has it that boys will not watch girls on television, but that girls will watch programmes for boys. Until recently, little girls were not thought to constitute a large enough market to justify the cost of the programming. In the 1980s, with the rise of home video-recorders and rental tapes, animated series specifically designed for girls were made for the first time. The shows *Strawberry Shortcake, The Care Bears, Rainbow Brite* (1983–7) and *My Little Pony* (1984–6) were denigrated as the trashiest, most saccharine products of the children's television industry. Yet these series were the first animated shows that did not require girls to cross-over and identify with males. I want here to take a close look at *My Little Pony,* a limited, toy-based series of videos unmistakably coded as feminine, as representative of children's animated series and their appeal on the basis of gender.

### The Boys' World of Children's Fiction

The preference for male characters in children's media has its origins in popular children's books from the nineteenth century. The marketing of children's books to the middle class began in the eighteenth century, with strongly moralistic books that were intended for boys and girls alike. As Elizabeth Segel has explained: 'Neither the Puritan aim of saving the child's soul nor the characteristic Georgian aim of developing good character seemed to require the distinction between girl-child and boy-child.' Instead, children's books of the late eighteenth and early nineteenth century 'clearly taught obedience, submission to authority and selflessness as the cardinal virtues of both girls and boys.' In the 1850s a division between domestic chronicles and adventure stories featuring male characters first appears.

> Before the boys' book appeared on the scene, fiction for children typically had been domestic in setting, heavily didactic, and morally or spiritually uplifting, and this kind of earnest family story remained the staple of younger children's fiction. The boys' book was, above all, an escape from domesticity and from the female domination of the domestic world. . . . The liberation of nineteenth-century boys into the book worlds of sailors and pirates, forests and battles, left their sisters behind in the world of childhood – that is, the world of home and family.[1]

The differentiation between boys' and girls' books coincided with the nineteenth-century expansion of the book market and the attempt to expand sales through segmentation.[2] Pulp fiction in the form of romances for girls developed later than boys' action stories. The rise of girls' popular romances coincided with the growth of the middle-class 'cult of domesticity' and the notion of separate worlds for male and female. In fiction – as in ideology – boys belonged in a public world of work and adventure, girls in a domestic world of personal relationships. According to Segel, from the outset of a gendered distinction in popular children's literature boys shied away from girls' books, while 'girls were avid readers of boys books from the start'.[3]

Decades later, Walt Disney set the standard for gender representation in children's motion picture productions. In adapting fairy tales and literary sources, he handed out a few starring roles to young women: Cinderella, Sleeping Beauty, Snow White, and more recently Ariel in *The Little Mermaid* and Belle in *Beauty and the Beast*. In each case, however, the heroine was innocent and selfless and the story placed her in a situation of enforced passivity whether through physical confinement, muteness or death. Any deviance from these characteristics immediately marks a female character as villainous in Disney's universe. Disney's best-known animated film characters, and the most fanciful, were always male: the Dwarfs, Jimminy Cricket, Bambi, Dumbo, Peter Pan. All the popular cartoon characters, at Disney and at Warners and Hanna-Barbera, were males: Mickey Mouse, Donald Duck, Tom and Jerry, Daffy Duck, Elmer Fudd and Bugs Bunny, Coyote and Road Runner, Silvester and Tweety. In many of the cartoons two male characters are locked in a sadistic game of entrapment and punishment. On the relatively rare occasions when female companions were used – Minnie Mouse, Daisy Duck, Petunia Pig – they were given human breasts, heavily made-up faces, short skirts and high heels. Sybil Delgaudio has characterised the gendered roles of the cartoons:

> The female as comic foil for the male is superseded by all-male rivalries in which comic incongruity is created by means other than sex differences . . . the cartoon seems to be a favorite place for the depiction of the pursuit/capture plot structure. When female characters enter the

> picture, they automatically take their places in line with the pursued, while the means of pursuit is changed to seduction and the end is clearly sexual.[4]

The striking difference between the female characters in the toy-based series of the 1980s involving licensed characters and the cartoons of the classic period is that the heroines are for the first time not pursued but pursuing – the initiators and actors on a quest. Strawberry Shortcake, My Little Pony and Rainbow Brite were not token female members of a male gang; and they are not drawn in the sexualised caricature of adult women familiar since Betty Boop.

One of the axioms of motion picture and television production (and of publishing) is that the female audience will take an interest in stories about male adventurers (the Western, the detective story, science fiction, action-adventure) while the male audience will not take an interest in stories about female adventurers (the romance, the domestic melodrama, the family saga). Thus female characters were rare on the science-fiction children's shows produced in the 1950s and the heroes were adult men such as *Captain Video and His Video Rangers* (1949–55), *Commando Cody, Sky Marshall of the Universe* (1955) and *Tom Corbett – Space Cadet* (1950–55).[5] These live-action shows were forerunners of the science-fiction and super-hero cartoon series produced in the 1960s and 1970s. *The Adventures of Johnny Quest* (a very successful show, intermittently aired between 1964 and 1980) was based on the characters Dr Benton Quest, anthropologist, his blond son Johnny, and his son's Asian companion Hadji. *The Fantastic Four* (1966–70) included one female, Sue Richards, on its team of superheroes. Sports and music series with a more comical bent featured a cast of male protagonists such as *The Monkees* (1966–72), *The Harlem Globetrotters* (1970–3) and *The Jackson Five* (1971–3). *Fat Albert and the Cosby Kids* (1969–77), one of the longest-running and most critically acclaimed children's television series (for its depiction of African-American children), counted not a single girl among its gang of seven living in the inner city. *Fat Albert's* attempt to deal realistically with childhood problems and feelings, and its positive messages emphasising self-esteem, were later borrowed by shows like *My Little Pony* and *Care Bears*.

Girls fared somewhat better in children's shows based on family situation comedies. Equal numbers of boys and girls enabled the battle-of-the-sexes theme to flourish on shows such as *The Flintstones* (1960–6), *The Jetsons* (1962–3), and *The Brady Kids* (1972–4). Only as teenagers, however, were girls given primary roles – as though it was beyond the writers' ability to create storylines that included girls without some element of heterosexual flirtation. Thus animated shows followed the conventions of *Archie*, with its long-standing rivalry between Betty and Veronica, even though the Saturday-morning television audience was in large part made up of young, pre-adolescent girls. Judy Jetson loved to dance and chase her rock idol. *Pebbles*, born in 1963, was given a love interest in Bamm-Bamm Rubble, the boy next door, while still a toddler. When she was given her own show, *Pebbles and Bamm-Bamm* (1971–6), the screenwriters accelerated her development so as to make her an adolescent.

Throughout the 1970s teenage girls appeared as tokens on shows like *Hot Wheels*. A few popular series featured teenage girls, notably *Josie and the Pussycats* (1970–6), featuring the sweet redhead Josie, the brainy black girl Valerie and the scatterbrained blonde Melody; and *Samantha the Teenage Witch*, based on an *Archie* character. *Josie* was a landmark for its establishment of the comedy adventure or 'let's get out of here' format involving teenagers menaced by supernatural foes. *Scooby-Doo* – probably the most successful series of this type – originally featured two teenage girls, pretty Daphne and smart Velma, to complement the beatnik Shaggy and the straitlaced Fred.

Designers of children's commercials and promotional campaigns have also preferred male characters. The roster of mascots is entirely male: Captain Crunch (cereal); Tony the Tiger (Frosted Flakes); the elves Snap, Crackle and Pop (Rice Krispies); Sugar Bear (Super Golden Crisp); Ronald McDonald; Geoffrey Giraffe (Toys 'R' Us). Advertising men believe that a female trademark for a children's product will immediately turn away every boy in the audience; their belief is repeatedly proven to them by market research. Even in the world of educational programming for pre-schoolers, where combating sexism was explicitly placed on the agenda in the 1970s, we find ourselves in a man's world. Adult women all but disappeared in the 1960s as hosts and puppeteers – Shari Lewis and Lamb Chop, Romper Room and Fran of Kukla, Fran and Ollie – only Mister Rogers[6] and Captain Kangaroo remained. Big Bird and Bert and Ernie dominate *Sesame Street*.[7] All the beloved monsters are male: Snuffalupagus, Honkers, Grover, Cookie Monster. The two females in residence on *Sesame Street*, Betty Lou and Prairie Dawn, are human-looking muppets rather than more fanciful creatures, and they tend to be strictly bound to realistic, rather than fantastic, actions and storylines, as though the celebrated creativity of *Sesame Street*'s writers and puppeteers dried up when confronted with female heroines. Miss Piggy from the Muppet shows and films is an exception to this, but she is a figure bound to incite feelings of confusion and ambivalence in little girls, combining as she does a flamboyant willingness to break the norms of girlish behaviour with the obsessive pursuit of her romantic interest, Kermit, and an avid pursuit of beauty with a ridiculous, porcine appearance.[8]

## The Controversy over Toy-based Programmes

The girls' cartoons *Strawberry Shortcake, Care Bears, My Little Pony* and *Rainbow Brite* were produced in the 1980s during a boom in licensed characters in the toy industry. 'Those Characters from Cleveland', a firm established in the late 1970s to think up popular characters for the toy industry and its many licensees, chose as its first task the job of reaching – in some ways creating – the young girls' market, using interviews, focus groups and storyboards of character designs to determine what girls found most appealing. Before the 1980s, Barbie and Mary Poppins had been the only successful girls' licences. This effort was made because the market for girls' toys was underdeveloped and seen as a potential income producer. Innovations in girls' toys are relatively rare: season after season, toy-makers limit their new toy lines to baby dolls who mimic human babies in different or more realistic ways (in 1990 all the manufacturers planned dolls that soil their diapers). Perhaps this is because the industry's executives are overwhelmingly male. Whatever the reason, toy store owners consider the girls' market harder to buy for than the boys' market. For a brief period, the heyday of licensed characters portrayed on videos, there were many new toys for girls: Rainbow Brite and her friends the Color Kids (Canary Yellow, Patty O Green, Buddy Blue – a token male character); the Care Bears, each a different colour and emotion;[9] Strawberry Shortcake and her girlfriends in lime, lemon, orange and blueberry; She-Ra, Princess of Power (twin sister of He-Man); and a lengthy procession of My Little Ponies.[10] Significantly, the process of first designing characters using the tools of market research and then producing a cartoon was labelled by Tom Engelhardt as 'The Strawberry Shortcake Strategy', suggesting the special link between licensed characters in the 80s and the girls' market. To a large extent these toy-based cartoons resulted from the discovery and exploitation of a marketing niche of girls in the 3–7 age group, produced by the overwhelmingly male orientation of classic cartoons, comic books and toys.

Many critics found these characters especially offensive because they were developed specifically for marketing purposes. Manufacturers wondered aloud why what they were doing was considered substantially different from what Disney had done since the 1930s in licensing the likenesses of cartoon characters for use by manufacturers of watches, clothes, cereal boxes, and toys. But the toy-based shows offended cherished notions of creative integrity. Engelhardt charged that 'for the first time on such a massive scale, a "character" has been born free of its specific structure in a myth, fairy tale, story, or even cartoon, and instead embedded from the beginning in a consortium of busy manufacturers whose goals are purely and simply to profit by multiplying the image itself in any way that conceivably will make money'.[11] Action for Children's Television led the protest against these programmes and filed suit with the Federal Communication Commission to get them banned from television.

Some of the most virulent attacks on the licensed character shows were in fact diatribes against their 'feminine' appeal. One of the reasons they seemed so dopey, so contrived, so schmaltzy was that they borrowed from popular women's genres – the romance, the soap opera, the family melodrama. Engelhardt complained that 'a group of bossy, demanding, doll-like creatures dominate the relentlessly "happy" realm of girls' TV.' This remark reveals a lack of familiarity with the stories, which in fact concentrate to a large extent on unhappiness, suffering and feelings of worthlessness. One reason these programmes appeared so artificial to critics such as Engelhardt was that a willed, intentional act – the act of targeting the female consumer – was required to revise the dominant conventions of the twentieth-century children's story so as to centre on female protagonists and the conventional concerns and play of little girls. Engelhardt noted with irritation that in the absence of the adventure plots and special effects typical of boys' cartoons there is an emphasis on pro-social, pop psychology values: 'An endless stream of these happy little beings with their magical unicorns in their syrupy cloud-cuckoo lands have paraded across the screen demanding that they be snuggled, cuddled, nuzzled, loved, and adored, generally enticing children to lay bare their emotions so that they can be examined and made healthy.'[12]

Girls' cartoons, like women's soap operas, were about emotional life. Engelhardt argued that the proliferation of characters on these shows leads to personality fragmentation, and worried about the effect on the audience in a tone that recalls concerns for the mental health of the soap opera viewer:[13]

> If we all have trouble with caring or hugging, if intervention is called for, and if you also have to sell lots of licensed characters, then you have to present the managing (or healing) process as a highly complicated one that needs lots of cooperation by lots of highly specialized dolls, so specialized that instead of being complex individual personalities, they are no more than carefully labeled fragments of a personality: Tender-heart Bear, Share Bear, Cheer Bear, Grumpy Bear.[14]

But personality fragmentation is not an invention of 'Those Characters from Cleveland'. It can be found in early Disney films, such as *Three Little Pigs*, which was praised by critics for its original 'character differentiation'. The single adjectives used to designate the Seven Dwarfs of Snow White (Grumpy, Happy, Sleepy, etc.) are probably the first examples of this trick in animation. But Disney's work was enthusiastically embraced by critics, probably in large part because of his painstaking attention to animation.[15] (Today, Disney's work is the standard for the genre.)

The difference between Disney's animation and today's television programmes is above all that of style. The limited animation techniques used to produce children's television series were pioneered by Hanna Barbera in the late 1950s. The television series were made for a fraction of the cost of, and in a fraction of the time spent on, film cartoons. Characters stand in one place more, and the same background drawings are repeatedly used, now stored in memory with computer animation. Discussing the cartoons based on licensed characters, Stephen Kline complains:

> The cartoon creature who acts, thinks, and feels just as humans, but is simplified in form and personality provides a perfect vehicle for children's characterizations. The drawings appear infantilized. Characters' features and expressions are reduced to the simplest and most easily recognized by the young. Animators emphasize those features and expressions that children most quickly and easily identify with. Indeed, the characters rarely learn anything in these programs – their nature is inherent and fixed by their species-specific and immutable characteristics.[16]

Kline's criticism concerns simplification and fixed character types: he wants characters that change and grow, the individualistic, well-rounded characters of the nineteenth-century realist novel. But between the lines in these critiques one also hears a denigration of the emotional and psychological, and an irritation with the lack of action in these shows. These are precisely the same grounds on which adult women's genres have been denigrated. Engelhardt and Kline note with dismay that these cartoons submerge the child in a fantasy world unknown to the parents; they complain that they are too specific to the child's gender and age group; they ghettoise their viewing. But if the narrative situations and plots are as simple as Kline and Engelhardt claim, shouldn't a parent be able to catch on quickly? I read in these passages a father's irritation at the daughter's immersion in a programme and a fictional world just for girls. The licensed character shows were not essentially different from other animated programmes for children that had been around since the 1960s. What was new about them was that it was girls – and very young girls at that – who were being approached as a separate audience.

**My Little Pony: Toys and Videos**

My Little Pony toys are popular with girls as young as two and as old as eight. In 1990, most children had heard of them, seen other children with the toys, watched the programmes, seen commercials for the toys, discussed them with playmates at pre-school or daycare. This will not last forever; the licence is past the peak of its popularity. But in 1990 I had never met a girl between the ages of three and six who did not either already have a pony or want one.[17] Many girls collect ten, twenty, thirty ponies. According to Hasbro, 150 million ponies were sold during the 1980s.

According to Sydney Ladensohn Stern and Ted Schoenhaus, *My Little Pony* was the result of some 'blue sky' research with little girls. 'Hasbro asked the little girls, "what do you see when you go to bed and close your eyes?" and the answer was often "Horses".'[18] In 1982, Hasbro was surprised when half a million brown plastic ponies sold without any advertising. The next year they changed the ponies from brown to 'fantasy colours' and sold $25 million worth of them. Sales increased with advertising to $85 million in 1984 and $100 million in 1985, and with the production of the *My Little Pony* television shows and movie. Individual examples of My Little Pony are differentiated from one another in body colour, hair colour and decoration. The ponies are very kitsch, anthropomorphised creatures with brightly coloured flowing manes and tails and large blue eyes adorned with eye shadow, eye liner and thick lashes. The eyes are especially prominent because no other features are painted on the rubber body of the pony. There are two small indentations for nostrils, two rounded ears on top, and a curling, smiling line of a mouth, but except for the eyes ponies are a solid colour of moulded rubber. The poses vary slightly; but the ponies always stand very solidly on four broad-based hooves caught in stride. My Little Ponies are available in a range of pastels, and in colours such as bright turquoise, hot pink and deep purple. The palette of colours is based on the exclusion of brown and black (the colours of real animals) and of primary red, blue or green (the colours of boys' clothes and boys' toys). Each pony has a different name and a different decoration painted on the haunch which stands as a totem for its name (butterflies, stars, flowers). All ponies are made in China; all come with a brush; all cost between four and ten dollars. They are sold at K Mart, Target, Toys 'R' Us, Costco; never at upscale toy stores or stores which specialise in educational goods.

My Little Ponies appeal to girls as collectors, cultivating an appreciation of small differences in colour and design from object to object. The toys themselves are low-tech. The principle for line extensions is based on cosmetic changes, on distinctions of appearance and name. As with the consumer goods targeted at adult women, the shopper is encouraged to buy many different products in the same category. Colour or other design features (style) are the only area of diversification among objects that are essentially similar.[19] As with all fashions, conformity and individuality are involved here: choosing one's favourite pony means exercising individual taste while acquiring a toy that will look like all other ponies. This

*As seen in dreams: My Little Pony packaging from Hasbro.*

principle applies to most toys available to girls: there are relatively few successful brands or models (Barbie, Cabbage Patch), but there are hundreds of different styles within each brand.

Ponies live in an idyllic outdoor world of flowers, birds, butterflies, bunnies, and fun. The name on the package is written across a rainbow. The packaging emphasises that Ponyland is a world of miracles and magic, of helpful, laughing, playing ponies. Every package includes a cheerful story about the pony that emphasises its visually dazzling qualities and its physical agility:

> 'Rise and Shine,' Sunspot called to the sleeping ponies, but they only yawned and snuggled deeper into their beds. 'I know how to wake them!' she thought, flying into the air. She flew up to her friend, Mr Sun, and whispered in his ear. Smiling happily, she sent sunbeams into the ponies' bedroom windows. The sunbeams filled each room and sprinkled glittering flecks of sunshine on the ponies. They awoke with smiling faces, and cheerfully tossed some of the bright flecks on Sunspot as she skipped into their bedrooms.[20]

Being ponies, rather than baby dolls to be taken care of, these toys allow for a certain kind of freedom: fantasies of galloping, flying, swimming. They are not, however, for riding. Play involves being a pony yourself, not owning one as a pet. The ponies exist outside the world of mommies, grocery stores, automobiles, schools, shopping malls. All the ponies, like the groups of children who play with them, are girls, with the rare exception of a baby brother. Boyfriends and the attraction of the opposite sex, which figure so prominently in other toys for girls, have no place here. Neither the human characters from the animated series nor the villains are available for purchase.

The success of My Little Pony spawned many imitations. Mattel worked vigorously to launch a competitor. Its 'Little Pretty' line of kittens and puppies bore a strong resemblance to the ponies. Little Pretties were sold in sets: for example, the Little Pretty Polished Paws Kitty set included Catra, Peekablue Kitty, Bow Kitty, Happy Feet Kitty and Dixie Kitty. Mattel, whose fortune was made with Barbie, tried to combine Barbie's glamour and interest in the opposite sex with the animal motif. (The kitties are female while the puppies are male.) One package reads: ' "I'm a Polished Paws Kitty and I love to look pretty," sang Catra, as she pounced on a leaf. Just then her puppy pal Dixie ran up: "Quick, we're going to have our pictures taken for the newspaper!" Catra quickly polished her paws her favorite shade of red, then purring proudly pussyfooted it to the photographer'.[21] The 'Little Pretty' line has met with only limited success. One reason was that parents and children were resisting the obsessions with clothing and boys that characterise Barbie and her many imitations. My Little Pony has proved to be singular in the longevity of its success as a girls' toy licence. I believe this was due to the relative innocence of the concept and the depth of little girls' identification with the utopian world of the ponies. Many middle-class parents are offended by the kitschiness of the ponies' design, but at least they aren't Barbie.

*My Little Pony* and *My Little Pony, The Movie* were never part of the Saturday morning network schedule – they were one-shot specials and limited syndication offerings – but these shows live on long past their production dates (1985–6), as rentals at the home video store.[22] *My Little Pony* is the kind of video that girls pick out from the shelves at the video rental store: recognising from the pink boxes, the flowers and animals and rainbows, that this is for them. Progressive parents often try to divert their daughters from choosing such sex-stereotyped entertainment. One of my local video stores (staffed almost entirely by college graduates in film studies) stopped carrying *Rainbow Brite* in 1990 because they received too many complaints from parents. 'The children loved it but the parents hated it!' the manager told me.

*My Little Pony*, by contrast, plays its childlike and female orientation totally straight. No attempt is made to appeal to a broader audience, and this, I will argue, is the reason for its success. Something was gained and lost when marketers began exploiting little girls as a separate market. Little girls found themselves in a ghettoised culture that no self-respecting boy would take an interest in; but for once girls were not required to cross over, to take on an ambiguous identification with a group of male characters. In the following sections, I offer a plot synopsis of three videos, focusing on their borrowing from women's popular culture genres, their range of character types, and their psychological themes. Doing this has taught me above all that children's cartoons have complicated narratives. It was surprisingly difficult to summarise these videos, given the many twists and turns of plot that occur within half an hour. There is an important lesson in this: adults tend to think children's videos are simple and closed to any but a single interpretation, because adults rarely watch children's videos in their entirety. By describing each video at length, I hope to demonstrate both their complexity and their openness to a variety of interpretations. As with most television, children watch these videos with mixed levels of attention, focusing on what they consider the good spots, often letting their attention waver – perhaps while they play with their miniature plastic replicas of the characters on the screen.

> *Mish Mash Melee*: Four ponies – Dizzy, Gusty, Windwhistler and Shady – are playing soccer together. Shady is frustrated because she always misses the ball. The ponies begin quarrelling about the rules, and Gusty inadvertently blows the ball away with her magic unicorn's horn. Windwhistler takes flight, chasing after the ball, and the other ponies follow. They find themselves in a forest. Windwhistler explains that this is the 'mysteficent forest', the land of the Delldroves, gnomelike caretakers of the forest. The Delldroves are mute, male creatures with monkey features. They work all day making rough lumps of rock into smooth stones and replenishing the forest by making acorns sprout tree shoots by hitting them with a hammer. 'They are an orderly and well-balanced

society and they do all this work without any glory or reward,' Windwhistler explains.

While walking through the forest, Shady accidentally bumps the lever on a trap door and the ponies find themselves whisked down a series of chutes to an underground factory where the Delldroves do their work. There, the ponies slide down a series of conveyor belts and themselves pass through the assembly line. The monkey-workers fail to notice the ponies and hammer at them as though they were making stones. Meeting up at last, the ponies are discussing the need to leave the forest when one pony falls into a barrel marked 'Balance' which spills out coloured raindrops with faces on them. The raindrops, called 'Frazzits', overwhelm the production of the acorns, and Shady explains that these protoplasms will upset the ecological balance. A change immediately occurs: the workers now become destructive in their work, breaking acorns and pulverising stones. Meanwhile the ponies begin acting out of character: Windwhistler, usually serious, becomes frivolous and playful; Shady, usually self-absorbed, finds she can work as part of a team. Dizzy becomes 'not so scattered' and takes charge. She even sounds scientific: 'Multicoloured protoplasmic organisms are ruining the ecology of this place . . . did I say that?' The ponies join in a musical number to celebrate the changes, with the refrain 'Gee, but it's fun to be somebody else!' Afterwards, Dizzy organises a system for getting the Frazzits back in the box: Gusty blows them, Dizzy encases them in bubbles, Shady bats them back in the barrel with her hoof. There is one final task they must do before balance will be restored: they succeed in turning the barrel upside down. The Delldroves gather to tell them, 'We can't thank you enough, you saved our dell.' Windwhistler gives credit where it's due: 'Dizzy took control and now everything is back to normal.' Dizzy, who has resorted to her 'scatterbrained' personality, cries: 'I did? How did I do that?' And the group has a good laugh as the show irises out.

This episode employs a number of narrative conventions from science fiction and fantastic literature which are frequently used in the plots of contemporary children's cartoons: the escape of a contaminating substance (the Frazzits); the existence of a parallel or lost world (the Delldroves); the placing of familiar characters in altered states induced by changes in body chemistry or sometimes by the substitution of a mechanical double (the ponies' altered personalities when the Frazzits are released). In *Mish Mash Melee*, the altered state device from science fiction provides the motivation for the cartoon's obligatory musical number. All of the girls' cartoons include musical numbers where the characters express their true feelings of the moment. In boys' cartoons, none of the characters burst into song unless it is motivated by the story or deliberately bracketed as an interlude done in music-video style.

The ecological themes in *Mish Mash Melee* are common to a variety of boys' and girls' cartoons produced in the 1980s: *Rainbow Brite*, *He-Man*, *Ghostbusters*, *Thundercats*, *The Care Bears*. (In 1990 the theme became the mainstay of Ted Turner's *Captain Planet* series.) Animators render pollution and toxic waste as colourful enemies, which allows considerable artistic freedom in their visualisation. The vaguely environmentalist themes that emerge in the cartoons are usually inoffensive to parents, pro-social and relatively non-violent. Pollution can be seen as a contemporary interpretation of the images of blight and infertility that have typically motivated the hero's quest in the romance.[23] Often the cartoons portray the terrible effects of pollution, temporarily transforming the cartoon's setting into a wasteland: Ponyland is frozen or stripped of colour;[24] Rainbowland is turned brown; a ruined, smoking Manhattan under a sort of post-nuclear holocaust sky appears repeatedly in *Ghostbusters*.

In girls' cartoons, the threat of toxicity and the turning of a homeland into a wasteland often motivates a group to act together as a team, replacing the traditional figure of the hero setting off on a quest. Thus a set of cute, tiny girls (or furry female creatures) prove to be capable of nothing short of saving the world. Redemption often takes the form of a clean-up, rather than a direct battle with a villain using weapons. In *Rainbow Brite, Strawberry Shortcake, The Care Bears, Fraggle Rock* and *My Little Pony* there is a vision of work behind the scenes which typically represents natural forces in the form of the industrial factory. The colour in Rainbowland, for example, comes from 'Star Sprinkles', which are produced by midget mascots called Sprites who work in an underground operation that is a cross between a factory and a bakery, with a furnace and a conveyor belt where the Sprites press out stars with cookie cutters. In *Mish Mash Melee*, we find a typical attribution of natural processes (weathering of stones, or sprouting of trees) to industrial techniques and the assembly line. Underlying the forest floor is a factory. In *Fraggle Rock*, a society of miniature workers, called Doozers, exist parallel to the Fraggles. Doozers do nothing but build.

These images serve both to relegate all natural processes to industrial ones and to suggest a perfect society of workers: the Delldroves work all day without glory or reward. While the workers are represented as very tiny and non-human, they essentially represent adulthood. The girls' programmes take cognisance of work behind the scenes, the work that adults do; and sometimes express an admiration for the discipline, order and hard work that is constantly going on. This workers-behind-the-scenes motif is exclusive to girls' cartoons. On boys' shows magic, bravery, weaponry and combat produce the results: no imagination is wasted on the boring, sacrificial, repetitive work that adults might do. (And the main characters are themselves often already adults, as in *Thundercats, Ghostbusters* and *He-Man*, or nearly so, as in *Teenage Mutant Ninja Turtles*.) In the magical settings of the girls' cartoons, a less exciting, more mundane picture of adult work and responsibility is never far out of sight.

*Baby It's Cold Outside*: One morning the ponies Galaxy, Truly and North Star awake to find snow outside. At first they play happily in the snow, building a snowpony together. But Galaxy becomes worried when she notices that all the trees are frozen and the birds and butterflies have disappeared. Truly rejects Galaxy's concerns and tells her she's just spoiling the fun. The next scene take place on the North Pole, where a little boy penguin, Prince Edgar, has found a little duck friend, Sunny, who needs to fly south for the winter. When he brings Sunny to his father King Charlatan for assistance, the father freezes the duck because he disapproves of his son's friendship. The king explains his plan to rule the world with his new machine, the Magnifier, which turns the king's own icy stare into a force powerful enough to freeze the whole world. Thus King Charlatan will do away with any weaklings (like the duck) who cannot withstand the cold. Prince Edgar protests, but his father asserts his complete authority as king of all, ruler of the world. Back at Ponyland, Galaxy flies up to the other ponies with a more urgent warning. As she speaks, the rivers freeze over before their eyes, trapping the seahorses Surf Rider and Sea Shimmer. Next, the ever-present rainbow freezes. Galaxy lectures the other ponies on the seriousness of the situation and sends Surprise to find Megan, the human heroine of the series, a blonde, blue-eyed girl about eight years old. When Surprise arrives at Megan's house, Megan presents her with some wing covers which she knitted herself.

Waiting for Megan and Surprise to return, Galaxy bursts into a song of determination and courage: 'We're not gonna freeze, no sir! We're not gonna end up frozen! We're gonna hang in there together, gonna rise above the weather . . . we may be on the spot, we may shiver quite a lot, but no matter what we're not gonna freeze.' When Megan returns, they agree to go north to find the culprit. At the North Pole, Megan and the ponies find themselves trapped in a maze, chased by a big white gorilla whose job it is to keep out intruders. One pony, who has the power to disappear, tricks the gorilla, while the others press on. But at the end of the maze they are captured by the palace guard and thrown in prison. In a typical scene, they apply various kinds of problem-solving (can they tunnel out? bend the bars?) before Galaxy melts the bars with her unicorn horn. In prison, they encounter Prince Edgar visiting the frozen Sunny. He explains the situation to them and they decide to escape together by pretending they are his prisoners so as to make it past the prison guard. Before reaching the throne room, they encounter numerous booby traps the king has set, but they finally arrive at the locked door. One of the ponies breaks down the door. King Charlatan turns on Edgar in his rage and freezes his own son with his icy stare. Megan sings her argument with the king, as she boldly points her finger at him: 'How can you be so cold . . .?' During her song, we see flashback scenes of King Charlatan as a good father: giving the infant Edgar a bottle, cradling him in his arms, playing and sledding with him. King Charlatan is moved to tears, and his tears melt the ice around his son. 'Only you could break your own cold spell,' Megan explains. The king is reformed, convinced of the evilness of his plan. The ponies blast the magnifier with a magic ray which unfreezes everyone. Megan and the ponies smile approvingly at the scene of paternal love, then walk off into the sunset.

Both boys' and girls' animated series of the 1980s routinely associate villainy with technology, thus borrowing a strain of technophobia from science-fiction novels. Male and female heroes use different means to wrest the technologically based power from the villains. In boys' cartoons evil uses of technology – typically, the desire to take over the world and subordinate all others – are pitted against good uses of technology by the heroes. The audience hopes that the good guys' guns, lasers, swords or ninja weapons – combined with cleverness – will be sufficient to put down the bad guys. In girls' cartoons, direct conflicts employing weapons or evil machines are avoided. In *Baby It's Cold Outside* Megan tries to talk King Charlatan out of his evilness, while his power is turned against himself. Megan and the ponies encounter mazes, traps and other physical barriers on their journey to confront the villain. Overcoming obstacles and extricating oneself from a trap provide suspense, rather than direct, hand-to-hand or weapon-to-weapon battles. Once the villain is encountered, the heroines must shame him into admitting error and showing remorse. In *My Little Pony* the villains resemble those of the classic quest-romance, as described by Northrop Frye: 'The antagonists of the quest are often sinister figures, giants, ogres, witches and magicians, that clearly have a parental origin.'[25] The results in the girls' cartoons are rehabilitation, reform and reintegration into a community, rather than, as in the boys' cartoons, zapping away the villain for ever, or locking it in a 'ghost trap' or 'containment chamber' as in *Ghostbusters*.

In *My Little Pony*, as in *The Care Bears* and *Rainbow Brite*, threat is founded on feeling. Typically, emotional coldness is the real evil: King Charlatan's icy stare propels the machine that could take over the world. Feelings rule the world. All the childlike female heroines, whether as teams or as individuals such as Megan and Rainbow Brite, possess the acumen of psychotherapists and the bravery of saints. They demonstrate that most courses of action can be changed through increased self-knowledge, through understanding a deed's consequences, through remembering someone you love. Emotional insight turns out to be the most powerful force in the world; and all the heroines possess it to a superior degree and in abundant quantity. The villains are usually male (even in the case of an evil queen, her henchmen are always male); the healers are female. Often the villains are incorrigible, infantile figures, like the *Rainbow Brite* villains Murky, a short, balding, middle-aged man, and his companion Lurky, a big brown blob of a creature; or the bald Professor Coldheart of *Care Bears*. All men are babies in this world order, and hostility and aggression can be cured by a combination of firmness and kindness.

Absent in *My Little Pony* is one of the central figures of girls' fiction: the rebellious, headstrong, egocentric pre-adolescent who eventually gets her comeuppance. Like Madeleine or Pollyanna, these girls end up, as do many adult women in melodramatic fiction, bedridden from illness or accident. A number of series designed for a mixed audience of boys and girls, of the kind stamped with the approval of the National Education Association and shown on PBS, feature such a female as a permanent character in a predominantly male cast: Miss Piggy of *The Muppets* and Baby Piggy of *Muppet Babies*, Red of *Fraggle Rock*, Whazzat of *Zoobilee Zoo*. These female characters enjoy more latitude in their behaviour than does a figure like Megan – they get to be tomboys, or to be unapologetically narcissistic or selfish, but in the end there is usually punishment and remorse, and an explicit moral lesson about the dangers of selfishness. In *My Little Pony*, there are only mature big sisters who already know how to act like wise, sympathetic mothers. They are ever-prepared to deal with the feelings of all, to ferret out sorrow or inadequacy or coldness. There is a kind of power in Megan's position, when she stands up to the penguin father and lectures him about his coldness. Though she does not break many rules of femininity, she is allowed the privilege of being always right. Unlike the more rebellious heroines who are eventually chastised for their selfishness and immaturity and lack of consideration, moral rectitude is always with the ponies and their friends. The girls are always on the side of the angels.

*The Princess in the Glass*: This 45-minute episode (planned as an hour-long special for television) begins with Megan helping the ponies set up the pony Olympics. Gusty, Galaxy and Pegasus are doing exercise drills, but Shady repeatedly fails. Shady wanders off in dejection: 'I can't play like Pegasus, I don't have any special powers like Gusty and Galaxy, and I can't even make it through a simple jumping drill like any self-respecting earth pony. Everyone thinks I'm useless and they're probably mad at me for messing things up.'

Meanwhile, a middle-aged princess-pig, Porcina, discovers that her magical cloak is wearing thin. Porcina has the power to turn all things into glass, which she likes to do because she can then admire her own image in everything around her. Porcina is dressed in a pink negligee, eats chocolates, and carries with her a pink pet with a long and phallic snout, something like a ferret. Her henchmen, the Raptorians, are a cross between dogs and birds who speak with urban, thug accents. Porcina has sent the Raptorians to find something to repair the cloak with. Flying around, the Raptorians spot the ponies playing and get the idea to use the ponies' hair for the replacement cloak. Porcina communicates with the Raptorians while they are away via her hand-mirror, which functions as a kind of walkie-talkie television. After Porcina orders them back to the castle, the Raptorians reveal in conversation among themselves that they hold the princess in contempt and want to take things over for themselves. Back at her palace, Porcina rummages through one of the rooms in her castle, a terribly messy room which looks like a garage. When the Raptorians return with news of the ponies, she bursts into song: 'Look at me, look at me, soon the whole entire world will look at me, I will make the world a looking-glass for everyone to see.' In the course of the number she undergoes a series of costume changes that link her with movie stars: Porcina with fruit on her head as Carmen Miranda and in a tuxedo as Marlene Dietrich. The Raptorians sing a mocking chorus to Porcina's song, adding snide lyrics about Porcina's appearance: 'Yes, make the world a looking-glass and you'll get a big surprise,' the head Raptorian sings with a nasty laugh.

Back at Ponyland, Shady is still dejected, talking it over with Lickety Split, Hearthrob and Gusty: 'What can I do that's of use to anyone?' she asks. One pony suggests practice, the other suggests having more fun, dressing up, but Shady wanders off again: 'You don't understand, I want to help in the rescue effort.'

At the evildoers' headquarters, the Raptorians display the ponies and their hair for Porcina's approval: 'Just what I needed to repair my cloak.' Then she gives her orders: 'First, hair must be absolutely squeaky clean: through the wash with them!' The ponies are tied down with ropes on a conveyor belt which takes them through an operation which resembles a car wash: first shower-heads, then dryer, then mechanical arms with towels, then curlers, powder, combing, brushing, curling and make-up. The ponies' appearance suggests that of prostitutes. They worry among themselves whether all the Raptorians want is their hair. The Raptorians cut their hair off; but when the angry ponies fix their gaze on them, it grows back immediately.

The Raptorians now reveal their plan: to get the cloak and turn Ponyland into glass so that they will have their own kingdom. They clamp the ponies to spinning wheels and sewing machines and order them to produce a cloak. The ponies sing a song of woe ('Our legs all ache/our backs may break/oh, how we wish we could leave'). On receiving the new cloak, Porcina is delighted. Preoccupied with her vanity ('Oh,' she exclaims, 'the cloak is so beautiful and I'm beautiful too'), she unthinkingly goes along with the Raptorians' request to turn Ponyland to glass by casting her spell through her mirror/TV. Finally the rescue team comes crashing in: Molly and Shady have been hanging back, but now Shady, who has been hoping she could do something special to save them ('If only I could help them all by myself'), hatches a plan. They will weave a substitute cloak, exchange it for the real one while Porcina is sleeping, and turn Ponyland back to normal. All the ponies, Megan and Molly sneak into Porcina's bedroom and the big confrontation takes place. The Raptorians order Porcina to turn the ponies into glass, but she immediately has a change of heart. Porcina explains: 'The ponies in my crystal orb didn't seem real but these are alive, I don't have the right.' Instead she turns the Raptorians to ice: 'Don't worry, they never felt it. They never felt anything, not about you or me . . . I guess I didn't see it.' Porcina is sent off with the Bushwoolies to be a groomer for them, and the ponies are happily returned to Ponyland. Megan praises Shady: 'Your bravery and good thinking came through when we needed it most.'

Shady's feelings of inadequacy form the backdrop for the formidable complications of plot in *The Princess in the Glass*, as they do in several other episodes and in *My Little Pony, The Movie*. Shady's often repetitive recitation of her own worthlessness provides the story's only breaks from the action. Many girls' cartoons focus on a character's wounded or resentful feelings, and often these feelings function as a catalyst in the plot by leaving a character so vulnerable and isolated that she is easily taken advantage of by the villain. Males such as Murky and Lurky in *Rainbow Brite* and the Raptorians in *My Little Pony* prey on the female feelings of inadequacy. One of the most common character flaws girls' cartoons' address is being too sensitive and self-critical. While there is always a cheery ending, characters often suffer from an underlying depression. But Shady is also ambitious, in a way: she wants to stand out from the crowd, to make a unique contribution, to gain some credit and recognition. Porcina has obviously gone too far in this direction: her narcissistic ambition has left her ridiculous and vulnerable.

Shady's voice is especially grating to adults: a high-pitched, singsong, nasal whine. Each of the ponies has one personality attribute that is primary: Shady's is feeling insecure and inadequate. She is unable to distinguish herself with a special talent; she is inept at sports; she inadvertently does the wrong thing; she causes trouble for her friends. If Shady represents a masochistic response to the problem of being a little girl, she at least represents an acknowledgment of that identity as problematic. The drama of the girls' cartoons regularly revolves around feelings of worthlessness: a narrative motivation unheard of – perhaps logically impossible – in the boys' cartoons.

Why is there this difference from boys' cartoons? Valerie Walkerdine has analysed the precarious position of girls in a world where the official word as handed down by liberal teachers is that gender is unimportant. To succeed in the classroom, girls must present themselves as active learners; but our culture symbolises activity as male, passivity as female. There may be an irreconcilable conflict between identifying with the female, and with the mother, and identifying with the part of the good student. Walkerdine argues that the failure to acknowledge the conflicts inherent in the role of the little girl, and these split identifications, can be especially harmful:

> Our education system in its most liberal form treats girls 'as if' they were boys. Equal opportunities and much work on sex-role stereotyping deny difference in a most punitive and harmful way. . . . A denial of the reality of difference means that the girl must bear the burden of her anxiety herself. It is literally not spoken. She is told that she can be successful and yet the painful recognition that is likely to result from the fear of loss of one or the other (her femininity, her success, or both) is a failure to be either, producing neurotic anxiety, depression or worse. . . . In a sense, then, rather than perpetuating the denial operating in the spurious circulation of needs, fulfilment and happiness, a recog-

nition of struggle, conflict, difficulty and pain might actually serve to aid such girls.[26]

Shady's feeling 'all wrong' seems to represent the very struggle Walkerdine suggests: Shady feels inadequate, and then she feels ashamed for feeling dejected. Male peers are not around to compete with; traditional femininity is validated. Megan's skills and achievements are those of the good mother. But the ponies, unlike the girls, are allowed to feel negative, sad, listless and insecure.

Most obviously, girls' cartoons present an unambiguous, segregated world of the feminine. Segregation by gender (within the audience, and among the characters), the display of traditional feminine behaviours and the use of kitsch aesthetic codes (pink and furry) in the girls' cartoons offended many television critics and child educators, whose position is usually implicitly informed by a liberal feminist political agenda. In *Feminist Politics and Human Nature*, Allison Jaggar has argued that rationality and individualism are the cornerstones of political rights in liberal political philosophy, so liberal feminism must assert the female capacity for both of these. Liberal feminists minimise gender differences. Liberal feminism looks forward to a future in which psychological differences between men and women, boys and girls will be much less pronounced, and education, once it is truly providing equal opportunities, will further enhance the female capacity for the development of reason. But female gender socialisation, as well as the work women are expected to do as adults, poses special problems for the liberal conception of individualism and rationality. As Jaggar explains:

> The instrumentalist strand within the liberal conception of rationality equates rational behavior with the efficient maximization of individual utility. To be rational in this sense it is necessary, although not sufficient, for an individual to be egoistic. . . . liberal theorists assume that all individuals tend toward egoism, even though they may be capable of a greater or lesser degree of limited altruism. While this model may provide a plausible approximation for the behavior of contemporary males, it is obvious immediately that it is much less appropriate to the behavior of women, who often find their own fulfillment in serving others.[27]

Megan and Molly encourage the ponies to voice their emotions, so that they can be cured of the negative ones. It is easy to see this aspect of the plot as simply parroting a therapeutic, self-help strategy made popular through television talk shows, talk radio, self-help groups and popular advice literature, as Stephen Kline has done. But rather than reinforcing the need for individual solutions to problems, *My Little Pony* emphasises the importance of the loyal community of females. 'I tried to be so helpful,' sings Shady. Molly assures her: 'Shady, it's not your fault.' The self-deprecating pony makes herself or others vulnerable to the more powerful forces of evil; but in the world of *My Little Pony* there is safety in numbers.

Shady's sulking may cause some ponies to be captured, but another group will come to their rescue. As Tania Modleski has said about the seemingly powerless heroines of the romance, 'victims endure'. In the end, the group rallies round to affirm the importance of each member. Like the members of a good family, Megan, Molly and the ponies learn to respect individual differences and to be vigilantly attentive to one another's feelings. The commitment to and sense of belonging in a group surpasses the individual's needs. This is the moral of the story.

*The Princess in the Glass* expresses a deep ambivalence towards those aspects of girls' socialisation that have to do with physical appearance. The most traumatic moment in the cartoon is when the ponies are tied down to have their hair washed and curled: a routine familiar to little girls in many different cultures. Porcina verbally directs this torturous exercise, but it is the sinister Raptorians who carry out the dirty work and seem to relish the ponies' distress. Hair care is such a traumatic and difficult aspect of gender socialisation that a host of consumer products have been developed and marketed which promise to make it a happier experience for parents and children: no-tears shampoo; headbands and neck rests to help keep soap out of eyes; cream rinses to take the pain out of combing wet hair. Feminists have seen hair grooming as the first lesson in submission for the sake of appearance. It is a long and troubled one, especially for African-American girls. The success of the My Little Pony toys may largely be due to the fact that they double as bath toys. Girls' play with ponies often involves doing to the ponies what mothers have done to them – washing hair, combing and brushing it, fixing it with ribbons and barrettes.[28]

Girls' animated series in the 1980s borrowed from popular genres for adult women. In *My Little Pony*, the ethos of the soap opera – that feelings are all-important – is combined with some conventions of the paperback romance, which, as Tania Modleski and Janice Radway have argued in their powerful work on this subject, are worthy of serious consideration by critics interested in the possibilities for producing popular feminist narratives. As in the soap opera, there is an emphasis on understanding the often mysterious codes of feelings. Unlike in the soap opera, the characters never appear in the domestic sphere. In *My Little Pony*, Megan is transported away from her real home to straighten out the world. Adventure comes with her departure from her home (when the ponies come to pick her up she is usually already out in the yard of her house). Megan's position is similar to that of the sympathetic heroines of soap opera: the mothers who worry over all their children's (read ponies') competing desires.[29] In the animated series there is a somewhat more affirmative order, a greater effectivity of female action than in soap opera. The axioms of popular psychology *work* here: revelations change evil-doers instantaneously and males can be quickly set right.

These cartoons dramatise the thrill of vulnerability found in the paperback romance, minus the romantic love. The ponies often find themselves wandering through a maze, a quest similar to the heroine's search through the mansion in the gothic romance. (Feminist critics have argued that the house represents the mother's body.[30]) The good characters in girls' cartoons resemble the heroine of the romance: modest, unassuming, average, flawed. In the end the heroine in the romance is loved for just who she is; so in the girls' cartoon the individuals in the group are accepted no matter what their feelings, no matter what mistakes they have made.

Tania Modleski has argued that a utopian strain exists in the traditional women's genres of popular culture – the soap opera, the gothic novel and the romance. A utopian element also exists in the girls' animated series. The animals live in a happy, playful world of love and friendship. When they are in danger, a coterie of friends always arrives to back them up; the word is more powerful than the sword. The viewer can shift between identifications with the humans Megan or Molly, or with the ponies themselves, and thereby acquire a long list of magical abilities, such as flying or disappearing. These are the pleasures to be gained by an identification with the universe of the girls' series.

The criticism of the toy-based shows as a practice made it harder to notice what was most unusual about many of them: that they were reaching out to the audience of little girls, and that this necessitated adapting the conventions of the cartoon in significant ways. Of course, not all the toy-based shows catered to the audience of girls in the same way; *The Smurfs*, for example, counted a lone female called Smurfette among its dozens of characters, and *The Smurfs* television series relied on standard male-adventure plots. *The Pound Puppies* used roughly equal numbers of male and female dogs, and mixed melodrama and detective fiction in its stories about locating dog owners or lost puppies. But marketing for girls brought about some interesting innovations in many of the animated television series: however crassly commercial the toy tie-in, shows like *My Little Pony* and *Rainbow Brite* created a utopian world in which females were dominant. It was hardly feminist, and it starred blonde, blue-eyed girls, but it offered much more than the literary and media fare in which girls are nearly always required to identify with boys and men.

In that respect, *My Little Pony* achieved something rarely accomplished in educational public television – the television fare most palatable to the intellectual middle class. Parents should understand, then, that for the little girl at the video or toy store to choose My Little Pony is to make a quite rational choice among the limited offerings of children's consumer culture. The choice is not made out of identification with an insipid and powerless femininity; but out of identification with the limited sources of power and fantasy that are available in the commercial culture of femininity.

NOTES

1. Elizabeth Segel, ' "As the Twig is Bent . . .": Gender and Childhood Reading', in Elizabeth A. Flynn and Patrocinio P. Schweickart (eds.), *Gender and Reading: Essays on Readers, Texts, and Contexts* (Baltimore and London: Johns Hopkins University Press, 1986), p. 171.
2. Increasing sales through segmentation is tricky; but with children's goods it works on a per family basis when brothers and sisters can no longer share the same clothes, books and toys.
3. Segel, ' "As the Twig is Bent . . ." ', p. 175.
4. Sybil Del Gaudio, 'Seduced and Reduced: Female Animal Characters in Some Warner's Cartoons', in Danny Peary and Gerald Peary (eds.), *The American Animated Cartoon* (New York: E. P. Dutton, 1980), p. 212.
5. My sources for this survey of female characters on children's television are George Woolery, *Children's Television: The First Thirty-Five years, 1946–1981* (Metuchen, NJ: Scarecrow, 1983), and Hal Erickson, *Syndicated Television: The First Forty Years, 1947–1987* (Jefferson, North Carolina: McFarland, 1989).
6. It is interesting to note that when Fred Rogers first appeared in 1955 on a show called *Children's Corner*, he worked behind the scenes as a puppeteer and a woman named Josie Carey hosted the show.
7. An exception to this is *Eureeka's Castle*, a programme for pre-schoolers on Nickelodeon, which was introduced in 1990 with the deliberate intention of winning the *Sesame Street* audience. The presence of a female lead offers both the possibility of some segmentation – getting the girls' and the mothers' attention – and lending an air of non-sexism to the show. Eureeka, however, remains more of a figurehead than a developed personality.

   As of the 1991 schedule, Nickelodeon seems to be orienting itself to girls in its daytime programming, with animated series like *The Little Bits* and *The Koalas* and the situation comedy *Clarissa Explains It All*. This mimicks the strategy of Lifetime, a cable network specialising in adult women viewers.
8. Miss Piggy has been read more positively by feminists Judith Williamson and Kathleen Rowe; I agree with these interpretations but do not find them pertinent to the experience of young girls.
9. The Care Bears were reintroduced in 1991 with a new, explicitly ecological bent to their characters: now they were interested in such things as kindness to animals and keeping the environment clean.
10. The girls' toys that were part of this phase outnumber the boys' toys, He-Man and the Masters of the Universe, the Transformers or the Thundercats. He-Man was merely a 'sword and sorcery' version of superheroes who were long familiar to the boys' toy and media market: Superman, Batman, Spiderman, etc. There was certainly nothing new about producing an animated series for boys whose licensed characters were 'tied in' with toy merchandising.
11. Tom Engelhardt, 'Children's Television: The Shortcake Strategy', in Todd Gitlin (ed.), *Watching Television* (New York: Pantheon, 1986), p. 84.
12. Ibid., p. 97.
13. See Robert C. Allen, *Speaking of Soap Operas* (Chapel Hill: University of North Carolina Press, 1985), and Ellen Seiter ' "To Teach and to Sell": Irna Phillips and her Sponsors, 1930–1954', *Journal of Film and Video*, vol. 41, 1989, pp. 150–63.
14. Engelhardt, 'The Shortcake Strategy', p. 97.
15. For a comprehensive discussion of the critical reception of Disney's work and the elaborate care that went into the drawing of the characters' movement, see Richard Schickel, *The Disney Version* (New York: Simon and Schuster, 1968). Ariel Dorfman attacks the content of Disney on ideological grounds in *Of*

*Elephants and Ducks: The Empire's Old Clothes* (New York: Pantheon, 1983), pp. 17–63; and *How to Read Donald Duck: Imperialist Ideology in the Disney Comic* (London: International General, 1975).

16. Stephen Kline, 'Limits to the Imagination: Marketing and Children's Culture', in Ian Angus and Sut Jhally (eds.), *Cultural Politics in Contemporary America* (New York: Routledge, 1989), pp. 299–316.
17. My informal survey ranges from the children of university faculty to the children of low-income, unemployed families served by a free daycare programme I worked at in 1988–9.
18. Sidney Ladensohn Stern and Ted Schoenhaus, *Toyland: the High-stakes Game of the Toy Industry* (Chicago: Contemporary Books, 1990), p. 117.
19. Roland Marchand has noted that introducing a choice of colours became a standard advertising technique in the 1920s. Marketers began to suggest changes in colour schemes for bathroom fixtures, towels, sheets, fountain pens and kitchen cabinets and appliances once the market had become saturated. Colours going in and out of fashion helps to drive the market for many consumer goods bought by adult women. Roland Marchand, *Advertising the American Dream: Making Way for Modernity 1920–1940* (Berkeley: University of California Press, 1985), pp. 120–7.
20. Hasbro, UK, 1988.
21. Mattel, 1989.
22. For an animated series to be considered for network screening, at least sixty-five episodes must be made.
23. 'Translated into ritual terms, the quest-romance is the victory of fertility over the waste land.' Northrop Frye, *Anatomy of Criticism* (Princeton, NJ: Princeton University Press, 1957), p. 193.
24. The frozen blight is reminiscent of the winter Demeter causes while she grieves over the separation from her daughter Persephone; in cartoons the blight appears but the mother is always already absent.
25. Frye, *Anatomy of Criticism*, p. 93.
26. Walkerdine, 'On the Regulation of Speaking and Silence: Subjectivity, Class and Gender in Contemporary Schooling', in Carolyn Steedman, Cathy Urwin and Valerie Walkerdine (eds.), *Language, Gender, and Childhood* (London: Routledge and Kegan Paul, 1985), pp. 224–5.
27. Allison M. Jaggar, *Feminist Politics and Human Nature* (Totowa, NJ: Rowan and Allanheld, 1983), p. 45.
28. In this respect it is very similar to a lot of somewhat older girls' play with Barbie dolls. Part of the success of the pony line may have been the way that it extended this possibility to younger girls, who may not have had the rather formidable hand-eye coordination required to style a Barbie doll's hair and to dress her. It also places the hair care issue at some remove from its meaning in heterosexual romance.
29. See Tania Modleski's description of the 'ideal mother' as the place of the viewer of soap opera in 'The Search for Tomorrow on Today's Soap Opera', *Film Quarterly*, vol. 33 no. 1, Fall 1979. Modleski discusses both romance and soap opera in *Loving with a Vengeance: Mass-Produced Fantasies for Women* (New York: Methuen, 1982).
30. See Janice Radway, *Reading the Romance: Women, Patriarchy and Popular Literature* (Chapel Hill: University of North Carolina Press, 1984).

# MORAL KOMBAT AND COMPUTER GAME GIRLS

HELEN CUNNINGHAM

Today, perhaps the most important question that needs to be addressed in relation to children's audio-visual media is not *what* children are watching on television but what they are *doing* with the TV set. Television is no longer (if it ever was) a passive medium.[1] The age of interactive television is upon us.

In the early 1980s, when the video game was just beginning to emerge as an adjunct of the television entertainment system, most of the research undertaken suggested that playing video games was a predominantly male leisure pursuit.[2] In the late 70s and early 80s, when this research was carried out, video game-playing was not a home-based activity. Arcades were the place where game-playing took place and these arcades were populated by adolescent males.[3] A decade later, in the early 1990s, the second wave of game-playing has occurred primarily through the purchase of dedicated games consoles which are plugged into the home television set. The main companies in the console industry are Sega and Nintendo. This domestication of computer games has increased access to them. Firstly, access has opened up for a lower age group who previously could not play video games in arcades,[4] and secondly, as the context of games-playing has changed, female participation in games culture has increased. Young girls can now be found huddled around 'Gameboy' handhelds in the playground, and girls as well as boys now talk of 'Sonic' (Sega's trademark) and 'Super Mario' (Nintendo).

There are over 9.4 million computer game consoles in use in the UK[5] and the vast majority of these are used by children aged between seven and fifteen. Computer games are the new children's medium of the 90s – and have sparked a moral panic within the UK. Schoolteachers and psychologists have all spoken up against prolonged childhood exposure to this new medium.[6] The aim of this chapter is to question the recent changes within the computer games industry, the moral panic surrounding computer games culture, and the extent of the gendered nature of computer game-playing.

## Methodology

My own interest in computer games and the panic surrounding them began through observations of my ten-year-old sister and her involvement in computer games culture. The pleasure she found both in playing the games and in the wider culture of reading the gaming magazines, watching computer game programmes on TV, and identifying herself as a games player (her 'Sonic' T-shirt became her favourite item of clothing), was not explained by either the media panic or academic research, both of which portrayed game-playing as boys' culture.[7] This chapter was written at the beginning of my research into computer games and children's cultures, and is consequently exploratory and speculative. This research is based on informal interviews with my sister Julie and a group of her 'best friends', all of whom I knew shared Julie's enthusiasm for and enjoyment of computer games. The interviews took place in Summer 1993. Around this time the media hysteria over the effects of computer games on children's development was at its peak and most of the girls were aware of the debates. I told the girls that I was interested in computer games and wanted to talk to them about what they thought about game-playing. My position within this informal interview situation was shaped by my position as Julie's older sister. Most of the girls had known me for as long as they have known Julie, and they were aware that I also often play computer games. Although my status as adult was apparent, since I am Julie's sister (rather than a parent or teacher) my questioning and listening were not seen as critical or authoritative. This research cannot be seen as representative of young girls' involvement with computer games in general, but as documenting the culture of a group of lower middle-class ten-year-old girls. The parents of some of these girls were also interviewed, to ascertain their views on their daughters' participation in computer game cultures.

## The Computer Game Industry

Leslie Haddon[8] provides a detailed history of the development of the computer games industry, but this history ends in 1991, which is the year when Sega and Nintendo began their big push for computer game console sales to children in Britain. Prior to 1990 these two Japanese firms were unheard of in British homes, but three years on 60 per cent of children own a computer games machine and 80 per cent are said to play computer games regularly.[9]

Sega and Nintendo are the brand leaders who dominate the market internationally. Nintendo is the largest of the two companies worldwide, but in the UK Sega holds the largest share of the market. The Japanese and American markets for computer games are fast approaching saturation. The battle for supremacy in the computer game market is now taking place in Europe, where profit margins are much higher because of the higher cost of game cartridges.[10] Once a console has been purchased the game cartridges are incompatible – the console manufacturers have a monopoly. In Britain alone the market for the software (cartridges and discs) is worth about £755 million and is still growing.[11] In 1989 the computer games market was worth £78 million, but by 1993 sales of games, consoles, magazines and accessories totalled £1.1 billion.[12]

The games industry and other areas of the entertainment industry are joining forces. Computer games are often more profitable than movies. One game, *Super Mario Bros. 3*, has sold 14 million copies and has generated more money than the movie *ET.*[13] Nintendo now makes greater profits than all of the American movie studios combined.[14] Sega and Nintendo have licensing deals with film companies in order to use animated characters – including Disney cartoon characters – and many computer games are based on successful films: *Robocop*, *The Terminator*, *Jurassic Park* and *Aladdin* are just some of the films which have transferred to the games console. This cross-media licensing has not all been one way. The film *Super Mario Brothers* was released in 1993 and both *Super Mario* and *Sonic the Hedgehog* have their own cartoons broadcast on Sunday morning children's TV in the UK. The advertising industry has also expressed an interest in computer games as a medium for product placement. In December 1993 the game *Snapperazzi* was launched, devised by the *Sun* newspaper and sponsored by the pizza delivery chain Domino's Pizza and the Leaf UK brand Fizzy Chewits. In the USA sponsored games have featured 'Spot', the character in 7 Up's advertising.[15] Sponsorship and product placement within computer game software will probably increase since in Britain there is as yet no regulation of such practices.

It is not only the entertainment industry that has been affected by the rise of the computer game. Over the past five years Nintendo has made bigger profits than many of the international computer giants.[16] The microprocessor within computer game consoles is similar to that used in many personal computers. When the chief executive officer of Apple computers was asked what computer company he feared most in the 90s, his reply – 'Nintendo' – was not altogether surprising.[17] These games consoles, at present used primarily for games-playing, are 8-bit and 16-bit computers, which with the addition of other pieces of hardware are capable of becoming more than just toys for playing games. Sega and Nintendo have had great success at getting children involved in computer technology, having put computers in the homes of 60 per cent of households with children. This entertainment-led technological revolution has been achieved not by cable TV or by any of the leading computer manufacturers, but by a blue hedgehog and a plumber in red dungarees.

Computer game culture was initially welcomed by many parents, any childhood contact with computers being seen as educational. If parents had worries over their children playing computer games, they were concerned about the cost of the cartridges more than about the content – *Sonic* and *Super Mario Brothers* appeared harmless.

As most children's first experience of computers is through computer games in the home, many of the parents I interviewed bought computer game consoles for their children believing that an active enthusiasm for computer games would be the first step towards computer literacy, and hoping that once the interest in game-playing waned the enthusiasm for computers and new technology would remain. Early familiarity with computers was seen as important for young children. This view was expressed particularly in relation to daughters. The parents I talked to were very aware of the need to encourage their daughters to be involved with new technologies. The occupations of these parents, many of whom worked in education, were perhaps a factor in shaping their views on the importance of children's access to technology. Many of them attempted to convince their children that a personal computer would be the most sensible and suitable piece of equipment to buy. These parents hoped that the computer would also be used for its 'real' purpose once the games had been mastered. However, when it came to purchasing the equipment, the power of Sega and Nintendo's advertising campaigns had convinced most children I spoke to that a 'SNES' or 'Megadrive' were the only credible consoles on which to play games.

Nintendo increasingly markets itself as a console which can be used for both entertainment and educational functions. 'Edutainment' is the word used in their promotional leaflets to parents. The 'Mario Edutainment Series' of software is promoted as relevant to the National Curriculum, and it also has other titles which are promoted as educational for pre-school children. The interactive and co-operative nature of computer game-playing provides the potential for computer games as a tool in children's early learning. This may be an optimistic view, however, because at present the main use these machines are being put to is games-playing, and none of these 'edutainment' games appears near the top of the game charts. The computer games industry is driven by commercial imperatives and the genres of games currently being produced are very profitable.

The industry is not likely to attempt to push consoles or software in any other direction until the market for entertainment games in the UK is saturated. Computer games have become part of 'youth culture' and the iconography of the games has been used in advertising, in 'Youth TV' programmes, and within club cultures. Computer games have been appropriated by young people and have been marketed to them as anarchic, rebellious and anti-establishment. Neither young people nor the games manufacturers want to lose their street credibility by being seen as too educational. Nintendo's 'edutainment' series reflects their marketing strategy, which appears very different from that of Sega. Nintendo, which is the market leader in the USA, has a wholesome family entertainment image. The version of *Mortal Kombat* available for Nintendo consoles did not contain the 'gore' codes to operate the notorious 'death moves'. As well as the 'edutainment' series Nintendo have produced a variety of leaflets for parents informing them of the educational benefits of Nintendo software.

Haddon documents the history of game-playing as being a young male preserve and sees no reason for this male dominance of gaming to change.[18]

*Relevant to the National Curriculum? Super Mario Brothers from Nintendo. Photo courtesy of D & O Communications.*

However, the move of computer games from 'street culture' in the arcades to 'bedroom culture'[19] in the home (which has been achieved through the dedicated games console) has transformed the experience of games-playing for young girls. This domestication of computer games has fed into girls' existing 'bedroom culture', and now both boys and girls spend hours in their bedrooms playing computer games with friends. As so often, when a new mass medium emerges it is accompanied by a moral panic.[20] The increasing popularity of computer games among young children has been accompanied by concern over the effects of this medium. These debates over the *effects* of computer games on young children have been very similar to past debates within television studies over the effects of television viewing.[21] The three main issues cited in the attacks on computer game-playing are firstly the addictive nature of game-playing, which is thought to hinder children in social interaction; secondly the violent content of the games; and thirdly the gender stereotyping within the games. I will discuss each of these in turn.

**Addiction to 'Kiddie Cocaine'**

Early fears about computer games concerned the ability of children who spent many hours alone playing computer games to interact socially with other children. Fears over the addictive nature of computer games were expressed. Reports of children who play computer games for up to six hours at a time, and the analogy of computer games to 'Kiddie Cocaine',[22] have contributed to these fears. The Professional Association of Teachers believes that computer games can discourage children from reading and writing and make them aggressive. Jackie Miller, deputy general secretary of the PAT, believes 'children's social and educational development is being affected by the games.'[23] Computer games are also accused of eroding traditional children's games, with fears of computers taking over children's lives.

These fears are not substantiated by my own research. The girls I interviewed claimed to play computer games for approximately one hour a day, and all talked of other hobbies and activities on which they spent far more time. Computer games were often regarded as being the 'last resort' when there was nothing else to do.

> SARAH: Games are good to play when you're bored.
> ALISON: It's good to play [computer games] when it's raining or late [at night] and you can't go out.

Julie pointed out that the amount of time spent playing computer games varied depending on whether a new game had recently been purchased:

> JULIE: I hardly play computer games at all now because I can do all my games and so it's boring. I only play about once a week now until I can afford a new game.
> EMMA: When I get a new game I play it loads.

This fascination with a newly acquired toy is not unique to computer games. Children can also be 'addicted' to other leisure pursuits.

> JULIE: Sometimes when I am reading I don't want to put it down and I just sit up and read for hours when my mum thinks I have turned the light out.

Fears over children's addiction to reading are not usually expressed. Perhaps fears over this addiction to a new technology have been voiced by an older generation who cannot understand the appeal of the games, preferring children to play traditional games. This generation gap, and parental ignorance of games, is often part of their appeal. Fears of this new technology are due to the hitherto unknown interactive nature of computer games; talk of virtual reality and cyberspace is often beyond the everyday knowledge of parents.

Computer games have been criticised for causing anti-social behaviour and for causing children to become isolated and unhealthy through spending many hours in a darkened room staring at the bright, fast-moving images on the TV screen. This removal of children from the streets by a modern-day Pied Piper in the form of a hedgehog or a plumber has come at a time when parental fears of letting children play in the streets have never been higher. This retreat into the bedroom has more to do with fear of strangers and fast cars than of any addiction to 'Sonic' or 'Super Mario'. The move to 'bedroom culture' was welcomed by many parents who were relieved that their children had taken up home-based activities rather than 'hanging around' in the streets.

The criticism that playing computer games leads to social isolation is a far cry from the fears expressed over video games in the early 1980s when video games were blamed for delinquency as arcades became the collective point for youths to hang around.[24] Ironically, now that computer games have increasingly moved into the individual player's bedroom, the games are seen as causing isolation. Yet among the children with whom I have carried out this research the majority played computer games with friends or family members. They all expressed the view that game-playing was more fun when it was a social activity. Even when children play games alone, knowledge of computer games leads to social interaction in the playground as children talk about the latest games and exchange tips and 'cheats'. Many children also write reviews of games for school magazines. Computer game-playing is a shared experience. The game player who has progressed furthest through the games' 'levels' and 'worlds' shares her tactics. The girls I interviewed talked about how they phoned each other when they came to a level they could not complete and pooled their knowledge. Computer games are a site of shared knowledge rather than of individual competition. This feature of games-playing could potentially be of great benefit in 'educational' games.

### Violence and Aggression in Game Play

The second main focus of the criticism of computer games has concerned the content of the games being played. When the narratives of the games are analysed they can be seen to fall into six main genres.[25] The two genres most popular with the children I interviewed were 'Platformers' and 'Beat 'em ups'. Platform games such as *Sonic* and *Super Mario* involve leaping from platform to platform, avoiding obstacles, moving on through the levels and progressing through the different stages of the game. Beat 'em ups are the games which have caused concern over their violent content. These games involve fights between animated characters. In many ways this violence can be compared to violence within children's cartoons where a character is hit over the head or falls off a cliff but walks away unscathed.

Controversy has occurred in part because of the intensity of the game play, which is said to spill over into children's everyday lives. There are worries that children are becoming more violent and aggressive after prolonged exposure to these games. As a computer game-player myself and also through my observations of Julie and her friends' game play, I have no doubt that playing computer games does involve feelings of intense frustration and anger which often expresses itself in aggressive 'yells' at the screen. It is not only the 'Beat 'em up' games which produce this aggression; platform games are just as frustrating when the character loses all their 'lives' and 'dies' just before the end of the level is reached. Computer gaming relies upon intense concentration on the moving images on the screen and demands great hand-to-eye co-ordination. When the player loses and the words 'Game over' appear on the screen, there is annoyance and frustration at being beaten by the computer and at having made an error. This anger and aggression could perhaps be compared to the aggression felt when playing football and you take your eye off the ball and enable the opposition to score. Yet the aggression felt in computer game play is vented on the screen and does not necessarily turn players into more aggressive and violent children. The annoyance experienced when defeated at a computer game is what makes gaming 'addictive': the player is determined not to make the same mistake again and to have 'one last go' in the hope of doing better next time.

Indeed the aggression generated in game-playing and focused onto the machine could be seen as *relieving* stress, tension and pent-up aggression. My own computer game-playing is my method of switching off from the day's pressures by focusing on 'Super Mario' and how to get past the boss character at the end of the level.[26] I am not alone in using computer games in this way. While I was researching the gendered image of computer games many female colleagues and friends have 'confessed' their enjoyment of game-playing as a method of switching off and so managing stress.

Some of the concern over the violence of computer games has been about children who are unable to tell the difference between fiction and reality and who act out the violent moves of the games in fights in the playground. But children have always played fighting games. I have childhood memories of Saturday afternoons spent watching wrestling on television and copying the moves of 'Giant Haystacks' and 'Big Daddy', trying in vain to overpower my brothers. This concern over the violent nature of popular culture is not new,[27] but Haddon suggests that it is the combination of violence and the new and as yet unknown powers of the interactive technology of computer games that is the cause of contemporary concerns. Haddon summarises the view put forward by many: '. . . concerns about the "violent" narratives of games, referred back to the underlying technology of the media . . . the experience of violence through mediating technology would de-sensitise users to aggression.'[28] Psychologists have put forward similar concerns. Professor Cary Cooper has commented: 'The problem with video games is that they involve children more than television or films and this means there are more implications for their social behaviour. Playing these games can lead to anti-social behaviour, make children aggressive and affect their emotional stability.'[29]

A theme behind this moral panic is ideological: law and order are seen to be weaker now than ever before, as more and more people report that they live in fear of violence. TV was blamed for this rising tide of violence, and now video and computer games are seen as inciting our children to violence. Each new form of popular cultural entertainment is seen as being more harmful than the previous one.

The manufacturers play down the violent nature of the games, claiming that violence in games reflects violence in society. Simon Morris, Sega UK's marketing director, points out: 'Violence is a problem that is part of our society and we are not to blame for that. Our games are produced as a result of consumer demand and we are just responding to what people want to buy.'[30] The girls I interviewed were well aware of this media concern that computer games cause violence and were very keen to express their rejection of this view.

> ELIZABETH: People were violent before computer games were invented.

The girls were aware of the media's coverage of computer game violence as being a problem which centred on boys rather than girls. Even so the computer games were not seen as the cause of boys' violence.

> EMMA: It's not playing games that makes boys violent, boys are already violent.
> JULIE: Boys are born violent.
> SARAH: Yeah, boys are just boys.

Although the girls did regard boys as being more violent than girls, they did not see this as an effect of the 'violent' games. The girls were quick to claim the 'Beat 'em up' genre as part of *their* game culture too.

**Gender and Computer Game Culture – Game Boys and Girls?**

The main focus of the media panic over the popularity of computer games among children has been the feared addictive nature of game-playing and the violent narratives of the games. Within this discussion of computer game culture the computer games industry, journalists and also many academics have portrayed game-playing as a predominantly male preserve. My research suggests that this is no longer true and that the gendered nature of game-playing is changing. A large number of girls appear to enjoy playing computer games. Female participation in games culture has significantly increased since computer game-play moved out of the arcades and into the home. This increase in girls' participation with computer games is encouraging. Most children's first experience of computers is through computer games, and it is vital that girls are included in these arenas where familiarity with new technology is established.

Angela McRobbie has posed the question of why girls are invisible in many accounts of youth cultures. She suggests that female invisibility is due in part to the media's concentration on violent aspects of youth culture.[31] This can be seen to be true within games culture. The girls I spoke to all mentioned platform games as being their current favourite game, rather than the more violent genre of 'Beat 'em ups'. Media concern has concentrated on 'Beat 'em ups' and the aggressive nature of *boys'* play rather than that of girls. However, the girls did indicate that they also liked to play the more violent games.

SARAH: I like violent games . . . especially the one where you kill and blood comes out.

The 'Beat 'em up' game *Mortal Kombat* to which I presumed Sarah was referring had only just been released amid a barrage of media publicity and all the girls were keen to play it. This popularity of 'gore' genres spread over into other media as every girl identified horror as her favourite type of book. The *Point Horror* series was mentioned by all as their current favourite reading.

Gender stereotyping within computer games is an issue that has been raised by many critics.[32] When human female characters are present they are often represented as the 'quest' to be saved by the male hero. In *Super Mario Brothers* the aim is to defeat 'Bowser' and free 'Princess Toadstool'. This gender stereotyping has to be acknowledged as a problem within the design of the games, even though it should be stressed that these games are still very popular among female games players. In the 'Beat 'em up' genre female characters are increasingly appearing and are not always weaker than their male rivals.[33] Patricia Marks Greenfield acknowledges the importance of involving girls in computer game-play as an 'entry point into the world of computers', and she suggests that 'there is an urgent need for widely available video games that make a firm contact with the fantasy life of the typical girl as with that of the typical boy.'[34] The vast majority of games designers are male and perhaps game design reflects this. Nintendo have attempted to engage with 'the fantasy life of young girls' and have marketed a Barbie game. This is a platform game in which Barbie travels through Mall World and Soda Shop World in her search for 'magical fantasy accessories' and ball gowns. This game was not well received by my young sister and her friends:

JULIE: I'd never buy that Barbie game, it's stupid.
SARAH: No way . . . I'd rather play violent games any day.

But Julie has never played with Barbie dolls and is probably too old to start doing so. Hopefully, as more female games designers enter the industry, a wider range of genres will develop and more female characters will be available within the existing genres. The most popular games for Julie and her friends were *Sonic, Sonic 2, Super Mario Brothers, Super Mario Brothers 3, Mickey Mouse in Castle of Illusion, Streets of Rage* and *Street Fighter 2.*[35] Although these games could all be described as action and adventure (and in some cases they are violent 'Beat em up' games), the playing of them should not be seen as gendered.

Although platform games appear to be the favourite choice among young children, both male and female, Julie and her friends enjoyed 'Beat 'em ups' and expressed pleasure in the violence of these games, enjoying being able to fight and win when playing against brothers or male peers. In most areas of society this violent and aggressive side of a girl/woman's nature has to be repressed in conformity to socially expected norms of what is acceptable 'feminine' behaviour. Playing violent games gives female players the chance to express this aggression in a safe context.

When playing these games the girls often chose to operate the male characters because they had 'better moves'. This operation of male characters by female players, and female characters by male players, could be seen as 'transgender identification',[36] but I do not believe that 'identification' adequately describes players' relationships with the characters on the screen. Computer game players choose characters to operate on the basis of the moves they can make or the special skills and functions they have.[37] Future research on computer games should perhaps concentrate on the experience of playing these games and how 'pleasures' are created.

Sega and Nintendo's success at getting consoles into children's homes has changed the nature of female participation in games culture. Haddon outlines how girls' experience of computer games differs from that of boys, documenting how 'girls would rely on brothers to inform them about the latest game' and how 'few girls played games in the various public sites'.[38] The explosion in computer game sales, not only to children but also to young adults, has increased access to computer games information. A number of children's television programmes have computer game review spots, and programmes such as *Bad Influence* on ITV and *Games Master* on Channel 4 are avidly watched by young children. Over fifty computer game magazines are currently available, many exclusively aimed at children, which provide reviews and ratings for new games and new consoles.

The public spaces in which games are available to be 'tested out' by young consumers have multiplied. These public spaces are quite often within shopping centres (department stores, electrical shops, record shops and also specialist computer game shops) and as such they are much more accessible to appropriation by young girls than arcades have been. Girls' knowledge of what new games are available is now potentially much greater. Reliance on brothers for information has decreased as other public sources of computer games information have evolved.

**Some Conclusions**

Computer games as a medium have a great potential for involving girls in new technology. The moving of computer games play from the arcades into bedrooms and shopping centres has significantly changed the experience of game-playing. This changing context has to be recognised in any account of computer game cultures. In expressing my thoughts on these issues I have generated more questions than I have answered. Computer games are a relatively new medium and it is difficult to predict how their popularity with my sister and her friends will be maintained as they grow older and develop new interests. In the absence of a larger study of patterns of computer game use among girls it is very difficult to assess how typical my sister and her friends are. A lot more research needs to be carried out on the appeal of games to females of all ages. The experience of playing games has been transformed since the days of *PacMan* and *Ms PacMan*. Gillian Skirrow's claim that 'the pleasure of computer games is gender specific . . . women do not play them'[39] is no longer valid.

Media interest in computer game-playing has ensured that game cultures are public cultures despite the domestication of the console. As games playing has become an activity of public concern and interest, the continuing portrayal of computer games as an activity only of boys is very worrying. As in so many accounts of previous youth cultures, female participants have been rendered invisible.

NOTES

1. For an overview of the debates over 'passive' and 'active' audiences, see Dennis McQuail, *Mass Communication Theory: An Introduction* (London: Sage, 1987).
2. For accounts of video games which put forward this view, see Gillian Skirrow, 'Hellivision: an Analysis of Video Games', in Colin McCabe (ed.), *High Theory/Low Culture: Analysing Popular Television and Film* (Manchester: Manchester University Press, 1986), and Leslie Haddon, 'Electronic and Computer Games: The History of an Interactive Medium', *Screen*, vol. 29 no 2, 1988.
3. The most extensive research on the gendered nature of arcade game-playing is in S. Kaplan, 'The Image of Amusement Arcades and the Difference in Male and Female Video Game Playing', *Journal of Popular Culture*, vol. 17 no. 1, 1983, pp. 93–8.
4. The minimum age to play legally in arcades in the UK is 16.
5. *Edge*, March 1994 (Future Publishing).
6. The Professional Association of Teachers has produced an information sheet outlining the potentially harmful effects of computer games: see 'Young People in the Firing Line', *Guardian Education*, 13 April 1993. For psychologist Dr Mark Griffiths' comments, see 'One in Five Children Addicted to Computer Games', *Guardian*, 15 December 1993. For Professor Cary Cooper's views, see 'Children of an Electronic God', *Guardian*, 27 April 1993.
7. Both Gillian Skirrow in 'Hellivision' and Leslie Haddon in 'Electronic and Computer Games' document the appeal of computer games for young boys.
8. Leslie Haddon, 'Interactive Games', in Philip Hayward and Tana Wollen (eds.), *Future Visions: New Technologies of the Screen* (London: BFI, 1993).
9. Catherine Bennett, 'Game Boys and Girls', *Guardian*, 2 December 1993.
10. The Monopolies and Mergers Commission in the UK is currently investigating the activities of Sega and Nintendo.
11. Sheila Hayman, 'Control Freaks: How to Play God in Simcity', *Arena*, Winter 1993–4.
12. Nick Cohen, 'This ain't no game', *GO*, October 1993.
13. Ibid.
14. David Sheff, 'Game Wars', *Esquire*, October 1993.
15. Meg Carter, 'Selling through Computer Games isn't Child's Play', *Independent on Sunday*, 5 December 1993
16. Nintendo made bigger profits last year than Sony, Microsoft and Apple Computers: see Sheff, 'Game Wars'.
17. Ibid.
18. Haddon, 'Interactive Games', p. 144.
19. For a discussion of young girls' bedroom cultures, see Angela McRobbie, *Feminism and Youth Culture* (London: Macmillan, 1991).

20. For a fuller discussion of this, see Kirsten Drotner, 'Modernity and Media panics', in Michael Skovmand and Kim Christian Schroder (eds.), *Media Cultures: Reappraising Transnational Media* (London: Routledge, 1993), pp. 42–62.
21. See David Buckingham, *Children and Television: an Overview of Research* (London: British Film Institute, mimeo, 1987).
22. Catherine Bennett, in 'Game Boys and Girls', suggested that 'after crack-cocaine they are one of the most perfect forms of capitalism ever devised.'
23. 'Video Games: Young People in the Firing Line', *Guardian*, 13 April 1993.
24. See Desmond Ellis, 'Video Arcades, Youth and Trouble', *Youth and Society*, vol. 16 no. 1, 1984.
25. These genres are: 1. Platformers: as the screen scrolls forward the characters have to leap from platform to platform (*Super Mario Brothers*, *Sonic the Hedgehog*); 2. Shoot 'em ups: hi-tech military games, the object of which is to defeat your opponent, often using military hardware; 3. Beat 'em ups: these involve fighting using hand-to-hand combat (*Streets of Rage*, *Streetfighter 2*); 4. Sports: these include football, golf and Formula 1 racing simulations; 5. RPG/Strategy: these are role-playing and strategy games (*Sim City*, *Zelda 3*); 6. Puzzlers: these include computer game versions of board games and other puzzle games devised for the computer (*Tetris*, *Lemmings*).
26. A common feature of 'platform' games, where a boss character has to be defeated in order to pass through to the next level of the game.
27. See Geoffrey Pearson, 'Falling Standards: a Short Sharp History of Moral Decline', in Martin Barker (ed.), *The Video Nasties* (London: Pluto, 1984).
28. Haddon, 'Interactive Games'.
29. See *Guardian*, 13 April 1993 and 27 April 1993.
30. 'Video Games: Young People in the Firing Line'.
31. McRobbie, *Feminism and Youth Culture*.
32. See Eugene F. Provenzo Jr., *Video Kids: Making Sense of Nintendo* (Cambridge, MA: Harvard University Press, 1991), and Marsha Kinder, 'Playing with Power on Saturday Morning Television and on Home Video Games', *Quarterly Review of Film and Video*, vol. 14, 1992, pp. 29–59.
33. 'Blaze' in *Streets of Rage*, 'Chun Li' in *Streetfighter 2* and 'Sonya Blade' in *Mortal Kombat* are all formidable females who are often chosen for their special moves.
34. Patricia Marks Greenfield, *Mind and Media: the Effects of Television, Video Games and Computers* (London: Fontana, 1984).
35. *Sonic* is a platform game featuring Sonic, a blue hedgehog whose aim is to free the Woodland Creatures who have been captured by Dr Robotnik. *Sonic 2* is similar, but Sonic is now accompanied by his friend Tails the fox. In *Mickey Mouse in Castle of Illusion*, Mickey has to rescue Minnie from the witch Mizrabel. *Super Mario Brothers* and *Super Mario Brothers 3* feature Super Mario and his brother Luigi in their adventures through the Mushroom Kingdom in their search for Princess Toadstool, who has been captured by Bowser. *Streets of Rage 2* is an urban 'Beat 'em up' in which various characters attempt to rescue their buddies who have been captured by an evil gangster. *Street Fighter 2* is another urban 'Beat 'em up'.
36. Marsha Kinder writes of her son's transgender identification when he plays Princess Toadstool in *Super Mario Brothers 2*.
37. Princess Toadstool can float for short periods of time.
38. Haddon, 'Interactive Games', p. 142.
39. Skirrow, 'Hellivision', p. 115.

# VERY NEARLY IN FRONT OF THE CHILDREN

## *The Story of 'Alternity'*

MARTIN BARKER

> 'It's new, it's now and it's *not normal!*' (cover slogan on the dummy of the new comic).
>
> My marketing plan makes play of the fact that in 1993 the UK economy is going to be a dangerous place. And here I am, proposing this venture. If it folded, it would wipe out more than half our profits.
>
> John Davidge, Managing Director, Fleetway Editions[1]

This is the story of a comic that nearly was but now might never be. A comic that was more than two years in the planning, and underwent more stringent market testing than any other I have ever heard of, went through three proposed titles (*Odyssey*, *Earthside 8*, and *Alternity*), but has not appeared. It is only rarely that we get to study failures; yet there are some things that can only be learnt through them. By happy accident, in this case I was able to observe the processes that were to lead nowhere.[2]

In late 1990 Fleetway Editions, one of the big two comics publishers in Britain, became worried about the decline of two of their titles: *Eagle* and *2000AD*. *Eagle* was first launched in 1950, the brainchild of Rev. Marcus Morris, who saw it as his implement simultaneously for opposing the 'harmful influence' of imported American comics and for making a certain kind of muscular Christianity palatable. From then until the late 1960s, the comic – even in decline – supplied a publishing role model for most mainstream boys' comic publishing. In 1968 Fleetway (then IPC) bought out Odhams Press and took over the *Eagle*, by now in terminal decline. In 1969, it died. But the company (or its Managing Director, John Sanders) felt strongly that in one character it had the nearest that British boys' comics had produced to Superman and Batman: Dan Dare, pilot of the future. Through the 1970s and early 1980s there were repeated attempts to bring the character and the title back to life. None really succeeded, but no one was sure why. In 1982 the new *Eagle* was launched, and it staggered on through the decade, partly by relaunches as it merged with (took over) titles such as *Battle-Action* and *Mask*. But by 1990 it was clear that this strategy (despite expensive TV advertising) was not building a secure reader-base.

*2000AD* had been born in 1977. A science-fiction comic, it soon became a flagship publication. While sales stabilised at around 100,000, the comic achieved a loyal fan following, a wide recognition for quality, and a new star in the firmament of comic heroes, Judge Dredd. Early on, the publishers realised that they had three different audiences: a large following of young boys, mainly buying at newsstands, who loved it for its violent adventure; a growing but still small number of American comic fans; and a smaller but loyal following of older comic fans, a good number of whom bought it through the developing network of comic shops. For the first ten years of its life *2000AD* managed to satisfy all groups. But in the late 1980s, under the editorial direction of Richard Burton, the comic began to change course. Burton identified a shift in his readers – away from the sci-fi, rock music and two-fingers rebelliousness of the older generation and towards computers (especially games), an interest in role-playing, and style cultures. The three readerships started to pull apart. Although readership figures are notoriously hard to get,[3] the comic was certainly slipping and, most worryingly, was failing to recruit new, younger (10–14) readers.

Faced with these problems, Fleetway took an unprecedented decision to try to find out why. It is important to signal just how big a step this was. Up to this time, it had been a matter almost of pride in the company that they didn't need research. Individual comics would poll their readers from time to time on the relative popularity of stories. But asking your existing readership tells you little about the many you are missing. Until recently, comic publishing was regarded as a fringe activity by large conglomerate publishers. High returns were not expected, safety was the prime rule; and on most occasions decisions on launches, mergers, closures, appointments and the like were made on the basis of in-house 'commonsense' knowledge – a body of understanding that comes from having been 'in the trade' for a long time.

So why does a publisher bring out a new comic at all? This is not a straightforward question: the reasons are complex and shifting. First, there is the balance and range of a company's products. Cultural production is by nature risky,[4] and a successful company has an imperative to spread the risk. If one comic goes through a bad time, others can bear the brunt for a time while remedial action is taken. Then there is 'market weight'. In order to have reasonable pull with distributors and retailers, a company is best placed if it is supplying a range of publications. Single-product companies have often suffered, except when they are at the height of a fashion (*Private Eye* suffered greatly from eccentricities of shelving in newsagents, for example). Thirdly, all companies exist within a structured market, in which they are rubbing shoulders with competitors who include major and minor players, specialists and generalists, each with a market image for certain *kinds* of product. This is no less true of cultural producers than of, say, biscuit manufacturers, and it affects judgments about perceived 'gaps in a market'. If a company does not move to fill a gap, what might be the response of competitors?

With comics, other more local factors come into play. British comic production has for most of its life been age-bracketed. This meant that a publisher hoped to hand on readers after, say, four years to its next age-group of publications. It was therefore standard for each group to advertise its 'neighbours'. For many years, also, D. C. Thomson and IPC competed with largely equivalent publications. If one was known to be launching a new publication, the other almost certainly had to respond.[5] A factor of real importance in this case was precisely the changes in these rules: D. C. Thomson was no longer a significant competitor, the marketing strategies of the two having moved apart. On the other hand, Fleetway was not directly challenging Marvel and D. C. Thomson, for whom there are quite other central imperatives.[6]

The reason for emphasising this point is that, for Fleetway, all the rules and expectations governing launches were changing, and changing fast. Market position, the nature of competitors, the nature of the audience, internal publishing traditions, age-bracketing, along with criteria for safe risk-spreading – all were changing. This is surely why the company spent so long agonising over this new launch – especially as the ownership of the company itself changed twice in such a short time. First (from 1987) as part of the Maxwell Group, then (from October 1991) as part of the Danish publishing giant Egmont, the company introduced new criteria, structures and procedures.[7]

### The Research: Phase One

The first phase of research was undertaken in early 1991 by Young Direction, a branch of Connexions, a London research bureau.[8] Using a number of groups of boys aged 9–13, the researchers explored their general leisure interests, and how comic-reading fit within that. Their broad conclusion was deadly to *Eagle*'s chances:

> The target audience of boys aged 8–13 is markedly different from previous generations of comic-readers. While they are still involved in traditional boys' activities such as clubs, organisations and sports, they are also strongly influenced by relatively new media such as the VCR and the satellite movie channels. These allow young people to access adult emotions and behaviour at a much younger age than was the case, say, 10 years ago. Their preferences for movies such as *Robocop* and *Lethal Weapon* reflect a taste for the anti-hero rather than the traditional goodies versus baddies scenario of children's films. In essence boys of 8–13 are growing older at a younger age.
>
> The change in young boys has impacted upon their expectations of action/adventure comics. The requirements of artwork, narrative and story content are that they mirror their preferred film values, providing similar levels of involvement.

Readers could best be understood within a threefold typology: aficionados (those who read – especially American – comics widely, collect them and are knowledgeable about them, and for whom there is a strong linkage between comic-reading and video and other preferences); appreciative readers (who buy other comics only occasionally, have a little knowledge of their forms and varieties, lead busier social lives, and count comics as just one filler of their leisure time); and uncommitted readers (occasional and hardly knowledgeable readers of comics, much more controlled by parents in all their leisure choices and more likely to be involved in traditional children's activities).[9]

On the basis of their findings, Young Direction recommended that any new comic should have the following: high production values – it must look and feel as good as videos; stories incorporating strands of violence and horror ('reality with a twist') but with caution about its graphic presentation; strongly identifiable characters; and an overall balance between action and humour. One comment is worth reflecting on, not least for its curious neutrality:

> The central character of a film or comic was often felt to be far more important than the simple blood and guts content. The 'anti-hero' of a *Robocop* or an Arnold Schwarzenegger film was by far the most favoured role. Much of the motivations of such characters was seen as centring on revenge or punishment without moral constraints. It was interesting to note that such feelings often impacted upon these boys' wider social attitudes. There was much talk of meting out punishment to perceived enemies; either individuals such as Saddam Hussein or societal elements such as muggers and drug-dealers.

The implications of this ought really, if taken seriously, to have led the researchers to a more subtle explanatory model than just 'earlier growing up'. Unfortunately, they could not escape a residual 'control-culture' model within which parental control of children's culture is thought of as the norm.

Finally, the researchers note that comic-reading generally has a definable place in their lexicon of pleasures. Except for aficionados, comics are largely seen as something with which odd moments of time can be filled, as an adjunct to other activities and pleasures.

With these findings to hand, the company began some serious in-house planning. A Publisher was appointed – Chris Power. This was a new kind of post, introduced by John Davidge when he joined the company in 1989. It devolves overall charge of the project on to one individual, usually with a financial planning background. Power had begun on the advertising side of papers like *NME*, then had progressed up through various levels to Senior Sales Executive. He had worked for IPC, then Maxwell, for fourteen years before taking up this post. His view of his qualities for the job is interesting, confirming my argument about the changes in the industry's imperatives: 'I tend to think it is an advantage to have come from outside, because my background is in magazine publishing, and for a long time comic publishing was like a cottage industry. You could actually get away with that twenty to thirty years ago, but now you only have to look at today's comics and they are far more magazine-like. Comics publishing has had to drag itself into the 1990s, and operate in the same business-like way that a national newspaper or a consumer magazine does.'[10] Power was responsible for a range of publications, from the dying *Roy of the Rovers* and *Buster*, through a series of 'licensed' titles such as *Thunderbirds* and *Teenage Mutant Hero Turtles*, to surviving monthlies from past titles such as *Whizzer and Chips*; and he would soon have an important new title in *Sonic the Hedgehog* (launched June 1993). *Sonic* was important because of its potential sales, but also because it arose from the new publishing strategies of Egmont.

In fact only two posts would be tied solely to our new comic: editor and sub-editor. All other work was spread across the company. The editor's position went to Glenn Rice, a young journalist who had learnt his trade on *Mizz* and *19*, though his post would be only freelance until the launch was confirmed.

Rice, with Steve MacManus, senior editor of the *2000AD* group, began to design the new comic, under the title 'Project Odyssey'. Between them, they constructed a list of writers who might wish to contribute to the new comic – some twenty people. This very short list indicates some real difficulties in finding new writers. Artists are not a problem – there is a steady flow of hopeful artwork submissions, especially to *2000AD*. Eventually eight proposals came in, and from these a dummy was constructed.

Rice's main task was an editorial framework:

> I took my lead from the Bill and Ted movies; and there is a tradition of fictional editors in British comics. I just thought we'll do an anglicised version of Bill and Ted, with a bit of Tharg in there; and basically get this guy who's like the hip bloke at school, the guy who's leaning on the wall going Tch, Tch, Tch. And then there was this thing came up in the research, that most of the kids watch videos; so I thought, OK, we'll have this thing which is not a comic, it's a programme, a pirate television programme, which I got from CBTV. . . . At the time it was an enormously popular kids' programme because it was illicit.[11]

The idea then was to present the comic as if it were a pirate TV broadcast, and try to evoke a sense of pleasure in doing something vaguely illegal. The editorial persona would then be the TV presenter – but creating him was a problem in itself: 'One of the hardest things for Glenn was choosing an artist to create his character. And something he said to me was, if it ain't hip they won't buy it. So he went for the hippest artist there is, Jamie Hewlett, to create a way-illegal "editor".'[12] Interestingly, the results were not popular, as follow-up research was to show.

*The first attempt at cover design, and the comic's title, were not popular with potential readers (left). Both were revised for the final dummy (right).*

**The Dummy**

If I had to sum up the first dummy issue, it would be that it had a lot of interesting ingredients, but ended up as a sampler among a melange of flavours. There were six stories:

– 'Tracer', a *RepoMan* lookalike, depicting a Japanese-looking Eddie Cassavetes who takes on dangerous jobs recovering stolen software and technology. The creation of Dave Stone, Eddie's first episode involves recovering some high-tech sports gear – only for him to discover that his target is a mad martial arts fanatic (something the company had neglected to tell him). Recovery involves wrecking the equipment, but Eddie doesn't care – it is fair payment for being 'setup'.

– 'The Burning Man' (John Wagner, with artwork by Carlos Ezquerra, both very popular through *2000AD*) begins with an assassination. We are viewing a sports arena through the eyes (and gun-sights) of the assassin (Johnny Goodnight, alias Mr Ecks) as he prepares a contract killing of a sports hero. As he leaves the arena, the job completed, we see him lurch with pain. Realising something is amiss, he consults a doctor, to learn that he has been infected with a rare toxin which will very painfully kill him within six weeks. He exits episode one, grimacing at the early spasms, to hunt whoever has done this to him.

– 'Alternity' (Mark Eyles, with two different artists because of the nature of the story) introduced Scott Glen, the son of a computer scientist who has invented a biological computer chip. When Scott 'saves' his father's invention from thieves by swallowing it, it implants itself in him and starts to grow and operate in him. Since it is a games chip, his brain is invaded by the games system and character – and the artwork for these parts shifts to a distorted, computer-generated style.

– 'Canned Heat' (John Wagner and Colin McNeil) was borrowed from *Robocop*, *The Terminator* and a dozen other cyberpunk films, to the extent of having a policeman remark at one point, 'They don't come any harder than Rocky Schwartzenberger.' Episode one, chock-a-block with vast machine-guns, blazing infernos and yells of defiance, effects the transformation of Rocky, via an appalling accident, from a no-nonsense policeman into a vast Dalek-like metal 'CyboCop', to his family's considerable consternation.

– 'Dinosty' (Pat Mills, a long-time *2000AD* writer,[13] with Chris Langley's artwork) was a dinosaur story. The dinosaurs were mock-aristocrats with a taste for fresh human flesh. Presented in mock-medieval style, the first episode set the scene for a story about a human who has found an ancient sword, fetchingly called 'Elvis', with the power to turn dragons into pacifists. The story, typically for Mills, had a high level of black humour: 'This is a true tale, my Lord,' reports the squire. 'It concerns the wild humans! They are in high spirits!' 'Good . . . good . . . happy meat is sweet meat,' replies a smirking lord.

Along with these went a small humour strip ('Mr Elephant Head', a spoof spy story), and some editorial pages.

The themes in these stories are not hard to discover – and perhaps there is something important in that fact. However they knew it,[14] the writers felt that they must walk a line between a number of story-qualities: heavy intertextual borrowings from film, television and computer gaming; parodic, 'alternative' forms of humour; violent action; American (and Japanese) references; and central characters who are loners, up against authority with only some primitive sense of justice to guide them. These themes are writ so large that it is almost as though the comic was saying out loud: we have no independent existence, we are here to fill the gaps around your other pleasures.[15] It was in danger of being a pastiche of every popular genre, with no core of its own.

The whole dummy evinces a tentativeness, rather like a sweets manufacturer testing a new flavour and packaging concept. 'We know we're still missing the key story, the "Judge Dredd" of *Alternity*',[16] one character who might 'live' and 'grow' beyond the comic and perhaps become a 'property' in wider senses. One result was that an additional story, 'Billy Whisper', was tested in the research. Billy is a Newcastle pop star who becomes President of the United States after World War III and who finds himself, with the maximum of cool, having to deal not only with his TV appearances and addresses to the nation, but also with the left-over aliens from the 1938 'war of the worlds' – Orson Welles had been lying, there really had been a landing . . . This story in fact proved one of the more popular with the research groups, particularly with the younger readers.

### The Research: Phase Two

Two further stages of quite different research were to follow. First, the company approached the business predictions firm Profit Impact of Market Strategy (PIMS). PIMS operate a large database, recording all aspects of more than 3,000 product launches by a great variety of firms. They use this to indicate what factors might aid or limit the success of the project. PIMS' report to the company is a fascinating document. Among the factors distinguishing 'winners' from 'losers' were: management's experience with their products; range of production; quality of product; extent of marketing; and willingness to spend on research. None of these is very surprising in itself. What is remarkable is the specificity of two particular recommendations PIMS were able to make to Fleetway. First, they advised them to double their planned marketing expenditure, from £180,000 to £360,000, if they wished to achieve their intended base of 60,000 readers (20 per cent penetration of the perceived market of 300,000 10–14 year-olds with a strong interest in action/adventure). Second, they predicted or (better) recommended a curve of publication:

> Lookalike analysis suggests that pursuing a rapid growth strategy is the way forward. In the short term, profit maximisation is an inappropriate goal. However, growth will attract others into the market. Given the nature of the life-cycle of comics, erecting barriers to entry is a fruitless exercise. Our lookalikes suggest that the prescription for the future is to go for growth until growth runs out, and then 'harvest' or 'milk' the business to generate cash. This is the point at which profit maximisation becomes the appropriate goal.[17]

There are remarkable implications in this for the ways in which we should explore the processes and patterns of cultural production. Of course, we may never know how far the company would have followed this specific advice – or how they would have interpreted that advice to 'go for growth' as long as it was possible, then to 'milk the business'. Nor can we know how exactly that might have affected the nature of the product. But we need to think through the implications of moves to a mode of operation in which specific production strategies may be steered by predictions from such a financial database.[18]

### The Research: Phase Three

The final phase of reader research was conducted by a different firm, The Research Business. Their brief was clear. Before launching the new title, Fleetway needed to be sure of its sales potential. The research was to have two phases: qualitative, to assess the acceptability of all aspects of the dummy magazine, right down to the logo, the persona of the 'editor', the colour of the cover, the balance of stories, and the usefulness of the imprimatur of *2000AD*;[19] and quantitative, to measure both the size of the overall market and how the typology of readers mapped on to it.[20]

The Research Business reported back to Fleetway on the qualitative phase of their research in March 1992. Overall, the response was a mildly equivocal 'yes'. Many of the boys liked the dummy, thought it different, and would consider buying it. But their many detailed criticisms enabled the report to recommend many specific changes. There was real unclarity about the 'editor', despite Hewlett's trendy artwork.[21] It just wasn't clear what kind of persona they were encountering. More than that, they felt the editorial page didn't connect with the rest of the comic. They found the stories quite uneven: 'Canned Heat' and 'Dinosty' were liked for their artwork, whilst the characters in 'The Burning Man' and 'Billy Whisper' won approval.[22] Criteria for artwork were quite precise: it had to be clean but dramatic, clear but challenging. Over-captioning and excessive dialogue were not liked. Much to the company's surprise, there seemed to be definite approval for black and white artwork, as long as it suited the story.[23] The title did not excite – 'Odyssey' was felt to be old-fashioned, and 'Earthside 8' confused the younger readers.

Guided by these criticisms, Rice set about revising the dummy. Out went 'Tracer' – not much liked at all (the artwork was seen as messy and too childlike in its primary colours); in came 'Billy Whisper'. The story-title 'Alternity' became the comic title *Alternity*. Hewlett's alien was replaced by the Navigator, a near horror-figure from the back page, and (most interestingly) in response to a criticism that the stories were not adequately signposted, each story was mast-headed with a fictional character who 'introduced' the plot – a change which harks back to, or rediscovers, what EC Comics did in their classic 1950s titles with the Vault-Keeper, the Old Witch and the Crypt-Keeper.[24]

**The Research: Final Phase**

Armed with this revised dummy, The Research Business went about the quantitative research, interviewing 545 boys aged 8–16 (selected with the requirement that they must be regular readers of at least one from a list of comics and magazines). The outcome was a 40-page report whose density of information can hardly be touched on here.

They put quantities onto the typology: aficionados, 9 per cent; appreciatives, 11 per cent; the remainder uncommitted. Whichever category they came in, most readers liked the comic.[25] Pleasure in the stories broke down into a number of semi-independent variables: interest in a central character; appreciation of artwork, pacing of the story; need to know what happens next; elements of action/adventure; and story-settings. Many boys did not understand the title *Alternity*, but interestingly this did not significantly interfere with their feelings about its suitability – it presumably had the right 'ambience'.

Of all the stories, while 'Canned Heat' and 'Dinosty' scored highest as favourite, 'Gameworld' (the new title for 'Alternity') got the highest overall rating. A small number of younger boys didn't like aspects of its visual presentation, in particular the panels where the computer starts extruding from Scott Glen's face. Also, Glen was not the most preferred central

*Above*: *The original E-Teen 'persona', not liked because he reminded readers too much of their 'spotty selves'.*

*Left*: *Promoted from the back page: The Navigator, but still not popular.*

*Below*: *The popular choice among the comic's 'presenters', and recommended for promotion to 'editor' by The Research Business.*

*Photos courtesy of Fleetway Comics.*

character. But overall, for its mix of qualities it scored a creditable 7.72 out of 10, on a scale between rubbish and brilliant.

The research concluded with a clear recommendation that Fleetway should 'proceed to launch'.

**Stopped in its Tracks**

And there the process stalled – not just for *Alternity,* but also for two other titles on which there had been some research: *Oh No!*, a humour title; and *Glory, Glory!*, a planned replacement for the lost *Roy of the Rovers.* Even carrying 'Project Odyssey' to this stage had cost the company more than £80,000, but that was peanuts compared with the predicted costs of a full launch, at £500,000. This level of outlay is not an automatic function of what it costs to produce any new comic. It is function of the kind of company Fleetway is, and its position within the larger pattern of international comic production. Where, in America, Marvel and DC now earn the majority of their earnings from the comics they produce for the direct sales market,[26] Fleetway still earn most of their money from newsstand sales. Their few forays into the more adult-directed, direct sales market (*Deadline, Crisis, X-Presso*) were close to disastrous. Consequently, the advantages accruing to the American publishers were missing for Fleetway. The American pattern included cross-advertising, the creation of 'team-ups' – building whole universes of characters which support each other's sales – and of course the simplicity of fewer outlets and a readership who can be expected to explore a range of publications (including, increasingly, looking also at publicity paraphernalia – preview and review magazines, fanzines and the like). All this reduces the risks associated with a new publication.

Fleetway have none of these advantages. To generate newsagent sales, their marketing budget had to include generous amounts for prime-time (children's) television advertising. There was also a lower ceiling on price than US publishers can expect, since Fleetway's readers would be making a move up from cheap comics like the *Beano.*

But one issue outweighed all others. This was in so many senses a British comic (see the quote at the head of this chapter); so were the other stalled titles. By the beginning of 1992, Fleetway had changed hands again. The Danish publishers Egmont bought the comics division from Maxwell for one central reason: Maxwell had won the right to the European distribution of Disney. Egmont wanted that, and bought the division to get it. But with this change in ownership, the criteria for an acceptable publication shifted. Even after all the research was in, Chris Power would have to make a presentation to Egmont's Fritz Ranstrom, now John Davidge's superior, and among his criteria would be that the comic ideally should be saleable in at least three countries. Why? The answer, I believe, lies in the logic of licensing.

Licensing is emerging as one of the prime ways in which media companies interconnect. When DC became part of Warner Communications, there is no doubt that a major motive was the acquisition of the 'properties'

*Setting a narrative agenda: Gameworld's play with the boundary between games and reality. Courtesy of Fleetway Comics.*

represented in particular by Batman and Superman.[27] Even then, a film, TV or comic company with a marketable 'property' will license aspects of associated merchandise to dozens of other companies, producing everything from lunch boxes, watches, T-shirts, pyjamas, plastic figurines, to games, sweets and ice creams. Most media companies also need to create one-off arrangements for marketing particular characters or storylines. This has enabled a number of smaller companies – for example, Dark Horse – to flourish at the margins of the American Big Two. The comic companies themselves have to make merchandising arrangements – a fact which Fleetway were slow to learn after the success of *2000AD* and Judge Dredd.[28]

Fleetway now have their own permanent licensing company, Copyright Promotions, which sets up arrangements for all kinds of merchandising. But in the other direction, the increasing importance of cross-media tie-ins means that Egmont have in place the structures for many-nation launches, and place greater importance on the production of multinationally acceptable publications. A typical product of these arrangements is of course *Sonic the Hedgehog*, a comic licensed by Sega and launched by Egmont in 1993 with an expected platform to European distribution within a year. All editions can be based on the same artwork with different language overlays. To do this effectively, a new infrastructure has to be in place, and that of course works directly against single-country launches. And indeed the costs are less – Chris Power estimated the launch costs for *Sonic* at half those predicted for *Alternity*.

A combination of high-risk economy, shifts in ownership and in publishing criteria, plus a new nervousness about how comics can find an audience: all these built wall upon wall in front of 'Project Odyssey'. It is now possible to say for certain that it will never surmount them.[29]

**The Lessons of a Non-result**

What can we learn from the experiences of this very shortlived comic? From among the many points that might be made, I would stress and recapitulate the following:

1. At the level of the publisher, they reveal the specificity of the production imperatives that run a company. Most of the time, these work 'on automatic'. Fleetway, however, was caught in the middle of a transformation from one *system* of production imperatives to another. We see here the local impact of one aspect of globalisation – a small company, used to working within a national tradition of publication, has to reorient itself *and its audience* to the wider demands of international ownership, production and distribution.[30]

2. At the textual level, we can see the rising significance of comic 'properties', yet how hard it is to produce them. One thing that really strikes me is that publishers *cannot* produce them to order – they only appear when creators are not really trying. With *Alternity*, the research process and the degree of dependence on readers' wishes were a guarantee

that the producers would actually be less creative than their readers. For good or ill, there needs to be an 'edge' between producer and receiver, if effective material is to emerge. There are, of course, larger issues about how and why, at certain points, cultural forms can emerge that encapsulate the experience or aspirations of a social group. We know very little, generally, about the conditions for this to happen successfully,[31] but it seems certain that they will not come out of such overtended phenomena as 'Odyssey' would have been.

The urge for contemporaneity is in fact self-defeating, because the comic itself in that case never *forms* the contemporary. The 'new' is always something external, something being chased, a veritable will-o'-the-wisp.

3. What do we learn about the readers? Many things, but I will comment only on one. It seems to me that the research commissioned by Fleetway reveals a curious tension and ambivalence in the boys they wanted to reach: between a considerable sophistication (in their closeness of reading and response to the dummy, the range of knowledge and references they brought to bear on it) and an inflexibility brought about by cultural and gender positioning (an overdetermined rejection of those things not immediately meeting their agenda). This suggests a complexity (imaginative freedom versus formulaic limitation) in reading responses which has been better researched, to date, in girls and women and deserves further exploration in boys and men.

NOTES

1. Conversation with the author, 20 February 1992.
2. I have been engaged for two years now in a large research project into the comic *2000AD*, covering everything from its production history to its audience. It was in the course of following up one avenue of this that I heard about the plans for the new launch, and asked if I could track it. The publishers Fleetway Editions have been very supportive. Thanks in particular to John Davidge, Chris Power and Steve MacManus.
3. One strong rumour had the readership falling as low as 60,000 in 1992; when asked, a company representative denied this strongly, insisting that it had actually risen recently. Certainly a major relaunch is taking place as I write this (June 1993).
4. On this, see the ground-breaking work of Nicholas Garnham, *Capitalism and Communication: Global Culture and the Economics of Information* (London: Sage, 1990).
5. And in this connection, rumours of 'industrial espionage' between the two companies were for many years legion.
6. Marvel in particular sell through 'cross-overs', that is, through stories in which characters from different comic worlds are set in conflict with each other. There are endless possibilities for such cross-overs, and reader-loyalty is built around keeping up with them. Marvel have been spectacularly keen to exploit these in recent years, leading to considerable speculation (in, for example, the American *Comics Journal* and the British *Comics International*) that they have been deliberately flooding the shelves of comics shops in the hope of displacing their smaller competitors.
7. Egmont was in fact known as Gutenburghus at the point where, in October 1991, it bought a 50 per cent stake in Fleetway Editions. At about the time it

bought the rest of the company, it changed its name to Egmont, as a more 'international' title. Egmont is itself a multimedia company, with interests in film, TV, book and magazine publishing, and with licensing arrangements with several American giants: Disney, Warner and Hanna-Barbera. Egmont likes to be known as a publishing 'house' because they take very seriously their image as a family-oriented company.

8. See their report to Fleetway, 'Project Sisyphus: A Report on a Qualitative Investigation into the Action/Adventure Comics Market', research conducted by Mark Ratcliff and Neil Dawson, May 1991.
9. I am struck by the close fit between this typology and that which I used in my research on the comic *Action* (see my *Action: the Story of a Violent Comic*, London, Titan, 1990). There, I distinguished Casual, Regular and Committed readers. In both cases, it has proved a revealing way to categorise readers. There is, though, a question which neither Young Direction nor I really pursued but which I would now regard as important. This is the *relations between* these types: whether they constitute a hierarchy in any sense, in which one group may *aspire to the condition of another group*, or recognise it as having a certain cultural cachet, or the opposite.

   Illogically, but rightly in my view, Fleetway ignored one possible conclusion from this. The report indicates that the Appreciative group is undoubtedly the largest; yet when following through this research, Fleetway chose to act on the assumption that most of its potential readers would favour strong linkage between a new comic and their interests in videos and computer games – something strictly found only in the 'aficionados'.
10. Chris Power, interview, 12 March 1992.
11. Glenn Rice, interview, 19 February 1992.
12. Steve MacManus, interview, 19 February 1992.
13. Mills has played a major role in a number of comics, including *Battle*, *Action* and *2000AD* (for IPC/Fleetway), and many other titles for other publishers. On the comics, see my *Action: the Story of a Violent Comic.*
14. I was assured by Glenn Rice that the advice to potential writers was very unspecific.
15. In this connection it is worth noting the comment in the final research report: 'In the longer term care needs to be taken with regard to the balance between originality in characters and the use of "tried and tested" concepts. *Alternity* must not be allowed to become a "copycat".' (The Research Business, 'Research into the Development of a New Action/Adventure Comic for Boys Under 14: A Final Report', October 1992)
16. Steve MacManus, conversation with author, 19 September 1992.
17. 'PIMS Start up Analysis of Project Odyssey', a report to Fleetway Communications, 1991.
18. Celia Lury's book *Cultural Rights: Technology, Legality and Personality* (London: Routledge, 1993) seems to me to provide an important handle on the general processes at work here.
19. See The Research Business, 'Qualitative Research into Project Odyssey', report presented to Fleetway Editions, 31 March 1992. My thanks to The Research Business for permission to quote from this and their other report.
20. See their final report, dated October 1992.
21. It seems that Hewlett's image presumed a capacity for self-parody that boys of 9–14 did not share. Chris Power told me that their reader groups felt the character was too like what the boys were trying to escape: a state of spotty gracelessness (interview, 3 July 1993).
22. The Research Business's final report includes a reader's quote relating to this story: 'Mr Ecks was a good character because you immediately dislike him.'

Being interested in theories of media influence, I have trouble thinking of much current thinking that can make sense of the complex relations implied by this one sentence.

23. This was in fact qualified in the quantitative research. It was more that, while they preferred colour art generally, they 'did not mind' some black and white among the rest.
24. On the EC Comics, see for example my *A Haunt of Fears: The Strange History of the British Horror Comics Campaign* (London: Pluto, 1984).
25. 26 per cent responded that they 'must have it', 29 per cent that they 'wish they could have it', 33 per cent 'would have it' but gave it low priority, the remainder (mainly older) positively would not want it. Interestingly, though, the researchers note a tendency for boys to try to 'upgrade' themselves to aficionados, claiming a commitment and knowledge they then could not sustain. On this, see note 9 above.
26. On this, see Roger Sabin, *Adult Comics: An Introduction* (London: Routledge, 1993), Ch.5.
27. See Roberta Pearson and William Uricchio, *The Many Lives of the Batman* (London: Routledge/BFI, 1991) for evidence on the extent of the merchandising. In the same period, the MacAndrews and Forbes Group bought Marvel Comics from New World Pictures for $82.5 million. What did they get for their money? 'The comic book company had come a long way from the days, thirty years earlier, when virtually its only asset was a desk with Stan Lee sitting behind it' (Les Daniells, *Marvel: Five Fabulous Decades of the World's Greatest Comics*, London: Virgin, 1991, p. 215). What Daniells doesn't tell (in this rather flatulent fan-book) is what they amounted to now. A bit of real estate in New York, some back artwork . . . and a large number of potential 'properties'. The issue of intellectual property is a vast one, on which not much has been written. Jane Gaines' book *Contested Culture* (London: BFI 1991) is an important first contribution. However, it argues almost entirely at the level of cultural consequences, whereas I want to argue that there are prior questions about forms and forces of production. See also Lury, *Cultural Rights.*
28. The emergence of Titan Publishers and Distribution, and the Forbidden Planet network of shops, was largely made possible by the relatively free rein they were permitted with the reprint albums of *2000AD* materials (a practice quickly constrained after the arrival of Davidge, and the reconstruction of management practices, at Fleetway in 1989).
29. At the time of first drafting this essay, there was an element of uncertainty. That element vanished when two of the stories commissioned for the dummy were used in other publications: 'The Burning Man' ran as a one-off story in a *2000AD* special in 1993; 'Dinosty' began a serial run in *2000AD* itself in January 1994.
30. For a fine introductory exploration of these processes in the comics industry, see Matthew McAllister, 'Cultural argument and organisational constraint in the comic book industry', *Journal of Communication*, vol. 40 no. 1, Winter 1990, pp. 55–71.
31. The founding study of such processes has to be Lucien Goldmann's *The Hidden God* (London: Routledge, 1964). In a fascinating reprise of this, Agnes Heller has argued that perhaps the conditions for such collective 'visions' no longer exist; see her essay 'Group interest, collective consciousness and the role of the intellectual in Lukacs and Goldmann', *Social Praxis*, vol. 6 nos. 3–4, 1979, pp. 177–92.

# INDEX


*2000AD*, 201, 205
*3-2-1-Contact*, 17
*A-Team, The*, 156
ABC, 21, 84
Action for Children's Television, 170
*Adventures of Tom Sawyer*, 95
Ahmadpoor, Babak, 104
*Aladdin*, 95, 109, 110, 111, 154, 190
*Alice in Wonderland*, 132
Allen, Woody, 77, 82
*Allsorts*, 34
*Alternity*, 11, 201–14
*American Film*, 115
*An American Tail*, 93
Andersen, Hans Christian, 144
Anderson, Louise, 122
Andrews, Julie, 95
*Andy Pandy*, 20, 36, 40–42, 43, 44
Apple Computers, 190
*Ashpet: An American Cinderella*, 123

*Back to the Future*, 76, 85
*Bad Influence*, 198
Barbie, 145, 197
Barnes, Edward, 48, 50, 51, 52
*Barney*, 17, 21
Barrett, Martin, 130
*Batman*, 79, 153, 156
*Batman Returns*, 79
*Batman: The Animated Series*, 84
BBC, 6, 8, 10, 17, 18, 19, 20, 21, 28, 34, 38, 40, 41, 49, 142
BBC Radio, 19, 36, 59
*Beano, The*, 211
*Beauty and the Beast*, 93, 111, 116, 118, 142, 167
*Beetlejuice!*, 84
Bentsen, Lloyd, 76
Bergman, Ingmar, 92
Bettelheim, Bruno, 12, 131, 132, 163
Bick, Esther, 135
*Big*, 76
*Big Breakfast, The*, 59
*Bill and Ben*, 41, 43
Bion, Wilfred, 134
Bird, Maria, 40, 41
*Bitsa*, 52
*Blue Peter*, 17, 20, 48, 50, 51, 58
*Borderlines*, 12
*Bremen Town Musicians, The*, 109
Brennan, Walter, 95
British Film Institute, 12
Brunsdon, Charlotte, 9
*Bullwinkle's Mooserama Show*, 85
Burton, Richard, 202
Bush, George, 76
*Byker Grove*, 30

Cant, Brian, 28
*Captain Planet*, 12, 62–73, 152, 177
*Care Bears, The*, 67, 159, 166, 176, 177, 179
Carnegie Foundation, 18
*Cartoon Time*, 58
CBS, 21, 84, 113, 152
Central Television, 23
Cerone, Daniel, 84
Channel Four Television, 21, 23, 34, 59, 198
*Chart Show, The*, 142, 149
Chicken Shed Theatre Company, 25
Children's BBC (CBBC), 23, 48, 60
Children's Channel, 21
*Children's Hour*, 36, 37, 43
Children's London Film Festival, 12
Children's Television Workshop (CTW), 18, 19, 22, 26, 28
*Children's Ward*, 30
Chilprufe, 38–9
*Cinderella*, 111, 118
*Clarissa Explains It All*, 86
Clausen, Erik, 98, 100
Clinton, Hillary, 20
Clinton, President Bill, 21, 75
CNN, 62, 66
Comstock, G., 27
Cooney, Joan Ganz, 18, 19

Cooper, Cary, 195
*Cosby Show, The*, 30
Costner, Kevin, 82
Craven John, 50
*Crossroads*, 49
Culkin, Macaulay, 77, 80, 96, 101

D.C. Thomson, 203, 211
*Daily Sketch*, 44
*Daily Star*, 22
*Danger Mouse*, 83
Danish Film Institute, 97
Davenport, Tom, 10, 112, 120–23
Davidge, John, 201, 204
*Dick Van Dyke*, 83
Dickens, Charles, 1
Dickens, Monica, 34, 35
*Die Hard*, 81
Dino-Riders, 156
*Disney Club*, 51
Disney, Walt, 7, 10, 12, 21, 59, 93, 109–12, 123, 124, 142, 144, 154, 167, 170, 171, 190
Dorfman, Ariel, 63
*Dr Quinn, Medicine Woman*, 85
Dukakis, Michael, 76
*Dungeons and Dragons*, 62, 72
Duvall, Shelley, 10, 112, 118

*Eagle*, 201, 203
Eastwood, Clint, 81
Egmont, 203, 211
Ellerbee, Linda, 87–8
Ellis, John, 25, 29
*Emperor's New Clothes, The*, 118
*End of the World Man, The*, 106
Engelhardt, Tom, 143, 154, 170
Estes, Clarissa, 163
*ET*, 7, 190
European Film Distribution Office (EFDO), 98, 107
Evans, Chris, 60
*Everywoman*, 42
Ezquerra, Carlos, 206

*Faerie Tale Theatre*, 118–20
Falch, Michael, 100
*Family Double Dare*, 85
Farrow, Mia, 77
Federal Communication Commission (FCC), 151, 170
Felgate, Cynthia, 15, 19, 25, 27
Fisher, Amy, 78, 82
Fleetway Editions, 11, 201
*Flintstones, The*, 168
*For Women*, 43
Ford, Gerald, 87–8
Ford, Harrison, 80
*Fortune*, 110
Fowles, Jib, 153
Fox Broadcasting, 84
Fox, David, 80
*Fractured Fairy Tales, The*, 123
*Fraggle Rock*, 177, 180
Frank, Kimberley, 82
*Free Willy*, 93
Freud, Sigmund, 127, 130, 131, 132
*Frog King, The*, 122
*Frog Prince, The*, 113, 118, 119
Frye, Northrop, 179
*Full House*, 30
*Fun House*, 50

*G.I. Joe*, 157
Gameboy, 188
*Gamesmaster*, 198
*Garfield and Friends*, 84
Garr, Terri, 119
Gettas, Gregory, 26, 27
*Ghost Train*, 50, 51
Ginsburg, Herbert, 18
GMTV, 53
*Going Live*, 50, 51, 59, 60
Gore, Al, 75, 76
*Grange Hill*, 23, 49
*Great Muppet Caper, The*, 112
Greene, Graham, 95
Greene, Sarah, 60
Greenfield, Patricia Marks, 197
Grimm, Brothers, 109
Gyngell, Bruce, 53

Haagensen, Christina, 99
Haddon, Leslie, 189, 191, 195
*Hans My Hedgehog*, 116
*Hansel and Gretel*, 122
Harris, Dr Miles, 128
Harris, Rolf, 58
Hart, Tony, 58
*Hartbeat*, 58
Hartley, John, 59, 60, 75, 80
Hasbro, 155, 172
Hays, Will, 93
HBO, 118
*He-Man*, 176
Henson Associates, 112
Henson, Jim, 10, 112–17
*Hey Dude*, 85
Himmelweit, Hilde, 36, 42
Holland, Patricia, 6
*Home Alone*, 7, 77, 79, 80–83, 89, 93
*Home Alone 2: Lost in New York*, 76, 79, 96, 101
Home, Anna, 18, 19
*Honey, I Shrunk the Kids*, 93, 95
*Hook*, 93, 95, 96
*Hue and Cry*, 96

Idle, Eric, 119
*Iftah Ya Simsim*, 26
Institute for the Intellectual Development of Children and Young Adults, 97
IPC, 201, 203
*Ipso Facto*, 23, 30
ITV, 17, 20, 21, 23, 34, 62, 142, 198
Iwerks, Ub, 109

*Jack and the Beanstalk*, 115, 120
*Jack and the Dentist's Daughter*, 122
*Jackanory*, 28
Jackson, Michael, 77, 82, 147
Jaggar, Alison, 183
Jarvik, Lawrence, 17
*Jurassic Park*, 190

*Karakum*, 96

Keats, John, 134
Kelly, Tommy, 95
*Khaneh-je Doost Kojast?* (see also *Where is My Friend's House?*), 94, 98
Kiarostami, Abbas, 97, 98, 103, 105, 107
*Kids' Club*, 84
Klein, Melanie, 133–34
Kline, Stephen, 143, 170, 183

*La Belle et la Bête*, 118
Labov, William, 18
Lane, John, 20, 22
*Lethal Weapon*, 203
*Like Father, Like Son*, 76
Lingstrom, Freda, 36, 40
*Listen with Mother*, 19, 36, 37, 40
*Little Mermaid, The*, 11, 84, 142, 144–50, 167
*Little Red Riding Hood*, 109, 115
*Live and Kicking*, 23
Llosa, Mario Vargas, 15, 16
*Loony Tunes*, 86
Lucas, George, 79
Luhmann, Nikolas, 68
Lull, James, 31
Lurie, Alison, 12

MacManus, Steve, 205
Madonna, 78, 82, 141, 147
Mallett, Timmy, 48, 51, 53–9
Marchetti, Gina, 158
Marvel, 203, 211
*Mary Poppins*, 95
Mattelart, Armand, 63
Maxwell Group, 203
McCulloch, Derek, 36, 37
McDonald's, 24, 56, 156
McRobbie, Angela, 196
*Me and Mama Mia*, 11, 98–102, 106, 107
*Megan*, 160
Meltzer, Donald, 134
*Mickey Mouse in Castle of Illusion*, 197
*Mig og Mama Mia* (see also *Me and Mama Mia*), 94
*Mighty Morphin Power Rangers*, 84
Minghella, Anthony, 115
Miskelly, Bill, 106
*Mister Rogers' Neighborhood*, 15, 21, 31
Modleski, Tania, 184, 185
Morley, David, 31
Morris, Simon, 196
*Mortal Kombat*, 191, 197
*Motion Picture Herald*, 94
Motion Picture Producers and Distributors Association of America, 93–4
*Mr Ed*, 83
*Mr Wizard's World*, 83
MTV, 17, 75, 83
Muffin Syndicate Ltd, The, 38
*Muffin the Mule*, 38–40
*Muppet Babies*, 86, 180
*Muppet Christmas Carol, The*, 93
*Muppet Movie, The*, 112
*Muppet Show, The*, 112
Murdoch, Rupert, 21
Murphy, Art, 79
*My Father Lives in Rio, 96*
*My Little Pony*, 11, 160, 166, 169, 172–85
*My Little Pony, The Movie*, 175

National Enquirer, The, 82
NBC, 21, 84
*Never Ending Story, The*, 123
*New Statesman and Nation*, 35
*New York Times*, 17
*Newsround*, 17, 23, 30, 50, 51
*Nick Arcade*, 85
*Nick News*, 87
Nickelodeon, 21, 76, 83–9
Nietzsche, Friedrich, 110
Nintendo, 80, 154, 155, 156, 188, 189–91
*NME*, 204
Noble, Grant, 48
Norris, Chuck, 81

*Observer, The*, 38, 40
Odhams Press, 201
Øst, Tammi, 100

*PacMan*, 199
Paik, H., 27
Palmer, Edward, 18, 27
Palmer, Patricia, 31
*Parallel Nine*, 50, 51
Peacock, Michael, 19
PeeWee Herman, 78
*PeeWee's Playhouse*, 86
Perot, Ross, 76
Pesci, Joe, 81
Peter Pan, 6, 47
Petersen, Leif Sylvester, 100
*Pipkins*, 23
Plato, 2
*Play School*, 10, 15, 16, 20, 22, 28, 31
*Playdays*, 16, 17, 19, 22, 24–5, 27, 28, 29, 30, 34
*Pob's Programme*, 23
*Point Horror*, 197
Poltrack David F., 152
Postman, Neil, 3, 26, 29, 30, 31, 142
Power, Chris, 204
Price, Judy, 84
*Princess and the Pea, The*, 118
*Princess Bride, The*, 123
Professional Association of Teacher (PAT), 193
Profit Impact of Market Strategy (PIMS), 208
*Puss in Boots*, 109, 118
Pyle, Barbara, 62

Quayle, Dan, 76

Radway, Janice, 184
*Rag, Tag and Bobtail*, 36
*Rainbow*, 23
*Rainbow Brite*, 166, 169, 176, 177, 179, 185
Ranstrom, Fritz, 211
*Rapunzel*, 122
*Really Wild Show, The*, 52
Reith, Lord John, (Reithian), 20, 31, 49
*Ren and Stimpy*, 77, 186
*Repoman*, 206
Research Business, The, 208, 209
Reynolds, Richard, 63
Rice, Glenn, 205, 209
*Roadrunner*, 152
*Robocop*, 135, 190, 203, 204

Rogers, Fred, 15, 24
Rose, Jacqueline, 6, 47, 48, 60
Rosenfeld, Herbert, 134
Rowland, W.D., 22
*Roy of the Rovers*, 205, 211
*Rugrats*, 86
Rustin, Margaret and Michael, 12, 132

Salomon, Gavriel, 26
*Salute Your Shorts*, 86
Schneider, Cy, 151, 166
Schoenhaus, Ted, 156, 172
Schofield, Philip, 60
Schoo, David and Sharon, 82
Schwarzenegger, Arnold, 80, 204
*Scooby-Doo*, 169
Scott, Jeffrey, 115
Sega, 188, 189–91, 213
Segel, Elizabeth, 166
Selznick, David, 95
*Sesame Street*, 10, 16–24, 26–32, 34, 112, 169
*Sesame Street Magazine*, 84
*Shining Time Station*, 21
*Sight and Sound*, 94
*Simpsons, The*, 84, 86, 163
Skirrow, Gillian, 199
*Sleeping Beauty*, 123
*Smurfs, The*, 159, 185
*Snapperazzi*, 190
*Snow Queen, The*, 118
*Snow White*, 109, 110, 111, 114, 118, 154
*Snow White and the Seven Dwarfs*, 109
*Snow White and the Seven Muppets*, 114
*Sonic, Sonic the Hedgehog*, 59, 188, 194, 197, 205, 213
Spielberg, Steven, 79, 93
Stallone, Sylvester, 80
*Star Trek*, 67
*Star Wars*, 156
*Stern, Daniel, 81*
*Stern, Sydney Ladensohn, 156, 172*
*Storyteller, The*, 112, 115–17
*Straw Dogs*, 81
*Strawberry Shortcake*, 166, 169, 177
*Street Fighter 2*, 197
*Streets of Rage*, 197
Strout, Richard, 35
*Sun Tots, The*, 152
*Super Mario, Super Mario Brothers*, 80, 188, 190, 194, 197
Superman, 62, 156

Taffel, Ron, 78, 82
Takashi, 115
Taurog, Norman, 95
*Teddy Ruxpin*, 159
*Teenage Mutant Hero Turtles* (see also *Teenage Mutant Ninja Turtles*), 7, 127, 205
*Teenage Mutant Ninja Turtles* (see also *Teenage Mutant Hero Turtles*), 12, 84, 127–30, 132–33, 135–39
*Teenage Mutant Ninja Turtles 2 and 3*, 139
Temple, Shirley, 6, 95
*Terminator, The*, 135, 190
Thames Television, 23
Thatcher, Margaret, 53
*Three Little Pigs, The*, 120, 171
*Thunderbirds*, 49, 205
*Thundercats*, 62, 72, 153, 176
*Tiny Toon Adventures*, 84
*Tom and Jerry*, 152
*Top of the Pops*, 142, 149
*Tots TV*, 34
Toys 'R' Us, 34
Tracey, Michael, 22
Troke, Jan, 42
Tsongas, Paul, 75
Turner, Ted, 62, 66, 177
Turner Broadcasting, 62, 63
Turner Entertainment, 10
TV-AM, 53

Valenti, Jack, 80
*Vice Versa*, 76
Virgin Films, 127
Vygotsky, L.S., 146

*Wacaday!*, 10, 48, 53–9
Wagg, Stephen, 49
Walkerdine, Valerie, 130
Warner Communications, 211
*Watch with Mother*, 7, 36, 37, 38, 42, 43–4
WGBH, 20, 24
*Where is My Friend's House?*, 11, 102–6, 107
Whitby, Joy, 19
*Whizzer and Chips*, 205
*Why Don't You (Switch off Your Television Set and Go and Do Something Less Boring Instead)?*, 52
*Wide Awake Club*, 53
*Wild and Crazy Kids*, 85
Williams, Robin, 20, 26, 95, 96, 120
Williams, W.E., 38, 40
Willis, Bruce, 81
Winnicott, Donald, 135
*Wizards, The*, 123
*Woman's Own*, 34, 35
*Wonder Woman*, 156
*Woodentops, The*, 36, 43

*You Can't Do That on Television*, 86
Young Direction, 203

*Zillions*, 83
*Zoobilee Zoo*, 180